Peterson's
SAT* Preparation Course
Homework Book

THOMSON

PETERSON'S

Australia • Canada • Mexico • Singapore • Spain • United Kingdom • United States

About Thomson Peterson's

Thomson Peterson's (www.petersons.com) is a leading provider of education information and advice, with books and online resources focusing on education search, test preparation, and financial aid. Its Web site offers searchable databases and interactive tools for contacting educational institutions, online practice tests and instruction, and planning tools for securing financial aid. Peterson's serves 110 million education consumers annually.

For more information, contact Peterson's, 2000 Lenox Drive, Lawrenceville, NJ 08648; 800-338-3282; or find us on the World Wide Web at www.petersons.com/about.

ISBN: 0-7689-2049-3

Printed in the United States of America

10 9 8 7 6 5 4 3 2 1   07 06 05

CONTENTS

Critical Reading

Writing

Note: Photocopying any part of this book is prohibited by law.

Math

Note: Photocopying any part of this book is prohibited by law.

Note: Photocopying any part of this book is prohibited by law.

CRITICAL READING

UNDERSTANDING DIFFICULT TEXT

> **Directions:** Read the sentence and put it into your own words. Then select the statement that best matches your paraphrase from the choices given.

1. Then bitter remorse was mine, for I thought I had been unfaithful, and therefore my little sister was to be called to the spirit land.

   A. I was bitter and angry with my sister for being unfaithful and dying.

   B. My sister was sad that I was unfaithful, and that's why she died.

   C. I thought that because I was unfaithful, my sister would die, and that made me very sad.

   D. My spirit was unfaithful which made my sister bitter and remorseful.

   E. I believed I was unfaithful, but since I was wrong, my sister died.

2. He and all the others were laughing, but when he saw me Zverkov assumed a dignified air and came toward me, without hurrying, and gave me his hand in a friendly but not effusive fashion, as if he were protecting himself from something by offering me his hand.

   A. Zverkov was in a good mood and he shook my hand enthusiastically.

   B. When he saw me, Zverkov got serious and came over and shook my hand cautiously.

   C. Zverkov laughed at me when he saw me and pretended to be friendly when he took my hand.

   D. Zverkov got terrified when he saw me and went to protect himself.

   E. Zverkov wanted to include me in a private conversation.

3. I am not unmindful that some of you have come out of great trials and tribulations. Some of you have come from areas where your quest for freedom left you battered by the storms of persecution and staggered by the winds of brutality. You have been the veterans of creative suffering. Continue to work with the faith that unearned suffering is redemptive.

   A. I don't know why some of you have suffered, but if you redeem yourself your suffering may end.

   B. Many people suffer to no end, but creative people suffer to be free.

   C. I think some of you may face great dangers in the future, but if you have faith you will come out of it all okay.

   D. I am aware that some of you have suffered greatly, but have faith that your suffering can make things better for you in the long run.

   E. Some of you have seen great suffering, but this experience will make you less likely to suffer in the future.

Note: Photocopying any part of this book is prohibited by law.

Directions: In the next three excerpts, you will find difficult words and long sentences. Analyze and paraphrase the sentences given. Then select the statement that best matches your paraphrase.

4. In continental Europe, of late years, the words patriotism and patriot have been used in a more enlarged sense than it is usual here in the United States to attribute to them, or than is attached to them in Great Britain.

   A. Lately in continental Europe, the words patriotism and patriot have a more expansive meaning than they do in the U.S. and Great Britain.

   B. Lately in continental Europe, the words patriotism and patriot have been used more often than they are used in the U.S. and Great Britain.

   C. People are more attached to the words patriot and patriotism in continental Europe than they are in the U.S. and Great Britain.

   D. People in the U.S. and Great Britain make no distinction between the words patriot and patriotism, as people in continental Europe do.

   E. People in the U.S. use patriotism in a larger sense than people in Great Britain or continental Europe.

5. Since the political struggles of France, Italy, Spain, and Greece, the word patriotism has been employed, throughout continental Europe, to express a love of the public good; a preference for the interest of the many over those of the few; a desire for the emancipation of the human race from the thrall of despotism. In short, patriotism there is used rather to express the interest felt in the human race in general than that felt for any country, or inhabitants of a country, in particular.

   A. People in France, Italy, Spain, and Greece express patriotic feelings for other countries more than they express them for their own countries.

   B. The human race in general is more important than the welfare of any single country.

   C. As a result of certain political struggles, people in continental Europe see patriotism as a feeling toward humanity as a whole, not just a feeling for a single country.

   D. People in continental Europe believe that all human beings are patriotic.

   E. People in France, Italy, Spain, and Greece have a more expansive definition of patriotism than people from other countries in continental Europe.

Note: Photocopying any part of this book is prohibited by law.

6. Laurels and statues are vain things, and mischie-vous as they are childish; but could we imagine them of use, on such a patriot alone could they be with any reason bestowed.

A. Those who want to reward patriots with awards and statues are childish and vain.

B. Awards and decorations are silly and maybe dangerous, but if anyone deserves them, this kind of patriot does.

C. Honoring someone with statues is silly, but all patriots deserve them anyway.

D. A good reason to honor a patriot with stat-ues and awards is when he alone did the patriotic deed.

E. Patriots should receive awards, but only for good reasons.

ANSWERS AND EXPLANATIONS

1. **The correct answer is (C).** "Bitter remorse was mine" is a tough phrase, but it's not impossible to figure out. You may know that remorse means sadness, or else you can infer from the context that the author is upset. Why is the author sad? The evidence signal word "for" tells you that the explanation is coming up: the author thought she was unfaithful, and the conclusion signal word "therefore" tells you what the author thinks will result from her being unfaithful—her sister will be called to the "spirit land." Perhaps you figured out that this is a fancy way of saying that her sister died, but even if you didn't, you still should be able to infer that it's not a good thing that results from the author's actions. Overall, (C) is the best paraphrase of the bunch. As for the others:

Choice (A): There's nothing about anger in the text. Also, the author is not speaking of feelings toward her sister, but rather of feelings about *what happened to* her sister.

Choice (B): "Bitter remorse was *mine*" means the author is sad, not her sister.

Choice (D): The speaker is the one who is bitter and remorseful, and she says nothing about her spirit. Rather, she talks about her sister being called to the *spirit land*—which is a poetic way of saying that her sister died. This is not an accurate paraphrase.

Choice (E): There's nothing here that suggests that the speaker's beliefs were incorrect or that being incorrect caused anything.

2. **The correct answer is (B).** In the first part of the sentence, the contrast signal word "but" indicates that Zverkov's laughing mood changed as soon as he saw the author. In the second part of the sentence Zverkov is described as "not effusive." Even if you don't know the meaning of the word, the author tells us that not being effusive is in contrast to being friendly. So you can assume that effusive is in the friendly word branch. This lets you know that something about Zverkov's manner was not friendly. Effusive actually means outgoing and enthusiastic. Zverkov's caution is indicated by the fact that he offered his hand as if he were protecting himself from something. We can tell that someone who shakes hands as if "protecting himself" can't be said to be enthusiastic about the handshake. All signs point to "cautious." As for the others:

Choice (A): Someone who shakes hands as if "protecting himself" can't be said to be enthusiastic about the handshake. Furthermore, Zverkov *was* in a good mood, but the contrast signal word "but" clearly indicates that Zverkov's mood changed as soon as he saw the author.

Choice (C): If you read carefully you will see that Zverkov was laughing before the speaker came in and changed his manner to a dignified, or more serious, mood when he saw the speaker. Nothing in the passage indicates that Zverkov pretended to be friendly. In fact, Zverkov's handshake is described as friendly, just not overly friendly.

Choice (D): Nothing indicates that Zverkov was terrified, just a little cautious and serious. This attempt at a paraphrase distorts the meaning of Zverkov's reaction.

Choice (E): If anything, Zverkov has set up a barrier between himself and the speaker.

3. **The correct answer is (D).** "I am not unmindful" is another way of saying "I am aware," and we get the sense from the context that the speaker is sympathetic and understands the suffering of the audience he's addressing. You can put aside, for the most part, the fancy language "storms of persecution" and "winds of brutality" and condense the second sentence down to the fact that their quest for freedom hasn't gone well (it has been "battered" and "staggered"). The third sentence reiterates that the people the author addresses have suffered greatly, but the fourth sentence is reassuring: such suffering is redemptive, meaning that it can redeem—that is, save them—in the end. (B) works as a paraphrase for this tough text. As for the others:

Choice (A): The author seems to understand the suffering of the audience he's addressing, and is not asking them to redeem themselves, but rather suggests that their unjust suffering will redeem them.

Choice (B): The speaker doesn't talk about creative people, only creative suffering. And by that, he means suffering that creates or produces something else—in this case redemption or reward. This paraphrase distorts the meaning of the word "creative" in this passage.

Choices (C) and (E): The author speaks of the suffering that has already taken place, not danger that may occur in the future.

4. **The correct answer is (A).** "Of late years" simply means "recently" or "lately," so the real difficulty turns out to be the phrases "in a more enlarged sense" and "than it is usual . . . to attribute to them." These phrases work together to describe how the words patriotism and patriot are used in continental Europe as opposed to in the U.S. and Britain. Once you see that a comparison is being made, it's easier to figure out what "a more enlarged sense" means: it means that these words have a broader, or more expansive (bigger), meaning in continental Europe than they do in these other places. (A) simplifies the wording nicely. As for the others:

Choice (B): The author is talking about differences in the way these words are used, not how often they are used.

Choice (C): Nothing in the passage suggests that people in continental Europe are more attached to the words themselves. The passage is about the differing use and differing meanings associated with these words in continental Europe vs. the United States and Great Britain.

Choice (D): The crucial distinction made in the passage is not between the words patriot and patriotism, but rather between two ways of defining patriotism.

Choice (E) makes the wrong comparison. It's continental Europe that's the subject here, not the U.S.

5. **The correct answer is (C).** It captures the gist of the text that comes after the phrase "in short." This valuable conclusion signal word phrase tells you that a summary of the first part of the sentence is coming up. Patriotism there (in continental Europe) means an interest in the human race in general as opposed to an interest in any one specific country. The rest of the text says the same thing, stressing a love of the public and human race above that of a specific people. (C) sums it up nicely. As for the others:

Choices (A) and (E): According to the author, the new meaning of the word "patriotism" is used in all of continental Europe, not just in France, Italy, Spain, and Greece. These countries are cited as places where political struggles took place that brought about the new meaning of patriotism the author describes. However, they are not the only places where the expanded meaning of patriotism is felt. The author's statement about patriotism speaks of the interpretation of those living in continental Europe, not just the people living in France, Italy, Spain, and Greece. These countries are mentioned for a different reason—namely, as the places where the political struggles took place that brought about the new meaning of patriotism the author describes.

Choice (B): While it plays off of the distinction the author makes between the human race and individual countries, (B) entirely leaves out the main topic of the excerpt, patriotism, and the way in which it is understood in continental Europe.

Choice (D): The passage makes no such claim. According to the passage, people in continental Europe define patriotism as a concern for humanity and a commitment to the common good, but there is no claim that all human beings feel patriotic toward one another.

6. **The correct answer is (B).** You may not know what "laurels" means, but it's lumped in with statues, and the author speaks of bestowing them on a certain kind of patriot. You probably know that statues are put up to honor people, so you could have figured out from this context that a 'laurel' is a kind of award too. Now, the author doesn't seem to like such awards, finding them "mischievous as they are childish"—but then we get the all-important contrast signal word "but," which tells us a shift of some sort is coming up. And here it is: If these honors *could* be given to anyone ("bestowed"), then the kind of patriot the author discusses would be it. (B) captures the gist of the author's thought. As for the others:

Choice (A): The author believes that laurels and statues are childish and vain, not the people who would reward patriots with them. In fact, the author doesn't mention such people at all.

Choice (C): The first part matches what the author says pretty well, but this paraphrase falls apart at the end. The author doesn't say that all patriots deserve statues, but rather that "on such a patriot *alone*" should statues and laurels should be bestowed. So only a special kind of patriot, the kind the author favors, should be rewarded with a statue—not *all* patriots, as (C) contends.

Choice (D): This paraphrase distorts the meaning of the word "alone" in the passage. In the passage, the author states that if honors are given, they should only be given to patriots who exhibit the characteristics described in the previous paragraphs. These patriots, *alone*, should be the ones to get awards. In this case, alone means only. The passage doesn't say anything about the patriots acting alone.

Choice (E) is too vague. Patriots might deserve awards, but for something more specific than "good reasons."

COMMON READING QUESTIONS

Questions 1–3 are based on the following passage.

Line Researchers claim that a new magnetic reso-
nance imaging (MRI) technique makes it possible to gauge people's reactions to political
issues and candidates by observing brain ac-
(5) tivity corresponding to a stream of sounds and
images projected inside subjects' goggles during MRI evaluations. For instance, a political
advertisement may cause observable activity
spikes in the amygdala, the part of the brain
(10) that reacts to danger. But what this may actually signify will still be up for interpretation,
bringing the more human elements of political "science" back into play.

1. According to the passage, an increase in
amygdala activity noted in response to an image of a political candidate most likely means
that the subject

A. likes that candidate

B. dislikes that candidate

C. is neutral to that candidate

D. senses danger in relation to that candidate

E. is pessimistic regarding that candidate's
chances for election

2. The author places the word "science" (line 13)
in quotation marks most probably in order to

A. demonstrate that MRI evaluations cannot
properly document the activity of the
amygdala

B. illustrate that science has no role in the
study of politics

C. emphasize the limitations of a purely scientific analysis of political opinions

D. discourage pollsters from using MRI technology to conduct political studies

E. refute the claim that political opinions are
related to brain activity

3. In the context of the passage, the amygdala
provides

A. confirmation that most people find politicians dangerous

B. an example that clarifies a scientific assertion

C. political images used for polling purposes

D. evidence that contrasts with the researchers' hypothesis

E. details regarding the part of the brain most
often analyzed by MRI techniques

Questions 4 and 5 are based on the following passage.

Line   In the early 1940s, radio executives needed a
       way to measure the popularity of their shows
       in order to set appropriate rates for advertise-
       ments. In 1941, Paul Lazarsfeld and Robert
(5)   Merton of Columbia University played radio
       programs for groups representing typical lis-
       teners, instructing them to push buttons indi-
       cating their opinions. Merton asked some
       participants to stay after the initial session to
(10)   discuss their views of the radio shows. These
       spontaneous discussions provided invaluable,
       in-depth feedback to the radio executives. Thus
       was born the "focus group," commonly used
       today to gauge public perception of entertain-
(15)   ment, advertisements, consumer products, and
       political issues.

4. According to the passage, 1940's radio execu-
    tives were interested in

    A. radio listeners' opinions regarding adver-
        tising rates

    B. using radio to promote politicians

    C. measuring public opinion of their products

    D. soliciting feedback from university profes-
        sors

    E. expanding radio content into other media

5. The author suggests that the button-pushing
    exercise described in the passage

    A. yielded the most important information
        from the radio listener study

    B. was not as valuable to radio executives as
        the discussions

    C. produced results that conflicted with the
        opinions expressed in the subsequent dis-
        cussions

    D. provided feedback that was meaningless to
        the radio executives

    E. was designed as a precursor to in-depth
        discussions

ANSWERS AND EXPLANATIONS

1. **The correct answer is (D).** Since the amygdala is the area of the brain that reacts to danger, an increase in activity in this region in response to a candidate's image most likely means that the subject experiences some sense of danger in regard to that candidate.

   However, since we do not know the *nature* of the danger signal, we cannot infer what this means in relation to the subject's feelings toward the candidate. The most obvious interpretation is that the subject dislikes the candidate and therefore feels threatened by the image. But since the results are open to interpretation, it's also possible that the subject *likes* the candidate, and that the sense of danger relates to a fear for his or her safety, or a feeling that the candidate is doing poorly and will lose the election. Without more information we can't be sure whether the subject likes or dislikes the candidate, so (A) and (B) are incorrect. (C) is also wrong: Given the danger signal, chances are the subject isn't indifferent toward the candidate, since something about his or her image sparked a reaction in the amygdala. We may not be able to tell exactly what the subject is feeling, but he or she is probably feeling *something* toward the candidate. (E) is also not inferable, since it's possible that the subject dislikes and fears the candidate and senses danger because he or she believes the candidate will win.

2. **The correct answer is (C).** Despite the impressiveness of the information generated by the MRI tests, the author believes that human interpretation is still necessary to put this information into context. Finishing this thought, the author places the word "science" in the phrase "political science" in quotes. Coming on the heels of the author's belief in the need for human interpretation, we can interpret the quotes as reinforcement of the idea that science cannot analyze politics all by itself.

   Choice (A) is incorrect. The author never questions the ability of MRI machines to measure what's going on in the amygdala. The question is what such activity *means*. (B) and (D) are wrong for similar reasons: The author does not disparage science's role in political analysis or attempt to dissuade pollsters from using it. He merely suggests that human interpretation is still necessary to make the information that science provides usable. Human elements must also come into play, but the author does not dismiss science's potential contribution to political opinion analysis entirely. As for (E), it's common knowledge that thinking originates in the brain, so it stands to reason that all opinions, including political ones, are related to brain activity. Nowhere does the author take issue with this notion, so placing "science" in quotes has nothing to do with this.

3. **The correct answer is (B).** The "scientific assertion" is that MRI technology can be used to gauge political opinions. The phrase "For instance" alerts us that an example is about to appear, and indeed the amygdala is presented as a specific example demonstrating *how* brain activity can be monitored in order to shed light on the subjects' reactions to political stimuli. The discussion of the amygdala thus helps clarify the researchers' assertion in the first sentence by providing a concrete example of how this process described might work.

   Choice (A) distorts the passage. The amygdala senses danger, and the polling concerns political candidates and issues, but nowhere does the author suggest that most people find politicians dangerous, or that the amygdala is somehow involved in confirming this. (C) is incorrect because the goggles supply the images, while the amygdala is a part of the brain that may react to them. As noted above, the amygdala example helps clarify the researchers' claim. It does not provide evidence that goes against their hypothesis (D). The fact that some interpretation may be necessary to evaluate the amygdala's activities doesn't invalidate the claim. Finally, the author never suggests that the amygdala is the most analyzed part of the brain, so (E) cannot be correct.

Note: Photocopying any part of this book is prohibited by law.

4. **The correct answer is (C).** The author states that radio executives wished to measure the popularity of their shows, which, presumably, entailed determining whether people liked them or not. They wanted to find out what the public thought of their shows.

Choice (A) is incorrect. The executives sought listeners' opinions on their shows in order to set advertising rates. They did not solicit opinions on the rates themselves, but rather on the factor (show popularity) that determined those rates. As for (B), the only place politics appears in the passage is as an example of one of the topics of modern-day focus groups. Nowhere does the author state or imply that radio executives had any interest in promoting politicians. (D), like (A), distorts the passage by inappropriately combining two elements of it. The radio executives *did* wish to solicit feedback, and university professors *did* help them do this. But nowhere does the author state that the executives wanted feedback *from* the professors who facilitated the study. (E) is incorrect because other media are never mentioned and are therefore beyond the scope of the passage. As far as we know, the radio folks are simply concerned with radio.

5. **The correct answer is (B).** Since the information garnered from spontaneous discussions proved "invaluable," meaning "priceless," one can infer that this important information was not conveyed by the button-pushing exercise alone. The fact that Merton spontaneously convened these sessions following the button-pushing exercise also supports the notion that the results of the button-pushing exercise did not fully satisfy the professors, and thus did not yield the same value as the subsequent discussions.

Choice (A) gets it backwards, as the "invaluable" and "in-depth" feedback from the discussions seems to be what helped the executives most. Furthermore, nothing suggests that the information received from the two parts of the study was contradictory (C), or that the feedback from the button-pushing segment was meaningless (D). The author merely suggests that more value came out of the discussions. As for (E), the fact that the discussions were "spontaneous"—meaning unplanned and occurring on the spur of the moment—suggests that the button-pushing exercise was not purposely designed as the first part of what became a two-part process.

OTHER READING QUESTIONS

Questions 1 and 2 are based on the following passage.

Line   Illiteracy—the inability to read—and aliteracy—
the ability but unwillingness to read—are on
the rise in the United States. This decrease in
the ability and/or desire to engage the written
(5)   word has been accompanied by an increase in
pictorial representations throughout society.
The words "Walk" and "Don't Walk" on traffic
signs are being replaced by pictures symboliz-
ing these actions. Companies are increasingly
(10)   advertising their logos unaccompanied by their
actual names. E-mail writers and online chat-
ters commonly pepper their messages with
"emoticons," little pictures such as smiley-faces,
to reinforce their sentiments lest the recipient
(15)   misinterpret their written expressions.

1. The author of the passage is primarily interested in

   A.   illustrating modern forms of corporate
communication

   B.   analyzing recent trends in literacy

   C.   evaluating the effectiveness of pictorial
representations

   D.   describing a shift in a society's mode of
symbolization

   E.   comparing literacy rates among nations

2. In line 4, *engage* most nearly means

   A.   interact with

   B.   marry

   C.   replace

   D.   desecrate

   E.   fit into

Questions 3 and 4 are based on the following passage.

Line   Travel once inherently included an element of
adventure, as people made their way by foot,
rail, or boat to their final destination. Modern
tourists, however, often wish to enjoy their
(5)   everyday habits and conveniences within the
setting of an exotic locale. Shuttled between
homogenous airports, planes, taxis, and hotels,
one can travel around the world and literally
experience nothing of it. Joining a tour, one is
(10)   led through an obligatory pre-planned proces-
sion of attractions, scripted right down to the
tour guide's patter. Thus, the tourist need never
experience the spontaneity or personal growth
that once accompanied the traveler's journey.

3. The author's attitude toward the tours mentioned
in this passage could best be described as

   A.   intense interest

   B.   derision

   C.   eager support

   D.   fright

   E.   cautious optimism

4. Which of the following best states the main
point of the passage?

   A.   Modern tourism replicates some but not
all of the excitement of travel from previous eras.

   B.   Traveling by foot and rail is the most efficient way to reach a final destination.

   C.   Travelers looking for spontaneity on their
trips should not take pre-arranged tours.

   D.   Modern tours are purposely structured so
as to limit the tourists' opportunities for
personal growth.

   E.   Modern tourism does not offer the same
experience as travel did in previous eras.

ANSWERS AND EXPLANATIONS

1. **The correct answer is (D).** The author asserts that as people are less willing and able to read, pictures are replacing or supplementing words throughout society. The author then provides three examples of this trend. It appears, then, that the author is interested in describing the shift underway regarding the way in which things in U.S. society are symbolized and represented. The shift from words to pictures represents this change in our manner of symbolization.

   Choice (A) is incorrect. The author mentions one example of corporate communication as evidence for a larger point. The passage is not primarily about how companies communicate. Similarly, while the author does point to a trend in literacy, he does not go on to analyze this trend, but rather describes a repercussion of it: the shift to pictorial representation. However, the author does not evaluate the *effectiveness* of such representations, (C). He merely asserts that they are on the rise as illiteracy and aliteracy increase. (E) is incorrect because no other nations besides the United States are mentioned or alluded to in the passage.

2. **The correct answer is (A).** The author begins by discussing a drop in the ability and desire to read, and then presents the sentence with the word in question: "This decrease in the ability and/or desire to *engage* the written word has been accompanied by an increase in pictorial representations throughout society." Since the author has already stated that more and more people can't or don't want to read, we can infer that he means they don't want to deal with, read, or struggle with writing. The author appears to say that some people don't want to have anything to do with the written word. In this context, "interact with" makes the most sense and best preserves the meaning of the sentence when substituted for "engage."

   Choice (B), "marry," has some relation to the meaning of engagement referring to a pre-wedding period, but marry is not the same as engage, nor does it make sense when read back into the passage. (E), meanwhile, plays off of another meaning of engage—namely, to connect or fit into place—which is also out of place in the context of the passage. "Replace," choice (C), better describes what pictures are doing to the written word. As for (D), "desecrate" is not a proper synonym for "engage," and in any case the desecration of the written word (that is, the opposite of finding it holy) seems to be increasing, according to the author. So the notion of a decrease in the desecration of the written word would tend to go against the point of the passage.

3. **The correct answer is (B).** To exhibit derision is to exhibit scorn or disdain, and indeed this author does disparage the tour activity as one in which people are led around passively according to a planned itinerary, with the entire "scripted" experience lacking in spontaneity. These factors add up to a strong show of disapproval of such tours on the part of the author, which automatically eliminates (C) and (E) from consideration. The harsh description she puts forth shows that the author neither supports nor is optimistic about such tours.

(A) is incorrect, as "intense interest" is too mild to represent the author's dislike of tours. Such a strong interest could very well imply a favorable opinion. The author may in fact be intensely interested in the issue of tours, but the correct choice must include something that indicates disdain for them. As for (D), while we can safely assume that the author would not wish to take such a tour, nothing indicates that fear of them. To the author, they simply do not seem appealing.

4. **The correct answer is (E).** The author describes how the traveler's journey once included an element of adventure that has largely been replaced by a tourist experience devoid of spontaneity and personal growth. Choice (E) accurately captures this sentiment while nicely summarizing the passage's final sentence.

(A) is incorrect, as there's little sense that the author believes that modern tourism offers any of the adventure or excitement of the travel of bygone eras. (B) is incorrect because the author is not primarily concerned with efficiency. If anything, traveling by foot and rail is less efficient than traveling by plane in terms of the time it takes to reach the final destination. But the author is concerned with the quality of the travel experience, not its "efficiency." (C) no doubt represents a sentiment with which the author would agree, but does not rise to the level of the passage's main point. The tour example is mentioned as evidence of the difference between modern tourism and past travel experiences, the main focus of the passage. As for (D), the author does not argue that tours are intentionally created to limit growth opportunities; she merely states that this is the effect they have.

Note: Photocopying any part of this book is prohibited by law.

UNDERSTANDING SENTENCE COMPLETIONS

1. Emily's success was partly due to her ——; she always believed that she would excel at any task she undertook.

   A. education

   B. insecurity

   C. conduct

   D. confidence

   E. preparedness

2. Edith Wharton's heroines often suffer great —— and are defeated by such challenges by the end of her novels.

   A. fortune

   B. hardship

   C. discord

   D. sympathy

   E. hysteria

3. Since previous delays had been very expensive for his company, the manager was —— to grant his contractors an additional extension.

   A. unwilling

   B. eager

   C. expected

   D. disposed

   E. forced

4. Research shows that speech patterns develop by ——, as babies attempt to repeat the sounds that they hear around them.

   A. assimilation

   B. imitation

   C. diversion

   D. memorization

   E. instinct

5. The cotton gin —— cotton harvesting in the nineteenth century by drastically increasing the speed and ease of gathering cotton.

   A. revolutionized

   B. initiated

   C. demoted

   D. marginalized

   E. hindered

6. Contrary to expectations, the project that introduced more fish into local streams eventually —— their population after competition for food became fierce.

   A. stabilized

   B. depleted

   C. expanded

   D. revived

   E. equalized

7. Laura's demeanor in the meeting was ——; her outward expressions gave no indication of her feelings.

A. off-putting

B. transparent

C. atypical

D. inscrutable

E. prevalent

8. The severity of a drought is often —— the water levels of local reservoirs since they depend on the rain for their water supplies.

A. predicted by

B. inconsistent with

C. accompanied by

D. indicated by

E. saturated by

9. The common loss of entire animal species —— some scientists, but others see it as a —— stage in the planet's development.

A. comforts..predictable

B. worries..recent

C. affects..reassuring

D. confuses..continuous

E. concerns..necessary

10. *Robinson Crusoe* is a novel that is dominated by its ——, the primary character who narrates his adventures that he experienced while on a deserted island.

A. villain

B. illustrator

C. audience

D. protagonist

E. ventriloquist

11. While the children's pranks were initially ——, their behavior became increasingly —— as they grew older.

A. simple..sedate

B. harmless..malicious

C. withdrawn..entertaining

D. destructive..foolhardy

E. conscientious..praiseworthy

12. Talent and perseverance are both —— traits, but the individual who has both is truly ——.

A. rare..insightful

B. valuable..abnormal

C. uncommon..exceptional

D. special..deprived

E. standard..daunting

13. Practically every sentence that Jonathan spoke was ——, leaving his correspondents confused and unsure of his meaning.

A. enigmatic

B. pensive

C. poignant

D. aesthetic

E. indulgent

14. Although the data from the poll was —— to the candidate, she —— her campaign for office.

A. surprising..reformed

B. promising..expanded

C. dissapointing..terminated

D. desirable..renewed

E. discouraging..continued

15. Larry was the object of an extensive —— campaign, receiving visits and proposals from various agents who wanted him to attend their schools.

- A. smear
- B. recruitment
- C. propaganda
- D. catering
- E. advertisement

16. The audit showed that the firm had —— its earnings for years; it had systematically underreported its profits in order to pay fewer taxes.

- A. withheld
- B. divulged
- C. misrepresented
- D. reprised
- E. consolidated

17. Although he is now remembered primarily for his contributions to geometry, Pythagoras was more —— in his own time as a philosopher.

- A. neglected
- B. denigrated
- C. vindicated
- D. renowned
- E. berated

18. One of the most pressing problems facing modern libraries is the lack of space, and —— shelves are becoming even more —— as libraries continue to acquire new books each year.

- A. uninviting..restricted
- B. crowded..cramped
- C. ample..alienating
- D. spacious..expansive
- E. compressed..rigid

19. The historian —— the inconsistent information she uncovered in order to fabricate a —— account of the event.

- A. emphasized..homogenous
- B. concealed..unified
- C. harmonized..mediocre
- D. categorized..disparate
- E. filtered..reliable

20. Even though members of the media claim to be —— when reporting news, most Americans feel that news reports are —— and represent the views of the reporter.

- A. objective..biased
- B. partisan..shoddy
- C. perceptive..equitable
- D. dispassionate..reliable
- E. erratic..slanted

ANSWERS AND EXPLANATIONS

1. **The correct answer is (D).** The key to Emily's success is the word in the blank, and conveniently everything following the semicolon describes what that missing word means. (Remember that the semicolon is a Green Light clue, so what follows it will give a definition or conclusion for what came before.) Therefore, we're looking for a word that would characterize Emily's faith in her abilities, and "confidence" fits the bill. While Emily's education, conduct, or preparedness might assist her, there's nothing in the sentence that specifically points to any of those qualities. "Insecurity" in (B) is just too negative, so (D) it is.

2. **The correct answer is (B).** If the heroines are defeated by "*such* challenges," then the word in the blank must be a synonym for challenges. The word "such" tells you that the challenges were mentioned earlier in the sentence, and the only place where that could have happened is in the blank. Also remember that the word "and" is a Green Light clue, which reinforces that the information in the second half of the sentence will logically go along with the information in the first half. "Hardship" is the closest synonym to "challenges" and is indeed the correct choice. (A) and (D) are too positive; one wouldn't be defeated by fortune or sympathy. Further, there's nothing in the sentence to suggest that the heroines suffer hysteria or emotional excitability. Finally, "discord" is appropriately negative, but there's no indication in the sentence that the challenges faced by the heroines have anything to do with conflict, or discord. (B) is therefore the right choice.

3. **The correct answer is (A).** We know that the manager has had to deal with several expensive delays, so it's safe to assume that he doesn't want to deal with more. The Green Light cause-and-effect clue "since" further supports that assumption. The word in the blank should describe the manager's reluctance to grant the extension, so look for a word that means something like "reluctant." "Unwilling" in (A) is perfect. "Eager" and "disposed" give us the opposite

of what we want, since both choices would suggest that the manager *wanted* to grant another extension. (C) and (E) are out because there's nothing in the sentence that points to them: we have no evidence that the manager was being ordered or was expected to grant an extension.

4. **The correct answer is (B).** We're looking for a word to describe the way that speech patterns develop, and since we're told that babies learn speech patterns by repeating what they hear, the word in the blank should mean something like "repetition." "Imitation" in choice (B) fits the bill. None of the other choices is directly supported by the sentence: "assimilation" means absorption, so that can't be right. Similarly, "diversion," "memorization," and "instinct" are fine words but none of them means "repetition." Since the sentence describes learning through repetition, or imitation, the word in the blank absolutely must describe that activity.

5. **The correct answer is (A).** Because of the cotton gin, cotton harvesting became much more efficient. So, since we're looking for a word to describe the very positive impact of the cotton gin on cotton harvesting, we'll look for a word that means something like "greatly improved." (C), (D), and (E) are out since they have negative meanings. We don't have enough information to say that the cotton gin "initiated" or began cotton harvesting, and actually the sentence suggests that the cotton gin improved a practice that already existed. Eliminate (B). That leaves us with (A), which is correct because "revolutionized" does describe a very favorable change.

6. **The correct answer is (B).** A project that added fish to streams had the unexpected effect of (blanking) the population of fish since the fish started to compete with each other for food. If the consequences of adding the fish were unexpected, and the fish were competing with each other for food, then their population must have decreased in the long term.

Note: Photocopying any part of this book is prohibited by law.

Looking for a word that means "decreased," you're left with "depleted" in (B). The other choices would not describe an unexpected consequence of adding fish to streams, so they cannot be right.

7. **The correct answer is (D).** The semicolon is a Green Light definition signal. Everything following the semicolon defines Laura's demeanor, so we're looking for a word that describes a demeanor that's hard to read and doesn't show what the person is thinking. "Inscrutable," or unreadable, works well. "Transparent" is the opposite of what we want; "prevalent," meaning very common, doesn't make sense as a type of demeanor; and "off-putting" and "atypical" are not perfectly consistent with the sentence. (D) it is.

8. **The correct answer is (D).** We know that the reservoirs depend on rain, and because of this the severity of a drought has some relationship with the water levels in the reservoirs. If the reservoirs depend on rain directly, then their water levels should show how much rain has been received, and therefore those water levels should be able to tell us how bad the drought is. We now have enough information to predict that the words in the blank will mean something like "demonstrated by." (B) is the opposite of what we're looking for, so eliminate it. (C) and (E) don't make sense in context—the severity of a drought can't be accompanied by or saturated by water levels. (A) might be tempting, but there's nothing to indicate that the water levels *predict* how bad the drought will be. Actually, the information we receive suggests that the water levels and the drought are determined by rain at the same time. That leaves us with (D), and since "indicated by" does match our prediction, it's the right answer.

9. **The correct answer is (E).** The sentence describes two reactions to the loss of entire animal species, and the phrase "but others" tells us that the reactions are different, since the word "but" is a U-Turn clue indicating contrast. We can't really predict what those reactions are (though it's a good bet that the first reaction to such a loss will be negative, since that's the ex-

pected reaction), so we should go through the answer choices and look for two words that describe quite different reactions. (A) and (B) do not describe a clear contrast (remember, you're not just looking for words that mean different things, but that describe *contradictory* or opposing reactions), so eliminate them. (C) presents something of a contrast, but not one that works, since if one is reassured then one is affected. The contrast doesn't hold up, so remove (C). (E) is correct because it describes a contrast: one group is concerned and the other is more comfortable with the development.

10. **The correct answer is (D).** Here we have a typical definition sentence: the word in the blank is defined by what follows, so we're looking for a word that describes the main character of a novel. "Protagonist" fits that description. Nothing tells us that this character is a bad main character in particular, and that's why (A) isn't right. Further, a primary character isn't necessarily an "illustrator," an "audience," or a "ventriloquist," but a protagonist is by definition the main character. That's why (D) is right.

11. **The correct answer is (B).** We can't really predict what happens to the children's behavior, though the word "prank" suggests that their actions weren't initially very serious. We do know that the children's behavior changes significantly as they age. The words in the correct choice must therefore contrast with each other, so eliminate (A), (C), and (E). "Simple" and "sedate," or calm, don't contradict each other. Similarly, "withdrawn" and "entertaining" aren't in any obvious way related to each other, especially not as opposites. Finally, "conscientious" and "praiseworthy" are both too positive to express a contrast. Upon closer inspection, you might see that (D) can be eliminated as well: "foolhardy," or careless behavior doesn't have to be different from "destructive" behavior. "Harmless" and "malicious," on the other hand, do contrast with each other, so (B) is the right choice.

Note: Photocopying any part of this book is prohibited by law.

12. **The correct answer is (C).** Normally, the word "but" indicates contrast. In this sentence, however, it signifies degree. Talent and perseverance individually are (blank), but together they are even more (blank). Since talent and perseverance are both positive qualities, the words in the correct choice will have positive meanings. Therefore, we can eliminate (B) and (D) since "abnormal" and "deprived" are too negative. We can look to the remaining choices for two words that describe the same quality, with the second word describing it more strongly (so something like "good…excellent" would work). You can eliminate (A) and (E) since "rare" and "insightful" describe very different traits, as do "standard" and "daunting," which means intimidating. We're left with (C), and since "exceptional" does mean "very uncommon," that's the right answer.

13. **The correct answer is (A).** If Jonathan leaves others confused, then his sentences must be confusing. Look for a choice that means "confusing" and you're left with "enigmatic," meaning unclear or difficult to decipher. A sentence can't really be "pensive," or thoughtful, or "indulgent." Finally, there's no indication that the sentences are "poignant," meaning touching or profound, or "aesthetic," meaning attractive. Only choice (A) is directly supported by the sentence.

14. **The correct answer is (E).** The word "although" in this sentence is a U-Turn clue that tells us that the sentence will contain a contrast: though the polling data suggests that the candidate should do one thing, she does the other. We can't predict what the poll said or what the candidate did, but we can still move on to the answer choices, knowing that the right one will give us two words that contradict each other. Only choice (E) would create a clear contrast in the sentence: even though the data was discouraging, the candidate nevertheless prolonged her campaign.

15. **The correct answer is (B).** Larry received visits from agents who were trying to attract him, and the word in the blank has to describe the agents' actions. "Recruitment" perfectly defines such wooing practices, since one who recruits another wants to attract that person to his or her school. There's no indication that Larry was "smeared" (A), meaning criticized, or received "catering," (D). It's not clear what a "catering campaign" would be, exactly. Even if one assumes, though one shouldn't, that "catering" means that the campaign was catered to Larry, "recruitment" still defines the actions of the agents more accurately. Similarly, "propaganda" and "advertisement" don't describe the agents' behavior as well as "recruitment" does. You wouldn't necessarily use propaganda or advertising to attract someone to your school, but if you're trying to attract them, then you are by definition recruiting them. That's why (B) is the correct choice.

16. **The correct answer is (C).** The semicolon is a Green Light clue: everything after the semicolon describes what the firm had done. So, we need a word for the blank that means "underreported." Our closest option is (C), "misrepresented," since to underreport is to misrepresent. If the firm had "divulged" its earnings, it reported them, and that's not consistent with the firm's actions as described in the sentence. "Reprised," meaning renewed, and "consolidated" don't have anything to do with underreporting profits, so they're out. Finally, the firm "withheld" information, perhaps, but it didn't withhold earnings in particular. Also, it's not clear what it would really mean to withhold earnings in any case—from whom were they withheld? Go with (C).

17. **The correct answer is (D).** The word "although" signals a contrast between Pythagoras' reputation in his own time and his reputation now. Now he's known mostly in the context of geometry (the Pythagorean theorem), so if his earlier reputation was different and had some relation to philosophy, as the sentence indicates, then he must have been better known as a philosopher in the olden days. Look for something like "well-known" and you're left with "renowned." (A), (B), and (E) are too negative; there's nothing in the sentence to suggest that his former reputation was negative. The contrast in the sentence is between *what* is he known for now and *what* he was known for then, not

between his favorable reputation now and his unfavorable reputation then. Finally, (C) is wrong because "vindicated," meaning "proven correct," again does not create the contrast that the sentence requires.

18. **The correct answer is (B).** While you always need to focus on the meaning of the whole sentence, that's particularly true in this case. If libraries lack space, then shelves must be pretty full to begin with. The acquisition of more books must only make the problem worse. Knowing that, we can predict that the word in the first blank should mean "full" and the second "more full." (B) meets those requirements. You can eliminate (A) because there's no indication that the shelves were "uninviting"; all we know is that there wasn't much space. "Ample" and "spacious," synonyms of each other, are both the opposite of what we need, taking (C) and (D) out of consideration. Finally, "rigid" doesn't mean "very full," but "immovable." That leaves us with (B).

19. **The correct answer is (B).** As it is, the sentence doesn't give us many hints; we're told that the historian did something with inconsistent information in order to make up ("fabricate") a certain kind of account. If the historian "uncovered" inconsistent information and then made up an account, she must have ignored the actual information she discovered. Look through the choices for a first word that means "ignored." (A), (C), and (D) aren't negative enough: if she made something up, then she must have dismissed the information she had. Also, if she fabricated the account, then the account must not be reliable, so we can eliminate (E). That leaves us with (B), which does indeed work for both blanks.

20. **The correct answer is (A).** We're given more information about the second blank, so that's a good place to start. The U-Turn clue "even though" alerts you to contrast in the sentence, so Americans must feel one way about the media, while the media itself feels differently. If Americans think that reporters are (blank) *and* "represent the views of the reporter," then the word in the second blank must mean something like "represent reporter's views." "Equitable" and "reliable" can be eliminated. Remembering the contrast, if Americans think that reporters are representing their own views, then members of the media must not agree. For the first blank, we can predict something that means "unaffected by their own opinions" or "unbiased." "Objective" describes that idea. "Partisan" means biased, and that's the opposite of what the sentence calls for. Finally, "erratic," meaning inconsistent, doesn't describe whether the reporters rely on their own opinions. (A) it is.

SENTENCE COMPLETION STRATEGY

1. Sometimes considered —— and outdated, the abacus continues to be used as a calculation device in many cultures.

   A. timeless

   B. antiquated

   C. historic

   D. indispensable

   E. premature

2. The book review was not only critical but ——; it passionately attacked both the novel and its author.

   A. forceful

   B. spiteful

   C. vivid

   D. constructive

   E. irrelevant

3. Novice rafters tend to —— the danger posed by the river because of its —— appearance, even though warning signs are posted around the area.

   A. underestimate..placid

   B. perceive..restrained

   C. exaggerate..deceptive

   D. belittle..rugged

   E. disregard..ominous

4. Because the novel vividly —— the negative consequences of pollution, it appealed to ——.

   A. revealed..legislators

   B. misrepresented..scientists

   C. downplayed..botanists

   D. concealed..conservationists

   E. portrayed..environmentalists

5. Although the computer is able to —— information that has been programmed into it, it is unable to innovate and —— new data.

   A. store..generate

   B. record..conceal

   C. remember..initiate

   D. process..inspire

   E. invent..recall

6. The aspiring artist was often —— by his inability to make his portraits —— the beautiful images in his head.

   A. misled..share

   B. heartened..evoke

   C. frustrated..resemble

   D. encouraged..recreate

   E. defeated..escape

7. While doctors recognize the benefits of early detection of illnesses, early symptoms are often so —— that they are difficult to ——.

   A. subtle..perceive

   B. distinctive..examine

   C. mild..ignore

   D. typical..review

   E. destructive..identify

8. The printing press was notably ——, producing few books until the invention of the moveable typeface allowed texts to be printed more ——.

    A. stilted..carefully

    B. refined..flawlessly

    C. inefficient..expeditiously

    D. sophisticated..hastily

    E. plodding..aggressively

9. Although domesticated cats may seem simply —— when they chase strings or bat balls, the —— demonstrated by such quick and adept movements makes them effective predators.

    A. playful..agility

    B. endearing..forethought

    C. instinctive..courage

    D. carefree..aggression

    E. threatening..vivacity

10. Because census reports are often inaccurate, researchers look to —— materials to —— the population more reliably.

    A. native..identify

    B. synthetic..determine

    C. additional..restore

    D. contradictory..gauge

    E. supplemental..measure

11. David frequently relocated and changed jobs, and this —— lifestyle made it difficult for others to stay in touch with him.

    A. heedless

    B. sporadic

    C. furtive

    D. itinerant

    E. deliberate

12. Jamie never doubted the veracity of her own opinions and was therefore —— the views of others which disagreed with her own.

    A. vehement towards

    B. accommodating to

    C. tempted by

    D. resistant to

    E. enamored with

13. The lawyer regularly complained that American society was too —— even while his business —— because of the steady increase in lawsuits.

    A. capitalistic..conspired

    B. forgiving..deteriorated

    C. litigious..prospered

    D. vindictive..suffered

    E. introverted..benefited

14 The committee decided that the annual bonus should no longer be —— but guaranteed within the terms of the employees' contracts.

    A. punitive

    B. equitable

    C. unconditional

    D. discretionary

    E. compulsory

15. The CEO was —— controversy after his company's disreputable trading practices were made public.

    A. impervious to

    B. steeped in

    C. unaccustomed to

    D. indignant with

    E. immune to

16. While the invention of e-mail led —— to —— the end of all personal interactions, the impact of the new technology was not so catastrophic.

A. promoters..foresee

B. naysayers..hasten

C. detractors..prophesy

D. enthusiasts..anticipate

E. cynics..euphemize

17. The survey sought to determine the relationship between exercise and eating habits, but it was criticized since the researchers questioned only those who never exercise, and who were therefore not —— the population as a whole.

A. inclined toward

B. accepted by

C. allied with

D. conducive to

E. representative of

18. In contrast to the flamboyant and colorful outfits that he usually wore, the pale green suit seemed —— to his colleagues.

A. repressed

B. eccentric

C. characteristic

D. outlandish

E. staid

19. Fans of traditional art featuring a range of colors were initially dismissive of the new —— paintings.

A. vapid

B. theoretical

C. vibrant

D. luminous

E. monochrome

20. While James Joyce is not best known for his sense of humor, many of his readers believe that *Finnegan's Wake*, for instance, is —— with ——.

A. replete..perspective

B. sparse..jovialty

C. bereft..levity

D. brimming..wit

E. permeated..satire

ANSWERS AND EXPLANATIONS

1. **The correct answer is (B).** The abacus is considered to be (blank) "*and* outdated," so the word in the blank will describe a trait that is similar to "outdated." Also, the opinion described by the blank and the word "outdated" contrasts with the information in the rest of the sentence, where we learn that the abacus is still useful. That means that the first blank will be filled with a word that means something like "useless" or "outdated." (A) and (D) are positive, so eliminate them. (C) is neutral, and that can't be right either; the view described at the beginning of the sentence is definitely negative. Of the remaining choices, (B) is correct because "antiquated" means old and useless. "Premature" describes a different idea; if the abacus were premature, that would mean that it was invented too early. Nothing in the sentence really suggests that, so stick with (B).

2. **The correct answer is (B).** Whenever you see the formula "not only...but (also)..." you know that the word or phrase following "but" expresses the same idea as that following "not only," but to a stronger degree (i.e., not only bad but evil). So, since the review "was not only critical but (blank), we know that the word in the blank must mean something like "very critical" or "excessively critical." The rest of the sentence defines the missing word more precisely: it must describe a personal and passionate attack. Choice (B), "spiteful" is the correct choice because it is very negative and suggests a personal attack. Choices (A) and (C) — "forceful" and "vivid" — might describe some of the character of the criticism, but neither is sufficiently negative given the rest of the sentence. "Constructive" is far too positive, and "irrelevant" makes no sense, since it doesn't describe a harsh, personal criticism.

3. **The correct answer is (A).** The phrase "even though" is a U-Turn signal, alerting you to contrast in the sentence. Indeed, we see that the novice, or new, rafters are acting a certain way "even though" warning signs are posted, so they must be ignoring those signs. If they aren't pay-ing attention to warning signs, then they must not be taking seriously the danger presented by the river. Look at the first words in the choices for one that means something like "underrate" or "downplay." You can eliminate (B) and (C). The rafters are making this error because of the river's appearance, and if the appearance leads them to minimize its danger, then the river must not appear to be dangerous. Therefore, look for a word like "safe." "Ominous," meaning threatening, and "rugged" are out, leaving us with (A). Read it back into the sentence and you'll see that it works perfectly.

4. **The correct answer is (E).** If the novel treats the negative effects of pollution "vividly," then it must be describing those effects, since "vividly" generally describes a true, realistic portrayal. Look for a word like "described" for the first blank. Eliminate (B), (C), and (D). If the novel is describing these negative effects well, then it must appeal to people who are concerned about pollution, and "environmentalists" better describes this group than "legislators." Legislators are not necessarily concerned about the environment, while environmentalists are by definition. That's why (E) is the correct choice.

5. **The correct answer is (A).** Let's start with the second blank: the computer cannot innovate, or act on its own, *and* it cannot (blank) new data. The word "and" is a Green Light clue, telling us that the word in the second blank will be compatible with "innovate," so look for something that means "create" or "make." "Generate" and "initiate" are the only remaining options. You might also keep (D) at this point, but it's not possible to "inspire new data." To inspire is to give hope, and data can't have hope. Also, it's impossible to "recall new data" because if the data is recalled, or remembered, then it can't be new. Returning to the first blank, we know that the first half of the sentence must describe a different idea since it begins with the word "although." If everything following the comma describes what the computer *cannot* do, then it makes sense for everything else to describe

what the computer *can* do. We know that the computer can't create new information but we're told that it can do something else with information. Our options are "store" and "remember." A computer can't "remember" since remembering requires a mind, so "store" is our only option. (A) it is.

6. **The correct answer is (C).** The artist is somehow affected by an "inability." That inability must have a negative effect on him, so look for a word for the first blank that is negative. Eliminate (B) and (D) because "heartened" is a synonym for "encouraged," and both are too positive. Moving to the second blank, we see that we're still dealing with the artist's inability. He can't make the portraits (blank) his mental images, so look for a verb that might make sense in this context. "Share" doesn't work since a portrait can't share an image. Also, the first word in (A), "misled," doesn't make sense in the context of the sentence, either. Finally, a portrait can't really "escape" an image, so (C) looks like the right choice. Read it in and you'll see that it does indeed work.

7. **The correct answer is (A).** The word "while" is a U-Turn clue, creating a contrast in the sentence: while doctors see the benefits of early detection, there appears to be some obstacle. The two blanks will work together, since they are both on the same side of the contrast. The right answer choice will contain two words that work together to create one idea, describing an obstacle to early detection. If the symptoms were "subtle" then they would be hard to "perceive" or see, so keep (A). "Distinctive" or very different symptoms would probably be easier to examine, so eliminate (B). Take out (C) since "mild" symptoms would be easy, not difficult, to ignore. The words in (D) aren't related to each other in any solid way—being typical doesn't make something easy or hard to review—so eliminate (D). Finally, (E) is out because a destructive symptom wouldn't always be hard to identify. It could be, but being destructive doesn't itself make something hard to identify. If something is subtle, on the other hand, it must be hard to notice, so (A) is correct.

8. **The correct answer is (C).** In its early state, the printing press produced "few books," so the first blank should be filled with something like "unproductive" or "slow." Eliminate (B) and (D) since both suggest that the early printing press worked quite well. The invention of the moveable typeface changed the situation, and since few books were printed before its invention, we can assume that more books were printed afterward. Looking for a word for the second blank that means "quickly" or "effectively," we can eliminate (A). If you're tempted by (E), try reading it into the sentence and you might see that "plodding," meaning "progressing slowly and with difficulty" doesn't really contrast with "aggressively." To print aggressively doesn't necessarily equal printing quickly. On the other hand, "inefficient" and "expeditiously" in (C) create a perfect contrast (the press wasn't productive and then it was), and that's why (C) is the correct answer.

9. **The correct answer is (A).** The sentence starts with the U-Turn clue "although," alerting you to contrast in the statement. Although cats seem (blank) when they play, what makes them able to play also makes them good predators. The word "although" points to the contrast between the two parts of the sentence, and because of it we can predict that the word in the first blank means the opposite of predatorial. Look for something like "harmless" and you're left with "playful" and "endearing," and perhaps "carefree." According to the sentence, the word in the second blank describes cats' "quick and adept movements" that are demonstrated when they play with strings or balls. Looking through our remaining options, we can eliminate "forethought" and "aggression." There's no indication that cats that are playing are thinking ahead, and playing with string and balls isn't really aggressive behavior. Also, "aggressive" doesn't describe "quick and adept movements," though "agility" does. That leaves (A), the correct choice.

10. **The correct answer is (E).** Census reports are inaccurate, so in order to (blank) the population "more reliably," researchers look to (blank) materials. Since we're told that the researchers want

to do something more reliably, and since we read that census reports aren't reliable indicators of the population, the researchers must be hoping to get a more reliable measurement of the population. Therefore, the word in the second blank should mean something like "count." Eliminate (C). You can also eliminate (A) because the point of census reports isn't to identify the population but to figure out how many people are in it. Back to the first blank, we know that the researchers can't be relying on the inaccurate census reports if they want accurate results, so they must be using other materials. Use "other" as a rough prediction and look through the choices: "synthetic," meaning either "compounded" or "artificial," and "contradictory" are off track. Only (E) remains, and since it makes sense when you read it in, stick with it.

11. **The correct answer is (D).** All we know about David's lifestyle is that he moved a lot and had a lot of jobs. Looking for a word that describes that lifestyle, we're left with "itinerant," a word that describes someone who moves around a lot. "Heedless," or careless, doesn't describe what we know about David's lifestyle. The same goes for "furtive," meaning secretive, and "deliberate." Finally, "sporadic," or irregular, doesn't really describe a kind of lifestyle. Only "itinerant" is consistent with what the sentence tells us about David's habits.

12. **The correct answer is (D).** If Jamie never doubts that her own opinions are correct, then she must not be very tolerant of people who disagree with her. The Green Light clue "therefore" confirms the direction of the sentence to be cause-and-effect. So, let's predict "intolerant of" and look through the choices. (B), (C), and (E) suggest that Jamie is somehow open to those different opinions, but that can't be the case if, as we're told, she never doubts that she's right. "Vehement" means emphatic, and that option doesn't work because it's vague. "Vehement" doesn't suggest disagreement or intolerance; it just describes a level of feeling. That leaves us with (D), and since "resistant to" matches our prediction and fits in well with the sentence, it's correct.

13. **The correct answer is (C).** If lawsuits are increasing, then our lawyer's business must be doing well. Look to fill the second blank with something like "increased." (A), (B), and (D) can be eliminated. A business can't "conspire" or plot; only people can do that. Also, you have to conspire to *do* something, so there are two ways that choice (A) doesn't work grammatically. If there are lots of lawsuits and the lawyer frequently complains about American society, then he must be complaining about Americans' love of lawsuits, even though he benefits from such lawsuits. "Litigious" describes someone who files a lot of lawsuits, so that works well. "Introverted" means shy, and it's not clear why the lawyer would complain about that. (C) it is.

14. **The correct answer is (D).** If the contracts should be guaranteed, then they must not be guaranteed already. The "but" points out a contrast between "guaranteed" and what the contracts are now, so we need a word that means "not guaranteed." "Discretionary" in (D) means exactly that. "Punitive" and "equitable" don't fit because they don't contrast with "guaranteed"; something punitive is used to punish, and "equitable" means fair. (C) and (E) are out because "unconditional" and "compulsory" basically mean "guaranteed." Only "discretionary" means "not guaranteed," and that's why it's the right choice.

15. **The correct answer is (B).** If the company's unethical practices have been publicized, then the CEO must have become familiar with controversy. Look for a choice that means "involved in" and you're left with (B). We know only that the company's problems went public; we don't know enough to say how they personally affected the CEO, whether she was "impervious to," "unaccustomed with," "indignant with," or "immune to" the controversy. All we can do is follow the signs in the sentence, and they lead to (B).

16. **The correct answer is (C).** The invention of e-mail wasn't "*so* catastrophic," so according to the logic of the sentence there must have been a group of people who thought that it would be. Those people must be described early in the

sentence, and it's easier to come up with a prediction for the first blank after we deal with the second. If this group of people worried that e-mail might prove "catastrophic," then they probably thought that it would lead to "the end of all personal interactions." Let's predict "expect" for the second blank and move to the choices. To "euphemize" is to substitute a word or phrase for another and weaken the original meaning (so a euphemism for war would be disagreement). That's not right, so take out (E). The other choices can stay for now. For the first blank, we need a word to describe people who thought that e-mail would have a catastrophic impact. "Promoters" and "enthusiasts" wouldn't describe such people. Read in the two remaining choices and you'll see why (B) can't work. Naysayers, or critics, would oppose the negative effects of e-mail; they wouldn't "hasten" them, making those bad consequences happen more quickly. (C) remains.

17. **The correct answer is (E).** We know that the survey was "criticized" and that the second half of the sentence explains why. If the researchers only questioned people who don't exercise, then the researchers surveyed a limited portion of the population. Therefore, the people surveyed must not have accurately represented the population as a whole. Now we can look through our choices for something like "indicative of." "Representative of" works: if only a certain group was questioned, then that group couldn't have represented the general population. The group must have been "inclined toward," "accepted by," "conducive to," and "allied with" the population (even though some of those phrases aren't grammatically great) since they are part of that population. The sentence doesn't describe the group's relationship with the *rest* of the population, but with the population, and people who don't exercise aren't separate from the population. So, whether you choose (E) directly or get to it by eliminating the other choices, (E) is the right choice.

18. **The correct answer is (E).** You don't even have to guess if there is contrast in this sentence—it includes the phrase "in contrast to"!

This particular outfit contrasts with the "flamboyant and colorful outfits," so it must not be flamboyant or colorful. Our correct choice will describe the opposite of flamboyant (meaning showy and extravagant), so we can start with a prediction of "plain." "Eccentric" and "outlandish" are synonyms, not antonyms, of "flamboyant," so we can eliminate them. We know that this outfit is not "characteristic" because it differs from the kind of clothes the person normally wears. Also, clothing can't really be "repressed," meaning something that's kept inside, like emotions. "Staid," which means sober and undistinctive, fits perfectly.

19. **The correct answer is (E).** People who like paintings with lots of colors weren't fond of these other paintings at first, so these other paintings must not have had a lot of colors. Look for something like "uncolorful" and you're left with "monochrome," meaning "of one color." If the new paintings were "vibrant" or "luminous," both meaning "bright," then they wouldn't really contrast with the colorful paintings that the people usually liked. Also, "vapid" means boring, and there's no indication that these paintings were boring (not having a lot of colors doesn't necessarily mean boring). Finally, there's no evidence that the paintings were "theoretical" or impractical.

20. **The correct answer is (D).** We're told that Joyce isn't well-known for his humor, and since this sentence creates a contrast between Joyce's reputation and the readers described in the second part of the sentence, then those readers must actually think that Joyce is funny. It's hard to predict words for the blanks individually, so look for two words that would work together to mean "funny." "Perspective" isn't funny, so (A) can be eliminated. If the novel is "sparse with joviality," then it would have little, not lots of humor. Eliminate (B). If the novel is "bereft" or lacking of "levity" or lightheartedness, then it wouldn't be funny. If the novel is brimming with, or full of, wit, then it would be funny. Keep (D). Finally, "satire" doesn't necessarily mean humorous; a satire can be funny, but it can also be critical. (D) is your answer.

PAIRED PASSAGES

The following passages are about hyperfiction, a recent form of writing that uses computer hypertext to construct fictional stories.

Passage 1

Line In his famous phrase "the medium is the message," Marshall McLuhan implied that all new communication technologies determine the kinds of ideas that can be channeled through
(5) them. It is no surprise then that our most recent and important communication technology, the computer, has radically altered the way stories are told. The computer makes extensive use of a navigation device called hypertext, a
(10) viewable text or image object that connects various screens or objects. The most common examples are the links that connect web pages on the Internet. Although such hypertext links are most often associated with surfing the Net
(15) for information or products, fiction authors have begun utilizing the power of hypertext for storytelling.

Hypertext has spawned a revolution in the art of narrative comparable only to the inven-
(20) tion of the novel. Much as the novel expanded the boundaries of expression above and beyond the capabilities of the essay, hyperfiction is breaking down the conventions of the book. Traditional books have a narrative structure in
(25) which the story proceeds in linear fashion from page to page in a fixed order. The reader may certainly fantasize along with the text and interpret it actively, but he or she never controls what happens next. Hyperfiction, on the other
(30) hand, contains numerous paths that the story can take, depending on the actions and choices of the reader. Digital narratives thus have no set plot, no fixed navigation, no predetermined length, and multiple potential storylines and
(35) outcomes.

The most far-reaching ramification of non-linear narrative lies in the nature of the meaning embedded in a hyperfiction story. In a book, the author weaves meaning through the por-
(40) trayal of chronological events. Meaning in non-linear narratives, however, is created through the user's interaction with the links connecting the story elements. Each reader is free to create his or her own story based on her unique
(45) preferences and disposition. Hyperfiction thus offers a vehicle for expressing our infinite desires and manipulating consciousness in a brand new way. Some future Shakespeare of the Digital Age will no doubt tap the unlimited
(50) potential of non-linear narrative and bequeath to us the means for discovering new truths and new beauty.

Passage 2

Line Last Sunday morning I arrived at a writing exposition exploring computerized non-linear storytelling. My dour demeanor throughout the day stood in sharp contrast to the arrogant
(5) enthusiasm of the new literary *avant-garde* hawking "hyperfiction" as the most glorious communication breakthrough since the printing press. And what exactly was their evidence for this astounding claim? Precisely that the
(10) stories of this new medium *have no point*—no definite plot, ending, or even meaning. At one point I could not help but interrupt the rapturous paeans to the form by wondering aloud what can possibly be good about a story
(15) with no determined plot or meaning? The reply, spoken as if to a naive child, was icy in its condescension. Why, it turns out that it is up to *me* to make meaning out of the "endless" possible paths of hyperfiction!

(20) At the risk of being labeled a literary fossil, I must point out that the notion of an "interactive story" contains a deep philosophical contradiction. True interactivity means that the reader affects the story's progression and even
(25) its ending. But the very act of telling a story presupposes that you have a story to tell. How

Note: Photocopying any part of this book is prohibited by law.

can we say that a writer tells a story when he or she cannot predict exactly what that story is in advance? Furthermore, when I read a book, (30) I do so to enter the world of the author. The thrill of reading comes from the interplay between the author's purposeful creation and my own personal interpretation. If meaning is based entirely on interpretation, this interplay (35) is destroyed. When I wish to create meaning, I write my own books, which happens to require skill, training, and perseverance. To simply assemble a bunch of random phrases, pictures, and sounds, code them into "paths," and then (40) put the burden of creating meaning (the hardest part of writing a story, mind you!) on the reader, seems to me a cop-out and an affront to common sense.

Millions of pages of literary criticism have (45) analyzed in the minutest detail the methods, skills, decisions, successes, and blunders of authors. There are generally-accepted standards for what constitutes effective writing. For example, if an author writes an implausible end- (50) ing, we would find fault with his or her book. Now along comes the hyperfiction "digerati" announcing that none of that matters. But if everything is subjective, and the burden of meaning creation is transferred to the reader, (55) then there are no qualitative standards by which one can evaluate a work of hyperfiction. How can something with no possible mistakes be considered art?

My experience at the exposition taught me (60) that it is not for nothing that "hypertext" begins with "hype." The genre gives me the unsettling feeling of looking in agonizing succession into a thousand random mirrors; in the end, I know I'm only going to see myself. Hyperfiction (65) encourages our narcissistic tendencies while subverting one of the main functions of literature: that of expanding consciousness beyond our own limited horizons.

1. The authors of the two passages would disagree most strongly about which of the following statements?

   A. Hyperfiction is likely to become very popular among the general public.

   B. Hyperfiction is a form of art.

   C. Future writers will embrace hyperfiction as a means of self-expression.

   D. Hyperfiction stories are comprised of a set of interrelated hypertext links.

   E. Writing expositions are the best way to showcase the potential of non-linear storytelling.

2. Both passages support which generalization about hyperfiction?

   A. Hyperfiction contains an inherent contradiction.

   B. The traditional novel will never be supplanted entirely by hyperfiction.

   C. The advent of hyperfiction represents a literary innovation as significant as the invention of the novel.

   D. Hyperfiction demonstrates the notion that every communication medium specifies the kinds of messages it can support.

   E. The reader creates the meaning of a hyperfiction story.

3. The approaches of the two passages differ in that only Passage 2 includes

   A. a description of the mechanisms of hyperfiction

   B. a prediction regarding the future of hyperfiction

   C. an account of the author's personal interaction with hyperfiction

   D. the testimony of an expert to support the author's opinion

   E. a comparison between the act of reading a hyperfiction story and the act of reading a traditional book

4. The final paragraph of Passage 2 suggests that the author of Passage 2 would

   A. agree with the author's assertion in Passage 1 that the most far-reaching ramification of hypertext lies in the meaning embedded in the story

   B. disagree with the author's assertion in Passage 1 that the novel expanded the capabilities of the essay

   C. agree with the author's assertion in Passage 1 that hyperfiction offers a vehicle for expressing our infinite desires

   D. disagree with the author's assertion in Passage 1 that someone will someday use non-linear narrative to express new truths and beauty

   E. not understand how the quote presented in the first paragraph of Passage 1 relates to non-linear storytelling

Note: Photocopying any part of this book is prohibited by law.

ANSWERS AND EXPLANATIONS

1. **The correct answer is (B).** At the end of paragraph 3, the author of Passage 2 says "How can something with no possible mistakes be considered art?" Clearly he feels that hyperfiction is not art. The author of Passage 1, on the other hand, predicts a future Shakespeare will use the power of non-linear narratives to give us a way to discover new truths and beauty. Combine that with her statement that "Hypertext has spawned a revolution in the art of narrative," and we can very reasonably infer that the author of Passage 1 does consider hyperfiction to be an art form. So (B) represents a point on which the authors would disagree. As for the others:

Choice (A): Neither author offers an opinion on whether the public will embrace hyperfiction, so we can't say the authors would necessarily disagree on this because we're not sure what they think about this. Certainly we can infer that the author of Passage 1 would like to see hyperfiction become popular, while the author of Passage 2 would prefer it didn't, but what they think will happen in this regard isn't discussed in either passage.

Choice (C): The author of Passage 1 seems confident that future authors will take up hyperfiction, although she doesn't say much about it other than that a future Shakespeare of this genre will emerge. However, despite his attack on the merits of hyperfiction, the author of Passage 2 never says whether he thinks writers will take to this new literary form. So we can't conclude that the two authors would disagree on this.

Choice (D): The author of Passage 1 specifically describes hypertext links, and the author of Passage 2 never mentions them but doesn't deny in any way that this is how hyperfiction works. So (D) doesn't represent a disagreement here.

Choice (E): The value of writing expositions for showcasing non-linear storytelling is outside the scope of both passages, so (E) is not what we're after here.

2. **The correct answer is (E).** The author of Passage 1 is explicit on the subject: "Meaning in non-linear narratives is created through the user's interaction with the links…" She also says that "each reader is free to create her own story based on her unique preferences and disposition." So clearly the author of Passage 1 believes that meaning comes from the reader. The author of Passage 2 doesn't like hyperfiction, and specifically for that very reason: because the meaning comes from the reader, not the author as he thinks it should in a legitimate story. He doesn't like it one bit, but the author of Passage 2 agrees with the author of Passage 1 that meaning in a hyperfiction is created by the reader. As for the others:

Choice (A): An inherent contradiction of hyperfiction is discussed in Passage 2 but not in Passage 1, so (A) is not a generalization common to both.

Choice (B): Neither author speculates on whether hyperfiction will eventually replace the book entirely, so (B) isn't what we're after here.

Choice (C): The author of Passage 1 seems to agree with the point in (C), but it seems as if the author of Passage 2 would not agree that the invention of hyperfiction rivals in importance the invention of the novel. So (C) does not contain the agreed-upon generalization we seek.

Choice (D) refers to the McLuhan reference at the beginning of Passage 1, but Passage 2 includes nothing about the kinds of messages that are unique to each communication mechanism.

3. **The correct answer is (C).** The author of Passage 2 writes about his personal experience with hyperfiction at the exposition, where he presumably encountered various examples of it. The author of Passage 1 does not relate any such personal interaction with the form; she simply tells us what she knows about it. No personal account is included in Passage 1, so (C) is correct for this Comparison question. As for the others:

Note: Photocopying any part of this book is prohibited by law.

Choice (A): Sure, a discussion of how hyperfiction works is part of Passage 2, but it's also a big part of Passage 1. No good.

Choice (B) has it backwards. Passage 1, not Passage 2, contains such a prediction—namely the bit about a future Shakespeare bringing the benefits of hyperfiction to the world.

Choice (D): Neither passage contains the testimony of an outside expert. The reference to Marshall McLuhan in Passage 1 doesn't count as support for the author's main argument, and the author of Passage 2 relies on his own experience as an author to make his argument against hyperfiction.

Choice (E): Both authors compare the experience of reading hyperfiction to that of reading a normal book. The author of Passage 1 is enthusiastic about what hyperfiction brings to the literary table, while the author of Passage 2 does not think the hyperfiction experience compares favorably to reading a book. We can't say (E) represents a difference in approach, since both authors make this comparison; they simply come to different conclusions.

4. **The correct answer is (D).** We can sum up the final paragraph of Passage 2 by saying that the author thinks hyperfiction is all hype and that it leads the reader to narcissistically get bogged down in his own limited world rather than expand his perspective. It is therefore reasonable to conclude from this attitude that the author of Passage 2 would emphatically disagree with the claim that some future Shakespeare will use this form to express new truths and beauty. What the author of Passage 1 sees as "unlimited potential," the author of Passage 2 sees as a dead end.

Choice (A): The author's attitude has little or nothing to do with the issue of the most far-reaching effects of hypertext. Whether the author of Passage 2 would agree with the notion in (A) is questionable, but we certainly can't say he would agree with it based on his argument in paragraph 4.

Choice (B): The author's final critique of hyperfiction is unrelated to the relationship between the novel and the essay as described in Passage 1.

Choice (C) represents an opposite wrong choice. The author tends to work against the idea that hyperfiction can express our infinite desires.

Choice (E): The author's opinion has nothing to do with the McLuhan reference in the beginning of Passage 1. The author of Passage 2 can attack hyperfiction and still understand perfectly well how different communication mechanisms are suited for different types of messages.

WRITING

VERB TENSES

1. Several years <u>after</u> the Soviets launched *Sputnik*,

A

    President John F. Kennedy <u>has</u> <u>announced</u> plans

       B   C

    <u>to send</u> U. S. astronauts to the moon. <u>No error</u>

D   E

2. The jockey <u>who</u> won this <u>year's</u> derby had <u>rode</u>

    A   B   C

    the winning horse in several races <u>earlier</u> in the

           D

    year. <u>No error</u>

  E

3. The Health Department <u>recommends that</u> all

        A

    children <u>be got</u> a blood test for lead at the age

    B

    <u>of</u> one <u>year</u>. <u>No error</u>

C   D   E

4. *The Night Before Christmas*, <u>which</u> is <u>commonly</u>

         A   B

    attributed to Clement Moore, was actually <u>wrote</u>

               C

    many years <u>earlier</u> by Major Henry Livingston,

     D

    Jr. <u>No error</u>

  E

5. After an <u>exhaustive</u> analysis of the company, the

    A

    consultants <u>concluded that</u> the range <u>of</u> services

      B   C

    <u>being</u> too wide and unfocused. <u>No error</u>

D   E

ANSWERS AND EXPLANATIONS

1. **The correct answer is (B).** The word "has," when used with the verb "announced," gives the impression that President John F. Kennedy recently announced plans to send U.S. astronauts to the moon. The first part of the sentence, however, implies that Kennedy's actions occurred well in the past. The correct sentence reads: "Several years after the Soviets launched *Sputnik*, President John F. Kennedy announced plans to send U.S. astronauts to the moon."

2. **The correct answer is (C).** The verb "had" indicates that the term has to be in the past participle, "ridden." The combination "had rode" is not possible. The correct sentence reads: "The jockey who won this year's derby had ridden the winning horse in several races earlier in the year."

3. **The correct answer is (B).** "Got" is the past tense of the infinitive form "to get." The sentence implies, however, that the Health Department has not yet administered the shots. The correct sentence reads: "The Health Department recommends that all children get a blood test for lead at the age of one year."

4. **The correct answer is (C).** The past participle form "written" is needed: using "wrote" in this case would indicate that the action happened only recently, but *The Night Before Christmas* was written many years ago. The correct sentence reads: "*The Night Before Christmas*, which is commonly attributed to Clement Moore, was actually written many years earlier by Major Henry Livingston, Jr."

5. **The correct answer is (D).** The use of the form of the verb "to be" is incorrect, because the whole of the sentence is in the past tense. The correct sentence reads: "After an exhaustive analysis of the company, the consultants concluded that the range of services was too wide and unfocused."

SUBJECT-VERB AGREEMENT

1. Every Monday there are always a long line of
        A   B

    store owners at the bank waiting
               C

    to deposit cash from their weekend sales.
              D

    No error
       E

2. The engineers who were chosen to speak at the
                  A

    convocation has been working in the field of
                B   C

    plastics manufacturing for 80 years collectively.
                                    D

    No error
       E

3. The artist's use of bold strokes and feathery

    details give her work a depth that inspires
           A   B   C   D

    respect and admiration. No error
                      E

4. Many developmental movement therapists

    believe that crawling on the hands and knees
           A

    help organize the brain for tasks such as focusing
     B   C   D

    and reading. No error
              E

5. The series of children's books written by Laura
                                      A

    Ingalls Wilder describe her life growing up in
                B   C

    the American plains during the 1800s. No error
                        D   E

ANSWERS AND EXPLANATIONS

1. **The correct answer is (B).** The problem here is one of subject/verb agreement. The verb "are" modifies a plural subject, but "long line" in (B) is singular. The correct sentence reads: "Every Monday there are always long lines of store owners at the bank waiting to deposit cash from their weekend sales."

2. **The correct answer is (B).** The problem here is one of subject/verb agreement. The subject of the verb phrase is "the engineers," a plural noun. The auxiliary verb used with plural nouns is "have." "Has" is the singular auxiliary verb. The correct sentence reads: "The engineers who were chosen to speak at the convocation have been working in the field of plastics manufacturing for 80 years collectively."

3. **The correct answer is (A).** The difficulty in this question is that it's easy to mistake the antecedent of the verb "give." The antecedent is "use" (singular), not "details" (plural). The verb and antecedent must both be singular. The correct sentence: "The artist's use of bold strokes and feathery details gives her work a depth that inspires respect and admiration."

4. **The correct answer is (B).** "Crawling on the hands" is a singular action, so it takes the form of the verb "helps," not "help" (plural). The correct sentence reads: "Many developmental movement therapists believe that crawling on the hands and knees helps organize the brain for tasks such as focusing and reading."

5. **The correct answer is (B).** The difficulty here is that you might be tricked into believing that "children's books" is the antecedent for the verb "describe," but the real antecedent is the singular "series." "1800s" is an acceptable way to indicate the nineteenth century. The correct sentence reads: "The series of children's books written by Laura Ingalls Wilder describes her life growing up in the American plains during the 1800s."

PRONOUNS: NUMBER

1. The director of security announced that,

   <u>effective</u> immediately, <u>all</u> security codes
     A   B

   <u>would be shortened</u> to make <u>it</u> easier to
        C   D

   remember. <u>No error</u>
           E

2. <u>At</u> the end of the rain-soaked game, most of the
   A

   remaining fans were <u>those who</u> <u>had brought</u>
                 B   C

   sufficient rain gear with <u>them</u>. <u>No error</u>
               D   E

3. The students <u>asked</u> the principal <u>if</u> <u>him and her</u>
            A   B   C

   could use the abandoned bathroom <u>on</u> the third
                              D

   floor as a darkroom for the school photography

   club. <u>No error</u>
        E

4. The students <u>had many</u> follow-up questions
               A

   <u>after</u> the seminar ended, but the professor was
    B

   in <u>too much of</u> a hurry to <u>answer it</u>. <u>No error</u>
       C   D   E

ANSWERS AND EXPLANATIONS

1. **The correct answer is (D).** "Codes," the subject of the clause "all security codes will be shortened to make it easier to remember," is a plural noun, and must be replaced by a plural pronoun. "It" is a singular pronoun. The correct sentence reads: "The director of security announced that, effective immediately, all security codes would be shortened to make them easier to remember."

2. **The correct answer is (E).** The sentence maintains consistency in person: "fans" is plural, and so the sentence uses "those" and "them."

3. **The correct answer is (C).** The pronouns "him and her" require a singular subject, but in this case, the subject, "the students," is plural. The correct sentence reads: "The students asked the principal if they could use the abandoned bathroom on the third floor as a darkroom for the school photography club."

4. **The correct answer is (D).** The trouble with this sentence is that you might confuse the correct noun antecedent to the verb. It is not "seminar," but "follow-up questions," a plural noun requiring the plural pronoun "them." The correct sentence reads "The students had many follow-up questions after the seminar ended, but the professor was in too much of a hurry to answer them."

PRONOUNS: CASE

1. Studies show that babies <u>which</u> sleep in the same
                                A

   room <u>as their parents</u> tend <u>to match</u> the rhythm
        B   C

   of <u>their</u> parents' breathing. <u>No error</u>
      D   E

2. <u>There was</u> an understanding <u>between</u> our
   A   B

   neighbors <u>and we</u> that we could borrow
             C

   garden tools <u>without asking first</u>. <u>No error</u>
                D   E

3. I wonder <u>if</u> my teacher will notice <u>that</u> the
            A   B

   winning entry in the pumpkin <u>growing</u> contest
                                C

   was grown by my <u>sister and I</u>. <u>No error</u>
                    D   E

ANSWERS AND EXPLANATIONS

1. **The correct answer is (A).** The pronoun does not match the subject in this case: people are always referred to with the pronoun "who." The correct sentence reads: "Studies show that babies who sleep in the same room as their parents tend to match the rhythm of their parents' breathing.

2. **The correct answer is (C).** "We" can only be used to replace the subject of a sentence (in this case, "understanding"), not the object ("our neighbors and we"). "Us" is the first person collective for the object of a sentence or a clause of a sentence. The correct sentence reads: "There was an understanding between our neighbors and us that we could borrow garden tools without asking first."

3. **The correct answer is (D).** The I/me question is one that many students struggle with, so whenever a sentence offers a combination like "my sister and I," it's important to scrutinize that part carefully. In this case, the best way to determine whether "I" or "me" is appropriate is to take out "my sister." You wouldn't say, "was grown by I," so "me" must be the correct usage. The correct sentence reads: "I wonder if my teacher will notice that the winning entry in the pumpkin growing contest was grown by my sister and me."

AMBIGUOUS PRONOUNS

1. Guillermo <u>gave</u> Ralph <u>a</u> video game that <u>he</u> liked
       A   B   C

   <u>very</u> much. <u>No error</u>
     D   E

2. <u>They</u> say <u>it's</u> going <u>to rain</u> all <u>week</u>. <u>No error</u>
   A   B   C   D   E

3. Scott handed Ben <u>his</u> jacket <u>as</u> <u>they</u> left
                     A   B C

   <u>the building</u>. <u>No error</u>
     D   E

ANSWERS AND EXPLANATIONS

1. **The correct answer is (C).** Does this sentence mean that Guillermo gave Ralph a video game that *Guillermo* liked very much, or that Guillermo gave Ralph a video game that *Ralph* liked very much? There's no way to tell—the meaning is ambiguous. The correct sentence reads: "Guillermo gave Ralph a video game that Guillermo liked very much" *or* "Guillermo gave Ralph a video game that Ralph liked very much." (Another possibility is to use "the former" or "the latter"—for example: "Guillermo gave Ralph a video game that the former liked very much" or "Guillermo gave Ralph a video game that the latter liked very much.")

2. **The correct answer is (A).** Watch out for the unspecified "they" on the SAT. Who, exactly, is "they"? In spoken language, there is nothing wrong with using "they" to mean "the powers that be," but on the SAT, pronouns have to have clear antecedents. A correct version of this sentence reads: "The weatherman said it's going to rain all week."

3. **The correct answer is (A).** Given our life experience, we might assume that Scott handed Ben's jacket to Ben—that's more likely to have been the case. However, what's to prevent us from thinking that Scott handed his own jacket to Ben—maybe Ben forgot his jacket that day, and Scott didn't need one? That's also possible. What we have is an ambiguous pronoun. A correct version of this sentence reads: "Scott handed Ben's jacket to him as they left the building."

MODIFIERS

1. <u>While</u> earning his Master's degree in education,
      A

    Paul <u>worked</u> <u>as</u> a nursery school teacher,
          B   C

    <u>supervising</u> young children all day long.
        D

    <u>No error</u>
      E

2. <u>Refusing to</u> bow to skepticism, Robert Fulton
      A

    <u>devoted</u> most of his life <u>to solving</u> the problem
      B   C

    <u>of navigation</u> by steam on a commercial scale.
      D

    <u>No error</u>
      E

3. <u>Having a sparse population, training missions
    are often flown over the Outer Hebrides by the
    Royal Air Force.</u>

    A. Having a sparse population, training missions are often flown over the Outer Hebrides by the Royal Air Force.

    B. With its sparse population, the Royal Air Force is often over the Outer Hebrides flying training missions.

    C. Because it is sparsely populated, the Royal Air Force, often on training missions, is over the Outer Hebrides.

    D. The Outer Hebrides are sparsely populated, the reason why the Royal Air Force often flies training missions over them.

    E. Because the Outer Hebrides are sparsely populated, the Royal Air Force often flies training missions over them.

4. Of all the romantic heroes in British literature, <u>the hero Fitzwilliam Darcy has captured more minds and hearts than any other in Jane Austen's novels.</u>

    A. the hero Fitzwilliam Darcy has captured more minds and hearts than any other in Jane Austen's novels

    B. Jane Austen's Fitzwilliam Darcy has captured the minds and hearts of more readers than any other

    C. Jane Austen created Fitzwilliam Darcy who has captured more minds and hearts than any other

    D. Jane Austen, with her hero Fitzwilliam Darcy, has captured the minds and hearts of more readers than any other

    E. Fitzwilliam Darcy has captured the minds and hearts of more readers than any other Jane Austen hero

Note: Photocopying any part of this book is prohibited by law.

ANSWERS AND EXPLANATIONS

1. **The correct answer is (E).** (A) might, at first, seem a little awkward, but it is grammatically correct. It means that during the time he was pursuing his Master's degree in education, Paul supervised young children.

2. **The correct answer is (E).** (A) might have distracted you in this question, but it is acceptable to begin a sentence with a gerund (a verb that ends in –ing.)

3. **The correct answer is (E).** The key to this question is understanding meaning from context. The point is that the Royal Air Force doesn't want to disturb the local population, so it uses the Outer Hebrides, which are sparsely populated, to run training missions. The original possibility, "Having a sparse population, training missions…" seems to indicate that the training missions have a sparse population. (B) indicates that the Royal Air Force has a sparse population. The same is true for (C). (D) has the meaning of the sentence correct, but it is awkward as written; in order for this sentence to make sense, you would need to write, "The Outer Hebrides are sparsely populated, which is the reason why the Royal Air Force often flies training missions over them." (E) is the only possibility that communicates the correct information and is not awkwardly written.

4. **The correct answer is (B).** To correct this sentence, you have to understand that Fitzwilliam Darcy is a character in a Jane Austen novel, and that Jane Austen is a British writer. This is possible to do without any outside knowledge, given that you know that Jane Austen is a novelist and that Fitzwilliam Darcy is a character. From here, you can determine that he is a character in a book she wrote; otherwise, why mention Austen at all? The only choice that communicates all of this information is (B). (A) indicates that Fitzwilliam Darcy has captured more minds and hearts than any other character in Jane Austen's novels, but the beginning of the sentence indicates that he's captured more hearts and minds than any other character in all of British literature. (C) is long and redundant; (D) indicates that Jane Austen has captured those hearts, not Fitzwilliam Darcy, and (E) indicates the same as (A).

Note: Photocopying any part of this book is prohibited by law.

PARALLELISM

1. You will never <u>be able</u> to finish your Ph.D. in
   　　　　　　　A

   <u>fewer than</u> 10 years if you do not set a concrete
   　B

   schedule for writing <u>one's dissertation</u> and stick
   　　　　　　　　　　　C

   <u>to</u> it. <u>No error</u>
   D　　E

2. She <u>was surprised</u> to discover that the present
   　　　　A

   she <u>received from</u> her biggest client was far
   　　　B

   smaller and <u>less</u> impressive than
   　　　　　　C

   <u>her next biggest client</u>. <u>No error</u>
   　　D　　　　　　　E

3. Nanotechnology allows scientists to continue the revolution in computer hardware <u>and they can repair</u> the human body at the atomic level.

   A. and they can repair

   B. as well as repairing

   C. so they could repair

   D. and the making of reparations to

   E. and to repair

ANSWERS AND EXPLANATIONS

1. **The correct answer is (C).** This sentence uses two different pronouns to refer to the same person. The writer begins by addressing "you," but in part (C) switches to "one." (B) might have distracted you because "less than" might sound better, but both fewer and less can be used in this situation. The correct sentence reads: "You will never be able to finish your Ph.D. in fewer than 10 years if you do not set a concrete schedule for writing your dissertation and stick to it."

2. **The correct answer is (D).** The parallel construction of this sentence is not upheld by part (D), which seems to indicate that the next biggest client is larger and more impressive than the gift received from her biggest client. What the sentence means to compare is the presents that each of the clients gave. The correct sentence reads: "She was surprised to discover that the present she received from her biggest client was far smaller and less impressive than the one from her next biggest client."

3. **The correct answer is (E).** Leaving the sentence as is introduces a redundant "they": it is already clear that the scientists are the ones doing the repairing. You should also always strive to preserve parallel structure. The first verb in the parallel phrase is "continues"; the second one should not end with an "-ing." You have no indication that the computer revolution will allow scientists to make repairs at the molecular level, so (C), which claims that the revolution will help scientists make atomic-level repairs, is not a possibility. (E) is the only answer that communicates the intention of the author and is grammatical.

WHAT MAKES A SENTENCE

1. Support for the military is at a 50-year high;

   <u>not since</u> World War II <u>has</u> so <u>many</u> high-school
      A   B   C

   graduates <u>enlisted</u> in the Army. <u>No error</u>
           D   E

2. Sea glass <u>is</u> an example of how <u>nature can turn</u>
          A   B

   destruction <u>into</u> beauty; ocean waves grind,
            C

   polish, and often <u>they reshape</u> pieces of
                  D

   broken bottles. <u>No error</u>
               E

3. The enthusiasm for Manet's "Le Déjeuner sur l'herbe" inspired a group of young <u>painters, and formed</u> the nucleus of the Impressionists.

   A. painters, and formed

   B. painters, having formed

   C. painters, having been forming

   D. painters, who formed

   E. painters that had been forming

4. Storms occasionally force closure of the Space Needle, <u>it was built for withstanding</u> a wind velocity of 200 miles per hour.

   A. it was built for withstanding

   B. which was built despite the withstanding of

   C. even though it was built to withstand

   D. yet it was built and withstands

   E. as it was built while withstanding

5. The League of Nations was formed after World War I in an attempt to secure world <u>peace; it had been in existence only six years, though, before</u> Germany and Japan withdrew.

   A. peace; it had been in existence only six years, though, before

   B. peace, but only six years later, though, was when

   C. peace; though having existed only six years,

   D. peace before, only six years later,

   E. peace, and six years were over, though, before

Note: Photocopying any part of this book is prohibited by law.

ANSWERS AND EXPLANATIONS

1. **The correct answer is (B).** Although you might be tempted to choose (A), a semi-colon is the same as "and," and so this clause is in fact connected to the first clause. The real error in the sentence is the incorrect form of the verb "to have." You need the present form "have" because the enlisting is occurring not in the past, but right now. The correct sentence reads: "Support for the military is at a 50-year high; not since World War II have so many high-school graduates enlisted in the Army."

2. **The correct answer is (D).** "They" is redundant in this sentence because it is already clear that you are referring to ocean waves; no additional pronoun is necessary. The correct sentence reads: "Sea glass is an example of how nature can turn destruction into beauty; ocean waves grind, polish, and often reshape pieces of broken bottles."

3. **The correct answer is (D).** The important thing in this sentence is to be clear on who or what "formed the nucleus of the Impressionists." As it is written, the sentence indicates that the enthusiasm for the Manet painting formed the nucleus, but only people can form the nucleus of a group. Therefore, you need the pronoun "who" after the comma. This makes it clear that the artists inspired by the painting founded the group.

4. **The correct answer is (C).** What you want to indicate in this sentence is that storms force the closure of the Space Needle, despite the fact that it was built to withstand heavy winds. The only possibility that accomplishes this goal is (C); the other possibilities do not indicate that there is any contradiction between the fact that the Space Needle closes for weather that it was meant to withstand.

5. **The correct answer is (A).** The original sentence communicates the irony of the League of Nations: that only six years after it was formed, Germany and Japan withdrew to start World War II. (B) is redundant: it uses both "but" and "though" to indicate the contradiction, and also adds an extra verb phrase, "was when." (C) indicates that Germany and Japan only existed six years. (D) does not communicate the meaning of the sentence: by adding "before," it indicates that the League of Nations was cognizant when it formed that Germany and Japan would withdraw. (E) has the same problem as (B).

NOUNS: NUMBER

1. Karl and Fred <u>decided</u> <u>to study</u> economics
                        A   B

   <u>in order to become</u>   <u>a businessman</u>.
            C   D

   <u>No error</u>
        E

2. <u>Throughout</u> history, <u>kings and queens</u> have
        A   B

   always been suspicious of <u>their</u> <u>sibling</u>. <u>No error</u>
                                  C   D   E

3. People tend <u>to act</u> according <u>to</u> <u>their</u> <u>belief</u>.
                    A   B   C   D

   <u>No error</u>
        E

ANSWERS AND EXPLANATIONS

1. **The correct answer is (D).** "Karl and Fred" is a plural subject; this sentence states that Karl and Fred—*two* people—decided to study economics in order to become *one* businessman. This cannot be—they have to become two separate businessmen. The correct sentence reads: "Karl and Fred decided to study economics in order to become businessmen."

2. **The correct answer is (D).** In this sentence, "kings and queens" stands for all the royal leaders our species has ever had. That set of people had to have had their own, specific *siblings*—they can't all have shared one sibling! The correct sentence reads: "Throughout history, kings and queens have always been suspicious of their siblings."

3. **The correct answer is (D).** As written, this sentence states that all people have only one belief. That's not plausible; people have multiple beliefs. The correct sentence reads: "People tend to act according to their beliefs."

ACTIVE VS. PASSIVE

1. <u>How often did he have to be told by Chris to clean his side of the room?</u>

   A. How often did he have to be told by Chris to clean his side of the room?

   B. How often did Chris have to tell him to clean his side of the room?

   C. He had to be told often by Chris to clean his side of the room?

   D. To clean his side of the room, he had to be told how often by Chris?

   E. How often by Chris did he have to be told to clean his side of the room?

2. <u>The students were given an exam by the professor.</u>

   A. The students were given an exam by the professor.

   B. To the students, by the professor, was given an exam.

   C. An exam was given by the professor to the students.

   D. By the professor, to the students, an exam was given.

   E. The professor gave an exam to the students.

ANSWERS AND EXPLANATIONS

1. **The correct answer is (B).** The original question is incorrect because it is written in passive voice. Choices (C), (D), and (E) do not correct this problem. Therefore, choice (B) is correct.

2. **The correct answer is (E).** The original sentence is incorrect because it is written in passive voice. The only choice that corrects the problem is choice (E).

Note: Photocopying any part of this book is prohibited by law.

ADJECTIVE VS. ADVERB

1. <u>Unlike</u> her contemporaries, Sor Juana Ines de la
   A

   Cruz did not want <u>to marry</u>, but <u>instead</u> entered
                        B   C

   a convent <u>voluntary</u>. <u>No error</u>
                  D   E

2. The <u>works of</u> Mark Rothko <u>capture</u> <u>eloquent</u> the
          A   B   C

   <u>tension between</u> form and emotion. <u>No error</u>
          D   E

3. <u>Regardless</u> of how <u>careful</u> people treat their
   A   B

   cars, each vehicle is <u>bound to</u> incur some sort
                             C

   of damage sooner <u>or later</u>. <u>No error</u>
                        D   E

ANSWERS AND EXPLANATIONS

1. **The correct answer is (D).** In this case, you need an adverb, not an adjective, to describe Sor Juana Ines de la Cruz's actions. Adverbs describe verbs; adjectives describe nouns. Since you are trying to describe something about how she entered the convent, you need the adverbial form. The correct sentence reads: "Unlike her contemporaries, Sor Juana Ines de la Cruz did not want to marry, but instead entered a convent voluntarily."

2. **The correct answer is (C).** You are trying to describe how an action is performed; therefore, you need an adverb and not an adjective (which describes a noun). The correct sentence reads: "The works of Mark Rothko capture eloquently the tension between form and emotion."

3. **The correct answer is (B).** Because you are attempting to describe how people treat their cars, you need the adverbial form of "careful," not the adjectival form. The correct sentence reads: "Regardless of how carefully people treat their cars, each vehicle is bound to incur some sort of damage sooner or later."

COMPARISONS

1. Her lecture <u>profiled</u> her extensive travels
    A

    throughout the West Indies, <u>describing</u> the
    B

    culture and customs <u>she</u> encountered <u>without</u>
    C   D

    passing judgments or invoking comparisons.

    <u>No error</u>
    E

2. Dr. Melendez <u>believes that</u> the <u>most</u> sensible of
    A   B

    the two treatment options <u>is</u> to adopt a radically
    C

    new regimen <u>of diet</u> and exercise. <u>No error</u>
    D   E

3. The way in which Puerto Ricans <u>speak</u> Spanish
    A

    <u>is</u> so different <u>from Argentineans</u> that a company
    B   C

    has published a new phrasebook <u>to help</u>
    D

    facilitate conversation. <u>No error</u>
    E

4. Graham Corporation <u>has sold</u> <u>more</u> steel pipe
    A   B

    fittings <u>than</u> <u>any</u> fittings manufacturer. <u>No error</u>
    C   D   E

5. For many a college graduate, <u>discovering a suit-</u>
    <u>able apartment is often more difficult</u> than se-
    curing a job.

    A. discovering a suitable apartment is often
       more difficult

    B. the discovery of a suitable apartment of-
       ten is more difficult

    C. there is often more difficulty in the discov-
       ery of a suitable apartment

    D. discovering a suitable apartment often has
       more difficulty

    E. to discover a suitable apartment is more
       difficult

ANSWERS AND EXPLANATIONS

1. **The correct answer is (E).** You might be tempted to decide that there is an error in (B), but if you eliminate some of the information in between, you would end up with the sentence "Her lecture profiled her travels, describing…" which is a perfectly acceptable usage.

2. **The correct answer is (B).** "Most" is used when comparing three or more things, but here, there are only two treatment options, so "more" is used to distinguish between them. The correct sentence reads: "Dr. Melendez believes that the more sensible of the two treatment options is to adopt a radically new regimen of diet and exercise."

3. **The correct answer is (C).** The sentence does not set up a proper parallel structure. In the phrase "so different from Argentineans," it is not clear what is being compared. It must be clear that the two things being compared are the way in which Puerto Ricans speak Spanish and the way in which Argentineans speak Spanish. The correct sentence reads: "The way in which Puerto Ricans speak Spanish is so different from the way in which Argentineans speak Spanish that a company has published a new phrasebook to help facilitate conversation."

4. **The correct answer is (D).** The problem with this sentence is that "fittings manufacturers" includes Graham Corporation. Therefore, you need the word "other" to distinguish Graham Corporation from the other manufacturers. The sentence, as written, says that Graham Corporation has sold more steel pipe fittings than any other manufacturer, including itself! The correct sentence reads: "Graham Corporation has sold more steel pipe fittings than any other fittings manufacturer."

5. **The correct answer is (A).** The author successfully establishes a comparison by using two "-ing" verbs (discovering and securing). (D) is the only other possibility that uses "discovering"; however, it also indicates that the discovering has difficulty when in reality, it is the person who has difficulty.

Note: Photocopying any part of this book is prohibited by law.

SENTENCE IMPROVEMENT STRATEGY

1. The Keel-billed Toucan, the national bird of Belize, has one of the largest bills and also the most dextrous of the bills in the bird kingdom.

    A. one of the largest bills and also the most dextrous of the

    B. not only the largest bill, but also more dextrous than any of the

    C. the largest bill and is also the most dextrous

    D. at the same time the largest and also the most dextrous

    E. one of the largest and yet the most dextrous

2. The Spaniards and Portuguese settled much of the Caribbean region in the 1490s and codfish was introduced responsibly by them to the area's cuisine.

    A. codfish was introduced responsibly by them

    B. had the responsibility to introduce codfish

    C. had the responsibility for the introduction of the codfish

    D. were the ones responsible for introducing codfish

    E. they were the ones who introduced codfish responsibly

3. Though liberal arts institutions have offered a wide array of courses of study, the neglect of most in including a curriculum of basic money management.

    A. the neglect of most in including

    B. most are neglecting to include

    C. most have neglected to include

    D. most show neglect by the lack of inclusion of

    E. most of them are neglecting the inclusion of

4. In a trial to ascertain if parental rights should be terminated, the judge's task is to determine whether a parent neglects the children or they are able to care for them.

    A. a parent neglects the children or they are able to care for them

    B. the parent neglects the children or is able to care for them

    C. the children are being neglected or they can take care of them

    D. children are, by a parent, being neglected or cared for

    E. a child is neglected and taken care of by the parents

5. A single drop of blood contains millions of red blood cells that constantly are delivering and removing oxygen and waste within the human body.

    A. cells that constantly are delivering and removing oxygen and waste

    B. cells are delivering oxygen and removing waste constantly

    C. cells, which constantly are delivering oxygen and the removal of waste

    D. cells, which, through oxygen delivery and waste removal, are

    E. cells, which are constantly delivering oxygen and removing waste

Note: Photocopying any part of this book is prohibited by law.

ANSWERS AND EXPLANATIONS

1. **The correct answer is (E).** The key here is to eliminate the choices that are redundant. The sentence, as written, is redundant because it contains the word "bill" twice. It needs to be set up in some sort of parallel construction, whereby you can communicate the information that the bill is both large and dextrous without repeating the word "bill" twice. The only two choices that fit these requirements are (D) and (E). (D) itself is awkward, because you don't require "at the same time" to have this sentence make sense. (E) accomplishes your purpose in the fewest words.

2. **The correct answer is (D).** The first question you should ask yourself here is how codfish can be introduced responsibly. If there is a way to introduce codfish responsibly, the College Board certainly wouldn't ask you to know it. It seems likely, then, that the writer means to say that the Spaniards and Portuguese were responsible for introducing codfish. The only likely option is (D). The sentence, as written, is in the passive form ("by them"). (B) leads you to ask, why were they given the responsibility, and by whom? (C) leads to much the same question. (E) is redundant; it adds a "they" when the antecedent is clear. So even if you believed there was some sort of process for responsibly introducing codfish, you could eliminate the other possibilities.

3. **The correct answer is (C).** The sentence, as it is written, is a fragment. It doesn't explain what the consequences of a lack of basic money management curriculum might be. It seems likely, then, that the subject of the sentence is the lack of a basic money management curriculum at liberal arts institutions. (B), while it does make the sentence complete, does not fit the tense of the sentence (i.e. "have offered"). You need an option that communicates the past tense. (C) does this.

4. **The correct answer is (B).** "Parent" is singular, but "they," the pronoun used to replace "parent," is plural. Your answer must consistently choose the singular or plural. (C) does not make it clear who the "they" is. (D) awkwardly adds the "by a parent" between commas and ends the sentence with the preposition "for." (E) links neglect and care with an "and," not an "or," when neglect and care cannot occur at the same time. Only (B) keeps number consistent: "is" is a verb in the singular form, making it clear that the verb refers to a singular entity.

5. **The correct answer is (E).** The first step is to know the difference between "that" and "which," and when to use both. "Which" is used when you have a non-restrictive clause; in layman's terms, you use "which" when the description that follows a subject is not necessarily the only description you could apply to that subject. In this case, this is exactly what you have. (C), (D), and (E) all use "which." You can immediately eliminate (D); the sentence does not make sense if you substitute it for the underlined portion. As for (C) and (E), the difference is the placement of "are." "Are" has to come before constantly because constantly describes are.

ERROR IDENTIFICATION STRATEGY

1. <u>Necessary</u> <u>for</u> a successful revolution <u>are</u> the
      A   B   C

    leadership of several strong individuals <u>who</u>
                                         D

    possess organizational skills and charisma.

    <u>No error</u>
      E

2. A conversation <u>between</u> two professional
                  A

    therapists <u>rarely</u> <u>result</u> in complete
              B   C

    <u>agreement about</u> the proper diagnosis.
            D

    <u>No error</u>
      E

3. Shannon's long program, <u>containing</u> three
                            A

    advanced-level jumps, <u>was</u> <u>as difficult</u>
                   B   C

    <u>as than</u> Yumi's. <u>No error</u>
      D   E

4. Louisa May Alcott received <u>only</u> modest <u>payment</u>
                            A   B

    for her first poem, "Sunlight," but her career

    <u>would later</u> bring her great fame <u>and end</u> her
         C   D

    financial worries. <u>No error</u>
                  E

Note: Photocopying any part of this book is prohibited by law.

ANSWERS AND EXPLANATIONS

1. **The correct answer is (C).** "Necessary," in this case, takes on the singular form, and you must replace the verb with the singular form "is." The correct sentence reads: "Necessary for a successful revolution is the leadership of several strong individuals who possess organizational skills and charisma."

2. **The correct answer is (C).** The antecedent to the verb in this case is "conversation," a singular noun. Therefore, you need the singular form of the verb "to result." The correct sentence reads: "A conversation between two professional therapists rarely results in complete agreement about the proper diagnosis."

3. **The correct answer is (D).** The problem with part D of this sentence is that it uses two words of comparison, making the meaning of the author difficult to determine. "Than" is usually used with "more" or "less," indicating that there is some difference between the two things being compared. "As" is used when the terms compared are the same. To improve this sentence making the fewest possible changes, eliminate "than," since the author seems to want to say that Shannon's and Yumi's programs were of equal difficulty. The correct sentence reads: "Shannon's long program, containing three advanced-level jumps, was as difficult as Yumi's."

4. **The correct answer is (E).** (D) is the distracter here: you might think that that the parallel construction of the sentence is not upheld, but in reality, writing "but her career would later bring her great fame and it would end her financial worries" is redundant. The meaning of the sentence as written is clear because it is understood that her career is what would bring her both great fame and end her financial worries.

Note: Photocopying any part of this book is prohibited by law.

MORE ERROR IDENTIFICATION PRACTICE

1. As <u>one scholar</u> <u>noted, the</u> office of the
          A   B
    presidency has a <u>long complicated history</u> with
                       C
    many <u>noble and ignoble</u> moments. <u>No error</u>
            D   E

2. <u>Today, as</u> he left for the <u>central office</u>, Kenneth
       A   B
    felt the uncontrollable urge <u>to change</u>
                        C
    <u>his busy life</u>. <u>No error</u>
      D   E

3. <u>Youth</u>, as the Greeks and <u>other early civilizations</u>
      A   B
    knew, <u>are best spent</u> as a time of learning
           C
    <u>and of recreation</u>. <u>No error</u>
        D   E

4. <u>How</u> people <u>naturally</u> divide <u>themselves</u> is
     A   B   C
    sometimes as important as the <u>way's</u> they
                          D
    feel united. <u>No error</u>
             E

5. <u>His father</u> often spoke of his <u>days, as</u> a
       A   B
    <u>younger man</u> in <u>pre-war</u> Warsaw. <u>No error</u>
      C   D   E

6. <u>Truthfully</u>, one <u>of the best ways</u> to get over
      A   B
    <u>a cold is</u> getting <u>alot</u> of sleep. <u>No error</u>
      C   D   E

7. In the eyes <u>of the law</u>, the defendant at a trial
             A
    <u>is to be</u> considered <u>innocent, until</u>
      B   C
    <u>proven guilty</u>. <u>No error</u>
      D   E

8. <u>Our coach</u> said the <u>high school center, towering</u>
      A   B
    above his basketball counterparts, had the
    look of a <u>"man</u> among <u>boys"</u>. <u>No error</u>
            C   D   E

9. Management recently <u>hung a sign above</u> the
                   A
    break room <u>door, which</u> most of us probably
             B
    ignored, that detailed <u>the federal laws in place</u>
                         C
    for worker breaks and <u>for employer obligations</u>.
                         D
    <u>No error</u>
     E

10. Kinetic <u>energy, one</u> of the more
           A
    <u>commonly-learned</u> and <u>least understood</u> terms
         B   C
    in physics, <u>is a way</u> of measuring the potential
                D
    of a body in motion. <u>No error</u>
                  E

11. <u>Throughout the course</u> <u>of the year</u>, the
         A   B
    committee was deadlocked on the
    <u>issue, some members even voted</u> for the
                C
    solution <u>of redistricting</u>. <u>No error</u>
             D   E

Note: Photocopying any part of this book is prohibited by law.

12. June of <u>2001, the</u> hottest <u>month that</u> <u>anyone</u>
               A   B   C
we knew <u>could recall</u>. <u>No error</u>
           D   E

13. On <u>paper there</u> was nothing <u>wrong with</u> the
              A   B
<u>artists' proposal</u> to build the statue
      C
<u>honoring the former governor</u>. <u>No error</u>
          D   E

14. Tales <u>of heroism</u>, the foundation <u>of much of</u>
           A   B
the early <u>greek</u> literature, still echo in many
         C
fictional <u>works today</u>. <u>No error</u>
        D   E

15. Finding work <u>right out of college</u> has become
                 A
the main priority for <u>soon-to-be</u> college
                   B
<u>graduates, eclipsing</u> world travel or
      C
<u>post-graduate</u> research. <u>No error</u>
      D   E

16. <u>Baseball</u> <u>has always been</u> a game for the
      A   B
<u>people not</u> a game <u>for the elite</u>. <u>No error</u>
    C   D   E

17. As the <u>astronauts</u> visit <u>to the moon</u> taught
          A   B
<u>us, the</u> ability to think big can bring about
   C
<u>remarkable</u> accomplishments. <u>No error</u>
    D   E

18. A <u>cadre</u> of security <u>personnel whisked</u> the
      A   B
player away after his <u>game-winner as</u> the
                   C
crowd got <u>even rowdier</u>. <u>No error</u>
        D   E

19. <u>Four-tenths</u>, or forty <u>percent, of</u> those polled said
      A   B
<u>they favored</u> amending the <u>states constitution</u> to
   C   D
allow for more governmental oversight. <u>No error</u>
                       E

20. <u>Among his many</u> memorable statements
      A
<u>to the crowd</u> was his admission that
      B
<u>he'd never read</u> his own book even after
    C
writing it and he believed it was

<u>normal and wouldn't you read it</u>? <u>No error</u>
           D   E

21. A kind word <u>from the older</u> of the two
               A
<u>men, arriving</u> at a particularly difficult time
   B
in <u>his managerment</u> of the ship, helped cheer
         C
<u>Captain Howard</u> up. <u>No error</u>
    D   E

22. The <u>pork industry</u>, of the nation's largest food
      A
<u>lobbies, have</u> most drastically increased <u>its</u>
    B   C
visibility <u>in recent years</u> in an effort to create
          D
new consumers in an era of healthier eating.

<u>No error</u>
  E

23. <u>Animal experts</u> have noted <u>that, in</u> carefully
     A   B

    controlled studies, cats retain information for a

    shorter amount of time <u>then</u> <u>dogs but</u> that
                          C   D

    cats have a faster recall time. <u>No error</u>
                                E

24. Watching the <u>window washers</u>
                  A

    <u>who clean skyscrapers</u> work is <u>nerve-wracking</u>
        B   C

    to anyone <u>with a natural fear</u> of heights.
                   D

    <u>No error</u>
      E

25. Tonight's show <u>by the senior class</u> was the
                 A

    first time <u>some parents</u> have seen <u>them</u> perform
             B   C

    in front <u>of a crowded room</u> full of people.
              D

    <u>No error</u>
      E

26. Art collectors have recently flocked

    <u>to galleries in New York</u> looking for work by
           A

    David <u>Pernice, an</u> artist with a fresh perspective
           B

    on the world and <u>one which</u> they believe will
                 C

    captivate art <u>viewers and critics alike</u>. <u>No error</u>
              D   E

27. The most popular condiment <u>in America</u> for the
                      A

    last few <u>years, as</u> researched by ad agencies and
          B

    consumer groups, <u>is somewhat</u> surprisingly,
                C

    the <u>Mexican</u> topping *salsa*. <u>No error</u>
         D   E

28. <u>Success, or</u> the measure <u>by which people</u>
       A   B

    judge <u>their life</u>, differs greatly among <u>groups,</u>
        C   D

    generations, and even individuals. <u>No error</u>
                            E

29. <u>Pigeons, considered</u> by many in urban areas
           A

    <u>a filthy nuisance</u>, are <u>actually quite</u> intelligent
        B   C

    animals <u>and highly</u> trainable. <u>No error</u>
          D   E

30. The overwhelming majority <u>of the population</u> of
                          A

    Canada, something like 80 <u>percent, lives</u> within
                       B

    90 miles of the border <u>with the United States,</u>
                    C

    a fact that irks some nationalistic Canadians

    <u>to no end</u>. <u>No error</u>
      D   E

31. The <u>olympic games</u>, a dramatic world stage
        A

    every four <u>years, have</u> struggled at times to
             B

    maintain high visibility <u>in America</u> when the
                   C

    television coverage is <u>in a different time zone</u>.
                     D

    <u>No error</u>
      E

Note: Photocopying any part of this book is prohibited by law.

32. While some <u>simply cannot properly</u> digest
                A

lactose, others develop <u>a intolerance</u>
                B

<u>over time</u>, despite the fact that as young
  C

<u>people, they</u> had no such problems. <u>No error</u>
   D   E

33. <u>With</u> three elevators servicing over 25 floors
  A

and probably <u>2000 people</u>, <u>James</u> new building
           B   C

was a far cry from his old apartment complex

<u>with its single escalator</u>. <u>No error</u>
       D   E

34. Despite a big <u>writeup</u> in the local <u>paper, the</u>
          A   B

art museum had a surprisingly difficult time

selling tickets <u>to its newest attraction</u>, an
          C

ancient <u>Egyptian</u> mummy. <u>No error</u>
     D   E

35. According to the tour <u>guide, stalactites</u> and
          A

stalagmites in the cave <u>system are limestone</u>
        B

deposits formed <u>over many years</u> as water
        C

<u>trickles</u> through cracks in the rock. <u>No error</u>
  D   E

36. Handheld devices <u>have become</u> so <u>omnipresent</u>
            A   B

that many people cannot remember

<u>how they managed</u> to live their lives before
     C

owning <u>them</u>. <u>No error</u>
     D   E

37. The <u>Mayan</u> ruins at Tulum, <u>Mexico, contain</u> a
     A   B

massive sundial that <u>use</u> pinholes of
          C

light to tell the time of day <u>as well as</u> the
               D

current date. <u>No error</u>
        E

38. Few Americans today, so far removed from the

event, <u>realized</u> the devastation that the Great
     A

Chicago <u>Fire, now</u> known <u>to have been started</u>
      B   C

by a single cow, caused

<u>to the nascent Midwestern city</u>. <u>No error</u>
      D   E

39. Rochester, <u>NY, calls</u> among its more famous former
         A

<u>citizens, the</u> suffragist Susan B. Anthony, the
  B

entrepreneur <u>George Eastman, and</u> the <u>renowned</u>
          C   D

opera soprano Renee Fleming. <u>No error</u>
           E

40. Compared to today's <u>high-powered</u>,
          A

<u>sleek compact</u> <u>models, the</u> original computers
  B   C

were rather inefficient, offering less power

and <u>much less memory</u> despite a much larger
     D

overall size. <u>No error</u>
     E

41. <u>Some economists</u> believe that airline travel
      A
<u>has, for years, boosted</u> the sales of daily and
      B
weekly magazines <u>due to an increased wait time</u>
                     C
<u>at airports</u>. <u>No error</u>
  D   E

42. In recent <u>years flu</u> vaccines <u>have become</u> much
          A   B
more common and <u>are encouraged for</u> the
                C
elderly and <u>for young children</u>. <u>No error</u>
           D   E

43. The library now offers dedicated <u>study time</u>
                          A
for three hours <u>daily 12–3 PM</u> with tutors
          B
available <u>during finals week</u> <u>for extra help</u>.
        C   D
<u>No error</u>
  E

44. Since the drawbridge opens for boat <u>traffic, at</u>
                          A
5 PM every day, leave early <u>or you'll be</u> stuck
                   B
waiting <u>to cross</u> for the <u>better part of an hour</u>.
      C   D
<u>No error</u>
  E

45. <u>Expert rock climbers</u> <u>who hold</u> their entire
      A   B
weight with a single <u>finger, even</u> hanging upside
               C
down <u>for minutes at a time</u>. <u>No error</u>
     D   E

46. Dubrovnik, on the <u>Dalmatian coast, is</u> a city
                  A
built entirely <u>within the walls</u> of an ancient
            B
fortress, which is still visible <u>to this day</u>
                    C
<u>and which many tourists</u> come to visit
           D
each year. <u>No error</u>
         E

47. When the moving van <u>arrives, it</u> is important
                  A
that all the boxes are packed, that the furniture
is cleaned and wrapped, <u>and the</u> many loose
                  B
items <u>lying</u> around are <u>collected and boxed</u>.
      C   D
<u>No error</u>
  E

48. Long a staple of Hollywood's vision
<u>of the underground world</u>, fortunetellers have
        A
<u>become more accepted</u> over <u>time, with</u> some
      B   C
even consulting on crime <u>investigations though</u>
                D
generally to limited success. <u>No error</u>
              E

49. An amateur magician must remember that

most people, especially those who consider
A   B
themselves skeptics by nature, are loathe to

believe that magic is possible, even some
                                            C
children, who are usually more willing to
         D
believe in the unknown, are tough to impress.

No error
     E

50. Years ago, the government decided that
                    A
National Parks were unique resources
         B   C
in need of special protection. No error
     D   E

ANSWERS AND EXPLANATIONS

1. **The correct answer is (C).** Within a sentence are often found phrases with a series of descriptors, such as, in this case, a "long" and a "complicated" history. When such a list of descriptions is present and when the words describing the subject at hand, here "history," are not inherently a part of the item (such as "flu symptoms), a comma is needed to separate more than one descriptor. Thus, the correct way of expressing this is that the office of the presidency has a "long, complicated history."

2. **The correct answer is (E).** There is no error present in this sentence.

3. **The correct answer is (C).** This sentence suffers from a subject-verb agreement problem. Specifically, the subject of this sentence is "youth," which is a collective noun. Despite the fact that many different people may experience youth, the combination of all of them is singular. And like any singular noun, the verb tense, regardless of add-on phrases, should be singular also. Here, the correct verb usage for "youth" would be "is."

4. **The correct answer is (D).** Many writers confuse the possessive case, using an apostrophe plus an 's' when making a word plural, which generally requires adding only an 's' to a word. The possessive case is used to show ownership or belonging, whereas the plural is simply to denote how many are in question. This is the case in this sentence, where the writer seeks to express more than one "way," not "way's" ownership of anything. The apostrophe should be dropped, making it "ways."

5. **The correct answer is (B).** Some prepositional phrases add extra information to a basic sentence and therefore deserve to be set off with commas. There can be a tendency at times to overuse the comma with regard to prepositional phrases. Setting them off is not always needed. In this case, the father spoke of his days "as a younger man" in Warsaw before the war, but the preposition "as" does not require commas surrounding it.

6. **The correct answer is (D).** The answer to this sentence is fairly simple and the issue at hand is a common one. Unplanned changes in language due to popular usage, media, advertising, or e-mail have clouded the correct spelling of certain common phrases, in this case the phrase "a lot." The correct spelling of this phrase is in two words.

7. **The correct answer is (C).** Careful writers will sometimes err on the side of caution and assume that a complex sentence must be a series of clauses and therefore needs commas used throughout. This is not necessarily the case, however frustrating that might sound. One can easily overuse commas, as is the case in this question. Here, the defendant is considered "innocent until proven guilty," and no comma is needed after the word "innocent."

8. **The correct answer is (D).** The problem with this sentence is one of correct grammar usage, specifically the use of quotation marks. When quotation marks are used to quote someone and they fall at the end of a sentence, the period or comma should be placed within the quotation mark. In this case, it is correct to write that the coach said the center looked like a "man among boys."

9. **The correct answer is (E).** There is no error present in this sentence.

10. **The correct answer is (B).** Hyphens are a tricky punctuation, as their rules are solid, but because hyphens do not show up in spoken English, they are not well known. Sometimes, modifiers need to be hyphenated preceding a noun, as in the case of a "well-researched paper." However, the sentence here gives modifiers that do not require a hyphen. So the correct usage would be "commonly learned," without a hyphen.

11. **The correct answer is (C).** The subject of the sentence initially is that the committee was deadlocked. The second part of the sentence speaks of the issue's solution. These two differ-

Note: Photocopying any part of this book is prohibited by law.

ent subjects are combined into one sentence, connected only by 'and.' In reality, these should be two separate sentences, or one sentence connected by a semicolon. Thus, the answer is C.

12. **The correct answer is (A).** Look carefully at this sentence and you'll notice something's amiss. There is no verb for the subject, which is 'June of 2001.' Therefore, the question has given you a sentence fragment. Despite the fact that the latter half of the fragment has the verb 're-call,' the subject of the sentence is left hanging, only described as the hottest month anyone could recall. The correct sentence would read, "June of 2001 was the hottest month."

13. **The correct answer is (A).** Sentences that begin with an introductory phrase generally need to contain a comma to offset the phrase. Read the sentence aloud and you may hear the natural pause between 'paper' and 'there.' This is because of the way in which introductory phrases affect sentences, setting up a place, format, or situation in which the rest of the sentence's actions will unfold. The correct answer is (A); there should be a comma after 'paper.'

14. **The correct answer is (C).** In cases where an adjective or noun is referencing a specific group of humanity, the word requires capitalization. Here, 'Greek' literature is a specific label requiring specific capitalization.

15. **The correct answer is (E).** There is no error present in this sentence.

16. **The correct answer is (C).** In sentences in which one clause is dependent on another one, like the one in this question, it is essential to show this dependency by offsetting the clause with a comma. Above, the author says that baseball is a game for the common person, but wants to note that, specifically, it is not a game dominated by 'the elite.' Therefore, a comma is missing since "not a game for the elite" is not a complete, independent sentence.

17. **The correct answer is (A).** The question at hand gives a sentence that seeks to describe the impact of a visit several astronauts made to the moon. To do this, the writer must use the possessive case when discussing the visit to differentiate between simply a plural use of 's' and a possessive use of 's.' Thus, the word 'astronauts' needs an apostrophe following it, since the noun is plural and the visit belongs to all the astronauts.

18. **The correct answer is (C).** Here is a good example of the subtleties of correct comma usage. The sentence talks of the actions surrounding a certain player's last-second shot. A number of things are happening, but this sentence focuses primarily on the reaction of the security personnel to the crowd's raucous behavior. What did the cadre of security officers do? They whisked the player away. That is the essential information. Anything else is subordinate, even the reason for the whisking away. So in this case, it is essential to use a comma to set off the expression "as the crowd got even rowdier" since it is an added prepositional phrase.

19. **The correct answer is (D).** Sometimes a reader's eyes can play tricks on her, as is probably the case for many with a sentence like the one here. At first glance, it may appear nothing is wrong with the sentence. The construction is sound; the words seem right. But a closer look at the underlined sections, from which at least one answer is probably found, might show you the error here. According to the sentence, those polled favor amending the constitution of one or more states. Thus, the constitution of the state or states in question must be said to belong to a state or states. In this case, the error is that there is a missing possessive case. 'State's' needs an apostrophe.

20. **The correct answer is (D).** This is a run-on sentence. The first part of the sentence discusses the speaker's admission that he didn't read his own work. But the second part of the sentence speaks of the speaker's belief that this was normal behavior, followed by a writer's question to the reader. Normal behavior or not, there are as many as three sentences here merely attached with the connector 'and.' These should be separate sentences, or one sentence connected by a semicolon.

21. The correct answer is (C). Again, it pays to read carefully. The mistake in this question is very easy to see. It is also very easy to miss if you aren't paying close attention. Focusing on poor Captain Howard, even a good reader might gloss over the fact that 'managerment' is not a word. The correct word is management.

22. The correct answer is (B). Test-makers love to try and toss tricky questions in, but smart readers can catch them before they get too far along. Reading this complex sentence, it's easy to assume that 'food lobbies' are the main subject, because they are dubbed "the nation's largest" and because the word 'lobbies' resides right next to the conjugated verb. But aside from the comma between them, 'lobbies' and the verb to have are unconnected. The subject for this sentence is the pork industry, a singular noun. Thus, in an error of subject-verb agreement, the pork industry has drastically increased its visibility.

23. The correct answer is (C). You may have heard of homonyms before. Homonyms are words that sound the same, but that have different meanings. Some words may not be homonyms, but are so similar in sound or spelling that people get them confused. The words "then" and "than" are pronounced the same or very similarly by most people, rendering them difficult to notice, but they mean different things. 'Then' is a standard of time, as in, 'first one, then another.' 'Than' is a comparison word, more fitting for the sentence at hand than the word 'then.' The correct sentence in this case would read "a shorter time than dogs."

24. The correct answer is (E). There is no error present in this sentence.

25. The correct answer is (C). Even the best writers sometimes can write confusing sentences. One way in which this happens is when pronouns get confusing, such as in this question. We have here several plural nouns, all of which can be replaced with 'them.' However, if they are all replaced, it becomes the writer's obligation to make sure the reader understands clearly who is being discussed. The error in this question is a pronoun antecedent disagreement, spe-cifically that whom the word 'them' refers to is unclear. Thus, the answer is (C).

26. The correct answer is (C). Though it may seem relatively nitpicky, there are fairly specific rules for how to use the words 'who,' 'which' or 'that.' In the case of this sentence, the word "which" is used incorrectly, though it does not drastically alter a reader's understanding of the sentence. When referring to a named person, or to a person with specific talents, it is customary to use the word "who." The correct answer in this case is (C), as the sentence should read "one who they believe."

27. The correct answer is (C). Here is a case where reading the sentence silently to oneself can be a huge help. As you can tell, the phrase "somewhat surprisingly" is added on to denote to the reader an important distinction that salsa was an unexpected answer to the research done by advertisers and consumer groups. But as it is technically inessential information, it therefore needs to be offset with commas. Currently, only one comma is present. There should be a comma also before 'somewhat.'

28. The correct answer is (C). Though the true subject in this sentence is 'success,' the error is made a few words later, when the plural noun 'people' is used. The word 'people' has to, by logic, do things in the plural. Thus, the phrase that "people judge their life" must be changed to say that people judge their 'lives,' instead of the singular 'life.'

29. The correct answer is (D). This question requires a reader to remember that it pays to look closely at phrases sandwiched around the word 'and.' Here, a missing predicate verb makes the sentence out of balance. Pigeons are 'quite intelligent' and are 'highly trainable.' So the corrected sentence should read "and are highly trainable," to reflect this parallel structure. The answer is (D).

30. The correct answer is (E). There is no error present in this sentence.

31. The correct answer is (A). Certain nouns are always capitalized. They are known as proper nouns. Some are certainly known to most students, words or phrases such as White House, Super Bowl, or Oscars. The name of the world's athletic competition is also a proper noun requiring capitalization, as in Olympic Games.

32. The correct answer is (B). This sentence has a small but critical error in article usage. When placing an article in front of a word that starts with a vowel, it is always the case that the article 'an' is used. This question has a word that not only starts with a vowel, but that can survive with or without an article. So the sentence shown should read either 'an intolerance' or simply 'intolerance.'

33. The correct answer is (C). This question gives a nice, complex sentence that reads smoothly and looks pretty good, but it has one flaw that needs correcting. Whose building are we reading about in this sentence? James' building. The answer here is that there is a problem with the possessive case when it comes to James and his new building. The correct answer is (C).

34. The correct answer is (A). Unlike the more tricky questions that ask a reader to follow comma and grammar rules or pay close attention to sentence structure, this question is a straightforward one. The error present here is one of spelling. The word 'writeup' is misspelled. The correct way of using the word is as one hyphenated word (write-up).

35. The correct answer is (E). There is no error present in this sentence.

36. The correct answer is (D). This sentence has in its back end a confusing predicate pronoun 'them' whose actual antecedent is unclear. Are the people unable to remember managing their lives before handheld devices, or are they unable to remember managing their lives before owning their lives? The reference may seem easy when you break it down like that, which is exactly what you should do.

37. The correct answer is (C). Sometimes, a subject can get lost from its verb when there are multiple subjects at play. In this case, the reader focuses on 'ruins', and prepares for plural verb conjugation. Just as there is more than one subject present, there is more than one verb. The sundial discussed is a singular noun, and therefore 'uses' pinholes.

38. The correct answer is (A). When reading these sentences on a test, it is crucial to know that not only will there be errors of sentence structure or punctuation, but there will also be some seemingly simple errors. One of these issues that pops up periodically is that of subject-verb agreement. In this case, the subject of the sentence is 'Americans.' So look to find what the Americans are doing in the sentence. It turns out they are failing to realize what really happened in the Great Fire of Chicago. The word "today" tell us that this failure to realize is something that is still ongoing. So the error is that the verb is here in its past tense. The answer is (A), because the correct sentence would say that "Few Americans today...realize."

39. The correct answer is (B). Students, seeking to be careful writers, are often prone to overusing commas to be safe. But overusing commas is no better than under-using them, since it can still confuse a reader. In this sentence, we find out some of the famous Rochesterians. There is no need, when detailing a list of people, places, things, what have you, to begin the series with a comma. The sentence should flow smoothly from "famous former citizens" to "the suffragist Susan B. Anthony."

40. The correct answer is (B). Within a sentence are sometimes found phrases in which a series of descriptors are present, such as, in this case, "high-powered," "sleek," and "compact" models. When such a list of descriptions is present, and when the words describing the subject at hand, here "models," are not inherently a part of the item (such as "flu symptoms), a comma is needed to separate the various descriptors. Thus, the correct way of expressing this sentence is that the new models of computers are "high-powered, sleek, compact models."

41. The correct answer is (E). There is no error present in this sentence.

42. The correct answer is (A). Sentences that begin with an introductory phrase need to contain a comma to offset the phrase. Read the sentence aloud and you may hear the natural pause between 'years' and 'flu.' This is because of the way in which introductory phrases affect sentences, setting up a place, format, or situation in which the rest of the sentence's actions will unfold. The answer is (A); there should be a comma after 'years.'

43. The correct answer is (B). There is little or no organization within this sentence. The most logical place for a break in the string of words and ideas is surrounding any extra information that is ultimately unnecessary or is merely added detail to already stated information. In this sentence, that added information is the precise time in which study time is available in the library. The correct answer to the question is (B), therefore. The sentence should include commas before '12' and after 'PM.'

44. The correct answer is (A). Folks often seeking to be more diligent writers are prone to overusing commas. But overusing commas is really no better than forgetting to use them, since it can still be disorienting to a reader. In this case, the prepositional phrase that begins with 'at' is not in need of special comma usage to offset it. Therefore, the best answer is (A).

45. The correct answer is (B). This sentence is a fragment, lacking a true verb, since the only verbs present are involved in prepositional phrases or are unaligned to the subject at hand, the 'expert rock climbers.' Replacing the word 'who' with a verb form of could, like 'can' would satisfy the basics of sentence structure. So the correct answer is (B).

46. The correct answer is (D). This run-on sentence has too many parts. The first parts of the sentence discuss the city of Dubrovnik's walls, which are still visible. But then the writer added on the fact that tourists come to visit the city to see the walls. However true, this last fact is tacked on. The last sentence can be a separate sentence. Right now, it is merely attached with the connector 'and'. These should be two separate sentences, or one sentence connected by a semicolon. The answer is (D).

47. The correct answer is (B). When a series of phrases is present in a sentence, it is often crucial to make consistent the wording of the entire series. This is an important point, even if it's tough to see sometimes. When this sentence lists the things that must be done in advance of the mover, the correct way of phrasing it would be to make sure "that" the furniture is wrapped, "that" the boxes are packed and "that" the many loose items are collected and boxed up. The missing 'that' in the final item of the series is a lapse in keeping the items parallel around the commas and throughout the series.

48. The correct answer is (D). Dependent clauses are often important information that cannot stand alone, as they describe or illuminate a sentence. Here, fortunetellers are noted to have been involved in actual crime investigations. But it is key to note that there is only a limited sense of success in their use. This final phrase is necessary, but dependent, and therefore needs to be offset with a comma. Hence, the answer is (D).

49. The correct answer is (C). This sentence is actually two full, complex sentences rammed together into a single one. Most of the time, this is called a comma splice, because there is only a comma connecting two completely independent clauses. The sentence that begins 'even some children' can stand by itself and should not be connected by the comma that is present in the underlined section (C).

50. The correct answer is (E). There is no error present in this sentence.

MORE SENTENCE IMPROVEMENT PRACTICE

1. Only one out of every 150,000 chemical compounds proves useful in the field of pharmaceuticals, and thus <u>many research scientists spend their entire careers to investigate drugs</u> that will never receive FDA approval.

A. many research scientists spend their entire careers to investigate drugs

B. many research scientists spend their entire careers investigating drugs

C. many a research scientist spends his or her entire career investigating drugs

D. many research scientists spend their entire career in the investigation of drugs

E. many research scientists investigate drugs in their entire careers

2. The mayor disappointed supporters when <u>he behaved differently than his campaign promises</u>.

A. he behaved differently than his campaign promises

B. he behaved different than his campaign promises

C. he behaved differently from his campaign promises

D. he behaved differently than the behavior of his campaign promises

E. his behavior differed from what he had promised in his campaign

3. Alexander Pushkin, one of Russia's great poets, had a great-grandfather who rose from slavery <u>to becoming a Russian general and favorite advisor of Czar Peter the Great</u>.

A. to becoming a Russian general and favorite advisor of Czar Peter the Great

B. to become a Russian general and favorite advisor of Czar Peter the Great

C. becoming a Russian general and favorite advisor of Czar Peter the Great

D. to being a Russian general and favorite advisor of Czar Peter the Great

E. and did become a Russian general and favorite advisor of Czar Peter the Great

4. Business executives who join corporate volunteer groups will find <u>that it is a good way to meet other businesses</u>.

A. that it is a good way to meet other businesses

B. it is a good way to meet other businesses

C. that it is a good way to meet other executives

D. it a good way for meeting other businessmen and businesswomen

E. that to meet other executives, this is a good way

5. <u>Just like to learn a new route helps people navigate the roadways</u>, learning a second language seems to help map new pathways in the brain.

A. Just like to learn a new route helps people navigate the roadways

B. Just as learning a new route helps people navigate the roadways

C. Similar to learning a new route helps people navigate the roadways

D. To learn a new route helps people navigate the roadways

E. Just as the learning of a new route helps people navigate the roadways

Note: Photocopying any part of this book is prohibited by law.

6. <u>Among art dealers after 1905, artistic rivals Henri Matisse and Pablo Picasso were the most marketable painters alive.</u>
   A. Among art dealers after 1905, artistic rivals Henri Matisse and Pablo Picasso were the most marketable painters alive.
   B. Among art dealers, artistic rivals Henri Matisse and Pablo Picasso were the most marketable painters alive since 1905.
   C. From 1905, artistic rivals Henri Matisse and Pablo Picasso were the most marketable painters alive among art dealers.
   D. From 1905 onward, art collectors found Henri Matisse and Pablo Picasso, two artistic rivals, to be the most marketable living painters.
   E. From 1905 onward, art dealers' most marketable living artistic rivals were Henri Matisse and Pablo Picasso.

7. <u>Any adult who does not take time for careful stretching before they engage in weekend activity</u> is prone to developing a back injury on Monday morning.
   A. Any adult who does not take time for careful stretching before they engage in weekend activity
   B. Any adult who does not take time to stretch carefully before engaging in weekend activity
   C. Any adult not taking time for careful stretching before engaging in weekend activity
   D. Any adult who engages in weekend activity without they take time for careful stretching beforehand
   E. Any adult who does not stretch carefully before engagement in weekend activity

8. After the experiment, in which teens slept while researchers shone light on the backs of their knees, <u>the teens performed better on a cognitive skills test the following day</u>.
   A. the teens performed better on a cognitive skills test the following day
   B. the teens' performance was better on a cognitive skills test the following day
   C. on the following day, the teens performed better on a cognitive skills test
   D. the teens' performance on a cognitive skills test the following day showed improvement over their previous test scores
   E. the teens performed well on a cognitive skills test the following day

9. The Washington, D.C. Humane Society <u>has develop a Visiting Dog program where pet owners show</u> school children how to handle pets with kindness and skill.
   A. has develop a Visiting Dog program where pet owners show
   B. has develop a Visiting Dog program for pet owners showing
   C. has developed a Visiting Dog program for pet owners to show
   D. have developed a Visiting Dog program where pet owners show
   E. for development of a Visiting Dog program where pet owners show

10. A comparison of monthly sales showed that salespeople perform best when they see their department managers working as hard <u>as them</u>.
    A. as them
    B. as they
    C. as they were
    D. as them working
    E. as their work

11. Audiences fell in love with Pavarotti's tenor voice, <u>reason being, he had a uniquely mellifluous yet expressive tone</u>.
    A. reason being, he had a uniquely expressive and mellifluous tone
    B. the reason being, he had a uniquely expressive and mellifluous tone
    C. reason being that he had a uniquely expressive and mellifluous tone
    D. because he had a uniquely expressive and mellifluous tone
    E. due to the fact that he had a uniquely expressive and mellifluous tone

12. During the strike, labor and management finally agreed to <u>bring in counsel to mediate between the dispute</u>.
    A. bring in counsel to mediate between the dispute
    B. bring in counsel to mediate among the dispute
    C. bring in counsel to mediate between the disputants
    D. bring in counsel to mediate of the dispute
    E. bring in counsel to mediate between the disputing ones

13. Customers <u>who intend buying inexpensive neckties will not find hardly any bargains</u> on the last day of the sale.
    A. who intend buying inexpensive neckties will not find hardly any bargains
    B. who intend buying inexpensive neckties will not find hard bargains
    C. who intend on buying inexpensive neckties will not find hardly any bargains
    D. who intend to buy inexpensive neckties will find few bargains
    E. who intend buying inexpensive neckties will find few bargains

14. The casting director explained that <u>either of the parts are acceptable</u> to recite at tryouts for a role in the movie.
    A. either of the parts are acceptable
    B. either of the parts were acceptable
    C. either part is acceptable
    D. either part was acceptable
    E. either of the acceptable parts

15. With one hundred dollars of his own money and $105,000 from seven limited partners, the business tycoon established an investment firm <u>and he grew to $26 million in assets within nine years</u>.
    A. and he grew to $26 million in assets within nine years
    B. and he grew it to $26 million in assets within nine years
    C. and grew to $26 million in assets within nine years
    D. whose assets grew to $26 million within nine years
    E. which grew to $26 million within nine years of assets

16. The traditional rule for polite introductions <u>is to present</u> the younger person to the older, as in "Mr. Tolkien, I would like to introduce my little brother Frodo."
    A. is to present
    B. is presenting
    C. is in presenting
    D. is the presentation of
    E. is that of presenting

17. In the summer of 1787, James Madison earned a reputation as "father of the Constitution" <u>due to he was interested in limiting</u> the government's ability to interfere in citizens' lives.
    A. due to he was interested in limiting
    B. due to his interest in limiting
    C. due to being interesting in limiting
    D. due to the interest to limit
    E. due to the fact that he was interested in limiting

Note: Photocopying any part of this book is prohibited by law.

18. <u>Widely used in hospitals, the properties of pe-troleum jelly are that it is</u> sanitary and hypoallergenic as well as odorless and color-less.
A. Widely used in hospitals, the properties of petroleum jelly are that it is
B. Widely used in hospitals, the properties of petroleum jelly is that it is
C. In wide use in hospitals, petroleum jelly has the properties of being
D. Widely in use in hospitals, petroleum jelly is
E. Widely in use in hospitals, the properties of petroleum jelly are

19. When Romeo first met Juliet, he felt that he <u>never saw another girl as fair as she</u>.
A. never saw another girl as fair as she
B. never saw another girl as fair as her
C. never seen another girl as fair as her
D. never seen another girl as fair as she
E. had never seen another girl as fair as she

20. Nomadic tribes herd their goats, sheep, and cam-els <u>while practice the art of dying wool and weaving intricate carpets</u>.
A. while practice the art of dying wool and weaving intricate carpets
B. while to practice the art of dying wool and weaving intricate carpets
C. which practice the art of dying wool and weaving intricate carpets
D. while practicing the art of dying wool and weaving intricate carpets
E. that practice the art of dying wool and weaving intricate carpets

21. Licking the spoon while baking cookies was always a favorite activity until the news media began to <u>caution against eating dough that con-tains raw eggs</u>.
A. caution against eating dough that contains raw eggs
B. caution against eating dough that contain raw eggs
C. caution against eating dough if it should contain raw eggs
D. caution against eating dough which con-tains raw eggs
E. caution against eating dough to contain raw eggs

22. In Region X, four out of five people alive today <u>has never traveled farther than 100 miles from their home</u>, and many do not have telephones.
A. has never traveled farther than 100 miles from their home
B. has never traveled farther than 100 miles from their homes
C. have never traveled farther than 100 miles from their home
D. have never traveled farther than 100 miles from their homes
E. have never traveled at least 100 miles from their home

23. From the 1950s onward, mass production of affordable vinyl record albums allowed <u>talented musicians' reaching of a vast audience</u>.
A. talented musicians' reaching of a vast audi-ence
B. talented musicians' reaching to a vast audi-ence
C. the reach of talented musicians to a vast audience
D. talented musicians to reach a vast audience
E. a vast audience to be reached by talented musicians

Note: Photocopying any part of this book is prohibited by law.

24. Some choreographers always <u>have their ballet students to hear intently to the music</u> before learning new dance steps.
- A. have their ballet students to hear intently to the music
- B. have their ballet students to hear intently the music
- C. have their ballet students to listen intently to the music
- D. have their ballet students listen intently to the music
- E. have their ballet students hear intently the music

25. When George Marshall retired from military service in 1945, <u>President Truman appointed he to be Ambassador to China</u>.
- A. President Truman appointed he to be Ambassador to China
- B. President Truman appointed him to be Ambassador to China
- C. he was appointed Ambassador to China by President Truman
- D. his appointment as Ambassador to China by President Truman
- E. President Truman's appointment of him to be Ambassador to China occurred

26. The music of Scott Joplin <u>evokes a positive response from both people</u> who are familiar with "Ragtime" as well as from those who are hearing it for the first time.
- A. evokes a positive response from both people
- B. evokes a positive response with both people from
- C. has evoked a positive response from both people
- D. earns a response positively from both people
- E. evokes a positive response both from people

27. Some of the hotel guests <u>would rather the hotel provides rooms that do not face the street</u>.
- A. would rather the hotel provides rooms that do not face the street
- B. would rather the hotel provide rooms that do not face the street
- C. would rather the hotel provides rooms that did not face the street
- D. would rather the hotel provided rooms that do not face the street
- E. would rather the hotel provide rooms not facing the street.

28. Ghandi married at the age of 13, studied law in England at age 20, and practiced law in South Africa for two decades <u>before he had returned to India</u>.
- A. before he had returned to India
- B. before he did return to India
- C. before returning to India
- D. before returned to India
- E. before the return to India

29. Writing in 1939, <u>Auden averred that great poetry can persuade</u> the human heart to experience optimism in the face of war.
- A. Auden averred that great poetry can persuade
- B. Auden avowing that great poetry persuades
- C. Auden vowed that great poetry would persuade
- D. Auden avowed that great poetry can persuade
- E. Auden avowed that great poetry might persuade

30. Flamenco guitarists depend on <u>flamenco dancers to provide rhythmic clapping as accompaniment</u> to the sound of the guitar.

A. flamenco dancers to provide rhythmic clapping as accompaniment

B. flamenco dancers to be providing rhythmic clapping as accompaniment

C. flamenco dancers' provision of rhythmic clapping accompaniment

D. flamenco dancers' providing of rhythmic clapping as accompaniment

E. rhythmic clapping as flamenco dancers' accompaniment

ANSWERS AND EXPLANATIONS

1. **The correct answer is (B).** The original contains a verb tense error: a present participle must follow the subject-verb construction *scientists spend*. (C) is unnecessarily wordy because it uses arcane language. (D) is incorrect because *career* should be plural since it refers to careers belonging to "many scientists," and (D) is also unnecessarily wordy because it uses *in the investigation of* rather than *investigating,* which conveys the same information more concisely. (E) is wrong because there is ambiguity over the antecedent of *their*.

2. **The correct answer is (E).** The original contains an error of comparison: it appears to say that the mayor behaved differently than [the way] his promises [behaved]. (B) fails to correct the original error and incorrectly uses an adjective rather than an adverb to modify a verb. (C) and (D) fail to correct the original error.

3. **The correct answer is (B).** The original is incorrect because an infinitive must follow the verb *rose*. (C) would be correct usage only if a comma separated it from the first clause of the sentence. (D) is incorrect because of incorrect parallelism; it equates the noun *slavery* with the verb *being*. (E) is incorrect because it changes the emphasis of the sentence, indicating that some information is missing.

4. **The correct answer is (C).** The original contains an error of parallelism. Business executives can meet other *business executives* but cannot meet other *businesses*. (B) contains the original error. (D) is incorrect because the preposition creates an error of idiomatic usage: *way to* should appear rather than *way for*. (E) uses awkward construction by separating *that* from its antecedent.

5. **The correct answer is (B).** The original contains two errors. *Just like* cannot precede an infinitive; also, to achieve parallelism, the underlined clause must use the gerund in order to pair with the second clause. (C) and (D) repeat the error of using the infinitive rather than the gerund. (E) corrects the original errors but uses unnecessary wordiness. In most cases, avoid the construction *the -ing of*, as generally this is a wordy synonym for *-ing*.

6. **The correct answer is (D).** The original contains a dangling modifier and vague wording. The use of "among" and the placement of the modifying clause implies that Matisse and Picasso were art dealers. *Alive* is not incorrect, but it detracts from the clarity of the sentence. (B) and (C) fail to correct the misplaced modifier. (E) changes the meaning by implying that Matisse and Picasso were rivals of the art dealers.

7. **The correct answer is (B).** The original contains two errors: it has a noun-pronoun error and unnecessarily cumbersome wording. (A) incorrectly pairs the singular subject *adult* with the plural pronoun *they*. *To stretch carefully* is more precise wording than *for careful stretching*. (C) avoids the pronoun error but uses cumbersome wording. (D) contains an ungrammatical construction: *without* cannot serve as a synonym for *unless*, and cannot precede the present tense. (E) is incorrect because engagement is a noun (meaning *a pledge to marry* or *an appointment*).

8. **The correct answer is (D).** The original contains an error of ambiguity, as *better* has no reference. (B) and (C) do not improve on the original construction. (E) avoids the original problem but changes the meaning. The correct answer, (D), clarifies the sense of the sentence.

9. **The correct answer is (C).** The original incorrectly forms the perfect tense *has developed*, and incorrectly uses *where* to refer to a noun that is not a place. (B) fails to correct the error with develop, and changes the meaning; (B) ambiguously indicates that the program is for the pet owners. You can eliminate (D) because it incorrectly changes the verb from singular to plural even though the subject *Society* is singular. (E) eliminates the verb, creating a sentence fragment, and also fails to correct the original problem with the word *where*.

Note: Photocopying any part of this book is prohibited by law.

10. **The correct answer is (B).** The original is wrong because it uses the direct object pronoun rather than the correct pronoun construction, which is *as hard as they [work]*. (C) corrects the pronoun error but sets the clause in past tense which is incorrect since *they see* sets the sentence in present tense. (D) contains the original error. (E) is wrong because it sets up an error in parallelism by comparing the verb "managers *working*" with the noun "their *work*."

11. **The correct answer is (D).** The original contains an expression that is not acceptable usage: *because* should replace *reason being*. You can eliminate (B) and (C) as soon as you recognize the outlaw expression. (E) corrects the problem but substitutes a wordy phrase; "due to the fact that" is an unnecessary paraphrasing of the simple words *because* or *since*.

12. **The correct answer is (C).** The original uses *dispute* as the indirect object of *mediate*, but this is incorrect because counsel can mediate between people, not between an indivisible entity such as *the dispute*. (B) fails to correct the original problem. In (D), the preposition *of* after *mediate* creates an unacceptable construction. (E) changes the meaning.

13. **The correct answer is (D).** The original contains two errors. An infinitive must follow the verb *intend*. *Not hardly any* is unacceptable usage; acceptable options are either *hardly any* or *few*. (B) fails to correct the *intend* error and changes the meaning by using *hard* as an adjective that modifies *bargains* rather than *any*. (C) fails to correct *not hardly*. (E) fails to correct the *intend* error.

14. **The correct answer is (C).** The original contains an error of pronoun subject-verb disagreement. *Either* is a singular subject and must pair with a singular form of the verb *to be*. (B) contains the original error. (D) changes the meaning because it places the action in the past. (E) is wrong because it fails to include a verb, thus forming a fragment.

15. **The correct answer is (D).** The original creates nonsense by using a personal pronoun between the subject *firm* and the verb *grew*,

thereby implying that the business tycoon grew. (B) is incorrect because it is standard English to *enlarge a firm* or *cause a firm to grow*, but not to *grow a firm*. (C) is wrong because it indicates that the business tycoon himself grew. (E) is wrong because *within nine years of assets* is illogical.

16. **The correct answer is (A).** The sentence is correct as written. It is correct idiomatic usage to state an infinitive after the *rule is*. You can eliminate (B), (C), (D), and (E) because these answers use other forms of the verb.

17. **The correct answer is (B).** The original is incorrect because the preposition *due to* requires the objective pronoun *him* rather than the nominative pronoun *he*. (C) uses a construction that corrects the original problem, but incorrectly uses the adjective *interesting* which changes the meaning. (D) creates ambiguity over *whose interest*. (E) corrects the problem but creates unnecessary wordiness.

18. **The correct answer is (D).** The original is incorrect because it uses passive voice and contains a misplaced modifier: it implies that the modifying clause refers to *properties* being in use, rather than to *jelly*. You can eliminate (B) because it contains the original error of passive voice. (C) corrects both errors but is unnecessarily wordy. (E) fails to correct the misplaced modifier.

19. **The correct answer is (E).** The original is wrong because it uses *simple past* to describe action that took place *prior* to simple past. Only (E) correctly places what he *saw* prior to what he *said*.

20. **The correct answer is (D).** The original contains an error in verb tense: to describe an ongoing action, it uses present rather than present participle. (B) substitutes the infinitive, which also is incorrect since the sentence requires a participle here. (C) and (E) insert a pronoun between the subject and its verb, incorrectly implying that the animals practice the art.

21. **The correct answer is (A).** The sentence is correct as written. (B) has a noun-verb disagree-

ment: *dough* is singular while *contain* is plural. (C) is incorrect because it contains an arcane construction that adds unnecessary wordiness. (D) incorrectly uses *which*, implying that all dough contains raw eggs and therefore the caveat is against eating all dough. (E) is incorrectly implies that "the containment of raw eggs" is a goal.

22. **The correct answer is (D).** The original uses incorrect subject-verb agreement. The plural subject *four* should use a plural verb. (B) is incorrect because it fails to correct the original agreement problem. (C) and (E) are incorrect because they incorrectly imply that four out of five people alive today all share one home.

23. **The correct answer is (D).** The original's use of possessive is an awkward construction that creates confusion. (B) does not improve on the original construction. (C) creates a different, equally awkward construction in its use of "the reach" as subject. (E) is incorrect because it uses passive voice.

24. **The correct answer is (D).** The original contains two errors. Correct idiomatic usage of *some choreographers have* requires the verb *hear* to appear in present tense rather than in the infinitive form. *Hear* is a vocabulary error in this sentence, as *hear* means *to engage in the passive reception of sound*, whereas the correct *listen* means *to make an effort to hear*. (You can insist that students listen, but you cannot make them hear.) Furthermore, for *hear* to appear correctly, the preposition *to* should not follow hear. (B) corrects the preposition error but fails to correct either of the two original problems. (E) corrects the preposition problem but fails to substitute *listen* for *hear*.

25. **The correct answer is (B).** The original incorrectly uses the subject pronoun *he* as the object of the verb *appointed*. (B) corrects the error by using the direct object pronoun *him*. (C) is incorrect because it uses passive voice. (D) creates a sentence fragment that lacks a predicate verb. (E) uses awkward construction and incorrect idiomatic usage, as it is incorrect to say that the *appointment occurred*.

26. **The correct answer is (E).** The original is wrong because of the placement of the adjective *both*; *both* incorrectly appears to modify *people* rather than *who are hearing*. You can eliminate (B), C), and (D) because they fail to correct the original promlem.

27. **The correct answer is (D).** The original incorrectly uses *provides* in present tense following *guests would rather*. If *would rather* refers to action by someone other than the subject, *provides* must appear in the past. Only (D) correctly places *provide* in past tense.

28. **The correct answer is (C).** The original uses the past perfect, creating confusion over the chronology. (B) uses an incorrectly wordy and arcane construction. (D) is incorrect because the preposition *before* interrupts the parallelism of the preceding list of verbs and therefore creates confusion: a correct logical option would be *before he returned*. (E) is incorrect because it creates confusion over the referent of *the*.

29. **The correct answer is (A).** The original is correct as written. The word *averred* (meaning to assert or affirm) is correct. (B), (D), and (E) are incorrect because they illogically substitute *avowed* (meaning to admit or acknowledge).

30. **The correct answer is (A).** The sentence is correct as written. (B) is incorrect because it uses unnecessarily wordy construction. (C) is incorrect because *provision* rarely appears as the object of a possessive pronoun and therefore creates confusion here. (D) contains incorrect idiomatic usage, *providing* should not precede the preposition *of*. (E) is incorrect because it changes the meaning.

MORE PARAGRAPH IMPROVEMENT PRACTICE

Questions 1–7 are based on the following passage.

(1) For centuries, musicians have played "acoustic" guitars, or ones that produce sounds through the vibrations of their strings. (2) They are made of light wood and have curved sides and a flat or arched top and back. (3) Guitar strings are made of bronze, nylon, or steel. (4) Most guitars have 6 strings, but some have 4 or 12. (5) The strings are fastened to the bridge, a small piece of wood on top of the instrument, extend along the finger board and are tied to tuning keys at the head. (6) Narrow metal strips called "frets" are located on the finger board below the strings. (7) To play the guitar, a musician must press the strings against the frets with the fingers of one hand. (8) The musician strums or plucks the strings with the other hand or with a plectrum, also known as a "pick."

(9) In the 1930s, guitar companies begin to commercially produce the electric guitar. (10) An electric guitar is essentially the same as an acoustical. (11) Except it also has an electromagnetic device that picks up the vibrations of the strings and translates them into electrical impulses. (12) An amplifier is used to modify the impulses, and loudspeakers change impulses back into sound. (13) An electric guitar produces a greater range of sounds than an acoustic guitar, although some people find the acoustic to be far more pleasant to listen to.

1. Given the context, which of the following is the best version of sentence 1?
    For centuries, musicians have played "acoustic" guitars, or ones that produce sounds through the vibrations of their strings.
    A. (As it is now)
    B. For centuries, musicians have played "acoustic" guitars: guitars that produce sounds through the vibrations of their strings.
    C. For centuries, musicians have played "acoustic" guitars, since they produce sounds through the vibrations of their strings.
    D. Guitars that produce sounds through the vibrations of their stings, or "acoustic" guitars, have been played by musicians for centuries.
    E. For centuries, musicians have played guitars that produce sounds through the vibrations of their strings or "acoustic" guitars.

2. Of the following, which version of sentence 4 makes the most sense?
    Most guitars have 6 strings, but some have 4 or 12.
    A. (As it is now)
    B. Most guitars have 6 strings, and some have 4 or 12.
    C. Some have 4 or 12 and most guitars have 6 strings.
    D. Most having 6 strings, guitars also have 4 or 12.
    E. Most guitars have 6 strings, although most are having 4 or 12.

3. Which of the following would be most suitable to insert after sentence 6?
   A. The tuning keys are used to adjust the tension of the strings.
   B. Some musicians play the strings on the fret board using their right hand rather than their left.
   C. Each fret marks the position of a specific tone.
   D. Different styles of acoustical guitar are used to make different types of music
   E. Some musicians prefer steel strings, while others prefer nylon.

4. In context, which of the following revisions is necessary in sentence 9?
   In the 1930s, guitar companies begin to commercially produce the electric guitar.
   A. replace "guitar companies" with "they"
   B. replace "commercially" with "commercial"
   C. replace "produce" with "production"
   D. replace "In" with "At"
   E. replace "begin" with "began"

5. What would be the best way to combine sentences 10 and 11, given the context of the passage?
   An electric guitar is essentially the same as an acoustical. Except it also has an electromagnetic device that picks up the vibrations of the strings and translates them into electrical impulses.
   A. An electric guitar is essentially the same as an acoustical since it also has an electromagnetic device that picks up the vibrations of the strings and translates them into electrical impulses.
   B. An electric guitar is essentially the same as an acoustical despite it having an electromagnetic device that picks up the vibrations of the strings and translates them into electrical impulses.
   C. An electric guitar is essentially the same as an acoustical, it also has an electromagnetic device that picks up the vibrations of the strings and translates them into electrical impulses.
   D. An electric guitar is essentially the same as an acoustical, but also has an electromagnetic device that picks up the vibrations of the strings and translates them into electrical impulses.
   E. An electric guitar is essentially the same as an acoustical: it also has an electromagnetic device that picks up the vibrations of the strings and translates them into electrical impulses.

6. In context, which is the best way to correct sentence 12?
   An amplifier is used to modify the impulses, and loudspeakers change impulses back into sound.
   A. remove the word "back"
   B. replace "impulses" with "impulse"
   C. add the word "those" after "change"
   D. add the word "all" after "modify"
   E. replace "An" with "The"

7. Which of the following revisions would improve sentence 13?
An electric guitar produces a greater range of sounds than an acoustic guitar, although some people find the acoustic to be far more pleasant to listen to.
A. An electric guitar produces a greater range of sounds than an acoustic guitar, although some people find the acoustical sounds to be far more pleasant.
B. An electric guitar produces a greater range of sounds than the sounds of an acoustical guitar, although some people find the acoustical to be far more pleasant to listen to.
C. An electric guitar produces a greater range of sounds than an acoustical guitar, although some people find the sounds of an acoustical to be far more pleasant to listen to.
D. Although some people find the acoustical to be far more pleasant to listen to, an electric guitar produces a greater range of sounds than an acoustical guitar.
E. An electric guitar produces a greater range of sounds than an acoustical guitar and some people find the acoustical to be far more pleasant to listen to.

Questions 8–14 are based on the following passage.

(1) Many people confuse the Belgian Malinois, a breed of dog that originated in the country of Belgium, with the characteristics of the German Shepherd. (2) Both dogs have many similarities that cause this confusion. (3) The Malinois and the Shepherd look similar in appearance. (4) A closer look will show differences that set the two breeds apart from one another. (5) The Malinois has a short-haired coat with longer hair along the back of the hind legs, while the Shepherd has an all-over long coat. (6) The Malinois is usually light tan in color, with darker coloration only on the face, but the Shepherd, while also light tan in color, tends to have large areas of dark color on its back and tail, in addition to on its face. (7) Both breeds of dog are about the same height and weight, but the Shepherd has a body type that is unique to its breed, its hindquarters appear to be lower than its shoulders, giving the illusion that it is walking uphill, even on flat ground. (8) It has a more standard conformation, with its hindquarters and shoulders standing at the same height. (9) Both breeds of dogs do, however, have similar personality traits. (10) They are devoted companions, have a tendency to be protective of their owners and their property, have strong herding instincts, and are very intelligent. (11) Both dogs are used for police work and as guide dogs for the sight-impaired. (12) Their loyalty, courage, and intelligence make them the perfect working dog or family pet.

8. Which of the following is the best version of the underlined portion of sentence 1?
Many people confuse the Belgian Malinois, a breed of dog that originated in the country of Belgium, <u>with the characteristics of the German Shepherd.</u>
A. with those of the German Shepherd.
B. with characteristics of the German Shepherd.
C. with the German Shepherd's characteristics.
D. with the German Shepherd.
E. with that of the German Shepherd.

9. Which of the following options is the best way to combine the underlined portions of sentences 3 and 4?
The Malinois and the Shepherd look similar in <u>appearance. A closer look</u> will show differences that set the two breeds apart from one another.
A. appearance, and a closer look
B. appearance, yet a closer look
C. appearance and closer looking
D. appearance, instead a closer look
E. appearance and looking closer

10. Which of the following is the best way to divide sentence 6 into two sentences?

The Malinois is usually light tan in color, with darker coloration only on the face, but the Shepherd, while also light tan in color, tends to have large areas of dark color on its back and tail, in addition to on its face.

A. The Malinois is usually light tan in color, with darker coloration only on the face. The Shepherd, while also light tan in color, tends to have large areas of dark color on its back and tail, as well as its face.

B. The Malinois is usually light tan in color, with darker coloration only on the face. So the Shepherd, while also light tan in color, tends to have large areas of dark color on its back and tail, as well as its face.

C. The Malinois is usually light tan in color, with darker coloration only on the face. Despite this, the Shepherd, while also light tan in color, tends to have large areas of dark color on its back and tail, as well as its face.

D. The Malinois is usually light tan in color, with darker coloration only on the face. Of course the Shepherd, while also light tan in color, tends to have large areas of dark color on its back and tail, as well as its face.

E. The Malinois is usually light tan in color, with darker coloration only on the face. However, the Shepherd, while also light tan in color, tends to have large areas of dark color on its back and tail, in addition to on its face.

11. Which of the following options is the best edit for the underlined portion of sentence 7?

Both breeds of dog are about the same height and weight, but the Shepherd has a body type that is <u>unique to its breed, its hindquarters appear to be lower than its shoulders,</u> giving the illusion that it is walking uphill, even on flat ground.

A. (As it is now)

B. unique to its breed. Its hindquarters appear to be lower than its shoulders

C. unique to its breed its hindquarters appear to be lower than its shoulders

D. unique to its breed: its hindquarters appear to be lower than its shoulders

E. unique to its breed and its hindquarters appear to be lower than its shoulders

12. Which of the following words or phrases best replaces the word "It" in sentence 8?

A. The Malinois

B. The Malinois and the Shepherd each

C. The dog

D. The Shepherd

E. They

13. In order to form two paragraphs, where would the most appropriate place be to place the separation in this passage?

A. after sentence 8

B. after sentence 7

C. after sentence 9

D. after sentence 6

E. after sentence 5

14. All of the following strategies are used by the author of the passage EXCEPT

A. using examples to illustrate a point

B. providing the reader with detailed information

C. quoting those whose opinions concur with the author's

D. articulating both similarities and differences of the breeds

E. supporting opinions by evidence or example

Questions 15–21 are based on the following passage.

The following passage is a student essay written on the topic of childhood immunization.

(1) A great debate over childhood vaccinations and the resulting problems is now brewing. (2) Many people feel they are bad. (3) A number of developmental disorders, such as autism, have been linked to the administration of vaccines. (4) Probably because of the presence of mercury. (5) However, others think they are important to have. (6) Since the risk of problems arising is so very small, many others think the benefits outweigh the risks. (7) Isn't it better to protect children from possible deadly diseases, such as measles, polio or hepatitis? (8) Since the risk of becoming paralyzed from the polio vaccine is only one in 2.7 million, it seems silly to not protect your child from this awful disease. (9) I guess the people who fought the vaccination requirements in places like schools and summer camps do have a point about all that mercury in the vaccine solutions. (10) If there is another way to make these vaccines without the unnecessary and harmful mercury, shouldn't the government do something about it? (11) I think vaccines are necessary (I know I don't want to get diphtheria or cholera), but they should be free from dangerous ingredients. (12) Especially ones that are not necessary. (13) But since the smallpox disease was completely wiped out by the widespread administration of the smallpox vaccine, you have to agree that mandatory vaccination is probably a good thing. (14) If just a few people decide not to get vaccinated, they will help diseases to stay alive.

15. In context, which of the following is the best version of sentence 1?
A great debate over childhood vaccinations and the resulting problems is now brewing.
A. (As it is now)
B. A great debate over childhood vaccinations and the resulting problems are now brewing.
C. A great debate over childhood vaccinations and the resulting problem are now brewing.
D. A great debate over childhood vaccination and the resulting problems are now brewing.
E. Great debates over childhood vaccination and the resulting problem is now brewing.

16. Which of the following revisions would make sentence 2 clearer?
Many people feel they are bad.
A. replace "Many" with "Most"
B. replace "feel" with "felt"
C. replace "people" with "folks"
D. replace "they" with "vaccines"
E. replace "bad" with "harmful"

17. In context of the passage, which of the following is the best way to revise and combine the underlined portion of sentences 3 and 4?
A number of developmental disorders, such as autism, have been linked to the administration of vaccines. Probably because of the presence of mercury.
A. have been linked to the administering of vaccines probably with mercury present.
B. have been linked to the administration of vaccines probably because of mercury being present.
C. have been linked to the administration of, with mercury in them, vaccines.
D. probably because of the presence of mercury in those vaccines, have been linked to the administration of vaccines.
E. have been linked to the administration of vaccines, probably because of the presence of mercury in those vaccines.

18. Which of the following, in the context of the passage, is the best version of sentence 5?
However, others think they are important to have.
- A. (As it is now)
- B. However, they think they are important to have.
- C. However, others think vaccines are important to have.
- D. However, they think vaccines are important to have.
- E. However, some think they are important to have.

19. In context, which is the best edit for the underlined portion of sentence 9?
I guess the people who fought the vaccination requirements in places like schools and summer camps do have a point about all that mercury in the vaccine solutions.
- A. (As it is now)
- B. the people who are fighting
- C. the people who had fought
- D. the people who will fight
- E. the people which fought

20. Which of the following sentences, if eliminated, would not affect the message of the essay?
- A. sentence 10
- B. sentence 11
- C. sentence 12
- D. sentence 13
- E. sentence 14

21. Which of the following provides the clearest rewording of the underlined portion of sentence 14?
If just a few people decide not to get vaccinated, they will help diseases to stay alive.
- A. they will support the life of diseases.
- B. they will enable these diseases to remain a threat to the population.
- C. enabling the life of diseases that threaten the population will happen.
- D. population-threatening diseases will be helped to live.
- E. the result will be the aliveness of these diseases.

Questions 22–28 refer to the following passage.

(1) Sundials, invented more than 4,000 years ago, are the oldest known instruments designed for telling time. (2) As the sun travels across the sky, it cast a shadow on the dial. (3) Sundials told time by measuring the length or the angle. (4) Other early timekeeping devices included hourglasses and water clocks. (5) These devices used either sand or water that flowed from one container into another at a steady rate. (6) By measuring the material in either container, one could tell how much time had passed. (7) The first mechanical clock was probably an invention present in China in the late 1000s, however, this invention was never fully developed, and later Chinese clocks were based on European models.

(8) The first European clocks were probably developed in the late 1200s. (9) They had no hands or dial; instead, they told time by ringing a bell. (10) The word "clock" comes from the French word "cloche" and the German word "Glocke," both of which mean "bell." (11) Modern clocks today range from small, inexpensive models to large, ornamental grandfather clocks with beautiful wood cases and complex chimes. (12) Traditional clocks, called dial clocks, have hands that show the time by pointing to numbers on a dial. (13) Other clocks, called digital clocks, show the time in digital

numerals on the clock face. (14) Many traditional clocks have chimes. (15) Some even have mechanical birds or dancing figurines that mark the hours or other intervals of time.

22. In context, which is the best way to revise sentence 2?
As the sun travels across the sky, it cast a shadow on the dial.
A. replace "As" with "If"
B. replace "travels" with "traveled"
C. replace "across" with "through"
D. replace "it" with "the sun"
E. replace "on" with "up"

23. Which of the following prepositional phrases, if added to the end of the sentence, would clarify sentence 3?
A. of the sky
B. of the angle
C. of the shadow
D. of the length
E. of the sundial

24. Which of the following is the best way to revise the underlined portion of sentence 7?
The first mechanical clock was probably an invention present in China in the late 1000s; however, this invention was never fully developed, and later Chinese clocks were based on European models.
A. The first mechanical clock was probably somehow invented in China in the late 1000s;
B. The first mechanical clock was probably some kind of invention in China in the late 1000s;
C. The first mechanical clock was probably in China in the late 1000s;
D. The first mechanical clock was probably invented in China in the late 1000s;
E. The first mechanical clock, in China in the late 1000s, was probably invented;

25. Which of the following is the best version of sentence 9?
They had no hands or dial; instead, they told time by ringing a bell.
A. (As it is now)
B. They had no hands or dial instead, they told time by ringing a bell.
C. They had no hands or dial instead they told time by ringing a bell.
D. They had no hands or dial; they told time instead by ringing a bell.
E. They had no hands or dial they told, instead, time by ringing a bell.

26. Which of the following choices would eliminate the redundant phrase in sentence 11?
Modern clocks today range from small, inexpensive models to large, ornamental grandfather clocks with beautiful wood cases and complex chimes.
A. replace "small, inexpensive models" with "inexpensive models"
B. eliminate the phrase "complex chimes"
C. add the word "oversized" in front of the word "ornamental"
D. replace "Modern clocks today" with "Modern clocks"
E. eliminate the word "beautiful"

27. Where is the most logical location for sentence 13, given the context of the passage?
A. (Where it is now)
B. after sentence 8
C. after sentence 9
D. after sentence 11
E. after sentence 15

28. If sentences 14 and 15 needed to be combined into one sentence, which of the following is the best way to accomplish this?

Many traditional clocks have chimes. Some even have mechanical birds or dancing figurines that mark the hours or other intervals of time.

A. Many traditional clocks have chimes, and some are even having mechanical birds or dancing figurines that mark the hours or other intervals of time.

B. Many traditional clocks have chimes, and some even have mechanical birds or dancing figurines that mark the hours or other intervals of time.

C. Many traditional clocks have chimes, but some even have mechanical birds or dancing figurines that mark the hours or other intervals of time.

D. Many traditional clocks have chimes since some even have mechanical birds or dancing figurines that mark the hours or other intervals of time.

E. Many traditional clocks have chimes, and some even had mechanical birds or dancing figurines that mark the hours or other intervals of time.

ANSWERS AND EXPLANATIONS

1. **The correct answer is (B).** Sentence 1 contains the definition of an acoustic guitar, but the way sentence 1 is structured leaves the reader guessing. Is the acoustic guitar an instrument that produces sound through the vibrations of strings, or do musician play two types of guitar: acoustic OR one that produces sounds through string vibration? Since this is unclear, choice (A) is incorrect. Choice (C) is not the best choice, because the word "since" implies musicians have been playing these guitars because they produce sound through string vibration, which is not at all the same as defining the word "acoustic." Choice (D) is problematic because it is in the passive voice, and choice (E) is incorrect because it contains the same ambiguity as choice (A). Choice (B) is the best answer. The colon signifies a definition is following and we are able to clearly understand the author's message.

2. **The answer is (A).** Sentence 4 is just fine as it is. We can eliminate choice (B) because of the word "and." Since we know that "most" guitars have 6 strings, the information about some having 4 or 12 should be joined to the preceding independent clause with a conjunction that expresses this difference, such as "but" or "however." Choice (C) has the same problem as (B), but also reverses the order of the clauses, which is awkward. Choice (D) is incorrect for a number of reasons: "most" is ambiguous, "having" requires the auxiliary verb "are" and it is unclear what "4 or 12" refers to in the second clause. Choice (E) is also incorrect, due to the verb "are having." The simple present tense, "have," is the proper form of this verb for sentence 4.

3. **The correct answer is (C).** Because sentence 6 has just defined the term "fret," the most appropriate sentence to follow is one that further elaborates the reason for having frets on the guitar. While all the choices are grammatically correct, choice (C) is the only sentence that would be a suitable addition, immediately after sentence 6, in this passage.

4. **The correct answer is (E).** This question asks you to make the one necessary correction in sentence 3. Choice (E) is the correct answer because the past tense of the verb "to begin" is the correct one to use in this context. The rest of the passage is in the present tense, but since the author tells us the electric guitar was produced "In the 1930s," we know this is in the past; therefore, the verb needs to agree. None of the other choices rectify this problem, and all of the other choices actually create new problems.

5. **The correct answer is (D).** Sentences 10 and 11 can easily be joined by using a conjunction that illustrates the author's point that the electric guitar contains something the acoustic does not. Choice (A) does not do this: "since" implies that an acoustic guitar also has this electromagnetic device, which it does not. We can eliminate choice (B) as well. The author is attempting to express how the electric guitar differs from the acoustic, not that they are the same "despite" the device unique to the electric version. Choice (C) creates one long, run-on sentence by joining the two sentences together with only a comma. Choice (E) is incorrect because it sounds as though both the electric and acoustic guitars have this same electromagnetic device.

6. **The correct answer is (C).** Sentence 12 may appear correct at first glance, but taking a closer look, we see that we actually have two independent clauses joined together by the conjunction "and." The second clause, "loudspeakers change impulses back into sound," is a sentence unto itself, unless we add the word "those" after "change." Now, we have a dependant clause that properly joins the preceding independent clause. Choice (C) is the only answer that creates that dependent clause. All the rest do not correct the problem, and many actually create new problems.

7. **The correct answer is (A).** The first problem we encounter in sentence 13 is the faulty comparison: the sounds of the guitars need to be

compared to one another consistently through-out the sentence. Second, the sentence ends with a preposition, something we also need to correct. Choice (A) rectifies both these mistakes, so this is the best answer. We can eliminate choices (B), (C), and (E) right away, since they all leave the preposition "to" at the end of the sentence. Choice (D) is the only other option left, but reversing the order of the clauses causes sentence 13 to be awkward within the context of the paragraph: sentence 12 discusses how the sounds of an electric guitar are made, so sentence 13 should begin with the clause about electric guitar sounds.

8. **The correct answer is (D).** Sentence 1 contains the error of comparing one dog with the "characteristics" of another. To correct this, we must use choice (D), which correctly compares the "Belgian Malinois" with the "German Shepherd." None of the other choices solve the problem, so (D) is the best answer.

9. **The correct answer is (B).** The second sentence (sentence 4) is acting as a contrast to the first: the author is telling us the dogs look similar, but a closer look shows that they are, in fact, different. All of the choices using "and" as a way to combine the sentences are incorrect (since "and" does not express the contrast), so we can eliminate (A), (C), and (E). We are left with (B) and (D), but choice (D) incorrectly uses the word "instead" as a conjunction, so we can eliminate this as well.

10. **The correct answer is (E).** Choice (A), while grammatically correct, does not clearly notify the reader that a contrasting characteristic of the Shepherd is following. The use of the word "but" in the original sentence clearly indicates the author's intent to do exactly this, so our revision needs to do the same. Choice (B) can be eliminated as well: beginning a sentence with "so" falsely links the coloring of the Shepherd to that of the Malinois, as though one were a result of the other. Choice (C) contains a similar error to that in (B): "despite" creates that same false relationship. Choice (D) is incorrect for the same reason as choice (A): "of course" does not clearly signify the upcoming contrast.

11. **The correct answer is (D).** Sentence 7 is currently a run-on sentence, so we can eliminate choice (A). By diving sentence 7 into two separate sentences, in choice (B), we fail to clearly convey to the reader that the unique body type is being described. Instead, it seems as though the Shepherd has both a unique body type (that is undefined) and also has hindquarters lower than its shoulders. Choice (C) is incorrect: eliminating the punctuation mark altogether does nothing to solve the run-on problem. We can also eliminate (E) because is poses the same problem as choice (B). Choice (D) is correct because the colon both signifies that the definition of that unique characteristic is following and eliminates the run-on sentence problem.

12. **The correct answer is (A).** Because sentence 7 tells us all about the unique body type of the German Shepherd, we know that the "more standard conformation" discussed in sentence 8 must be in reference to the Belgian Malinois. Choices (B) and (D) are incorrect because the author is not saying that the Shepherd is standard. In addition, choice (B) is a plural subject which would not agree with the singular verb "has." The same problem arises with choice (E), so we can eliminate this too. Because choice (C) is just as ambiguous as "It," we can eliminate this and choose choice (A) as our answer.

13. **The correct answer is (A).** This passage actually contains two distinct subtopics: the differences and similarities between the appearance of the Belgian Malinois and the German Shepherd, and the similarities in their personality traits. In order to properly divide this one passage into two paragraphs, the separation should be placed after sentence 8. Choice (A) is the only suitable way to keep each subtopic contained in its own paragraph.

14. **The correct answer is (C).** The author provides detailed descriptions of both the Belgian Malinois and the German Shepherd, so choices (A), (B), and (D) are incorrect. Choice (E) can also be eliminated because the author is of the opinion that many people confuse the two dogs due to their similarities and includes examples of those similarities in the passage. The only cor-

Note: Photocopying any part of this book is prohibited by law.

rect answer is (C): the author never quotes any supporting opinions.

15. **The correct answer is (A).** Sentence 1 may appear to have a subject-verb agreement problem, but this is not the case. The subject "debate" is singular and the verb "is" is in agreement, but because the plural nouns "vaccinations" and "problems" separate the subject and verb, it is easy to think that "is" should be changed to "are." We can eliminate choices (B), (C), and (D), since "are" does not agree with "debate." Choice (E) changes the subject to the plural "debates," but the verb is now singular ("is"), so the sentence is still incorrect.

16. **The correct answer is (D).** Sentence 2 is a little unclear: what do many people feel are bad? Vaccines? Most likely, yes, since that is the topic of this essay, but since the pronoun "they" could also refer to the problems arising from the vaccines, or even to the "people" themselves, we should replace the pronoun "they" with the noun "vaccines." Replacing "Many" with "Most," as in choice (A), does not make the sentence clearer. Choice (B) is incorrect because the author is writing in the present tense, so the past tense "felt" does not belong here. "People" and "folks" are interchangeable and changing this word in choice (C) does nothing to clarify the sentence. The same problem exists in choice (E): the two words are synonyms and don't help create a clearer sentence.

17. **The correct answer is (E).** Sentence 4 is actually a sentence fragment, so we can eliminate this problem by combining it with sentence 3 with a simple comma. In addition, the clause "probably because of the presence of mercury" is a bit unclear, so the best way to revise it is to clarify where that mercury is present. Choice (E) is the only correct answer. The rest of the choices fail to either clarify the statement about the presence of mercury, as in choices (A) and (B), or fail to properly join the dependent clause with sentence 3, as in choices (C) and (D).

18. **The correct answer is (C).** Once again we are faced with the ambiguous pronoun "they." Given that the preceding sentences mention both developmental disorders and vaccines, it

is impossible to tell to which one "they" refers. Choice (C) is the only one that solves this ambiguity problem. Choices (B) and (D) introduce a new ambiguity by replacing "others" with "they." Choice (E) is also incorrect because it does not eliminate the ambiguous pronoun.

19. **The correct answer is (B).** The question asks us to choose the best version in the context of the passage, which alerts us to consider the material in the preceding sentences. Since we know a debate "is now brewing" (sentence 1) and people "feel" vaccinations are dangerous (sentence 2), the action of those fighting the vaccinations in sentence 9 also needs to be in the present tense. Only choice (B) provides us with a verb in the present tense; the rest can be eliminated.

20. **The correct answer is (C).** Sentence 12 is the only sentence we can eliminate from this passage without loosing a pertinent portion of the author's argument. It is actually a fragment that is redundant, repeating a portion of the message in sentence 10 regarding the unnecessary ingredient mercury. All of the other sentences are important to retain, or we risk eliminating the information and opinion with which the author presents us.

21. **The correct answer is (B).** While there is nothing grammatically incorrect about sentence 14, it could be reworded to make its message a little clearer. Choice (B) is the only correct option: it restates the message of the author in a clearer voice and does not contain clumsy expressions or passive voice. The rest of the choices are awkwardly worded and should all be eliminated.

22. **The correct answer is (B).** Sentence 2 is problematic because the verb "travels" should not be in the present tense, as it is now. The action of telling time using the sundial takes place in the past, something we know from sentence 3. Since the verb "cast" in sentence 2 is in the correct past tense, we need only to replace "travels" with "traveled." Choice (A) can be eliminated: we can safely assume the sun is and was going to move across the sky on a daily basis, so using "if" seems very odd. Choice (C) is not incorrect (the sun can move either

"across" or "through"), but it doesn't correct our verb tense problem. Choice (D) is similar: it is not wrong to replace "it" with "the sun," but we still need to fix the verb. Choice (E) is definitely incorrect because shadows are cast "on," never "up."

23. **The correct answer is (C).** Because sentence 2 tells us the sun cast a "shadow," adding the phrase "of the shadow" to sentence 3 makes the author's message clearer. Choice (A) is incorrect because it is not possible to measure "the sky." Choices (B), (D), and (E) all should be eliminated: they actually make the sentence confusing and incorrect.

24. **The correct answer is (D).** The current wording of the first portion of sentence 7 is a bit odd, so we need to be sure we choose the clearest option to rephrase it. Choices (A) and (B) should be eliminated because of the phrases "probably somehow" and "probably some kind of," which do not contribute in any way to the message conveyed by the sentence. Choice (C) makes it sounds as though the first mechanical clock mysteriously appeared in China, and the structure of (E) is awkward and unclear.

25. **The correct answer is (A).** The best choice is (A); there is nothing incorrect about sentence 9. None of the other options clarify or improve the existing sentence, and they all actually contain one or more errors that should never be included in a proper sentence. Choices (B) and (C) eliminate necessary punctuation, and choices (D) and (E) place the word "instead" in the wrong location.

26. **The correct answer is (D).** The only redundant phrase in sentence 11 is "Modern clocks today," so by eliminating the word "today," we solve this style error. Choice (A) is not correct because we need to keep the word "small": it is not a synonym for "inexpensive" and is not redundant. Eliminating the phrase "complex chimes," as in choice (B), only removes important detail from the sentence and does not eliminate redundancy. Choice (C) actually adds a new redundant statement, and choice (E) poses the same problem as choice (B).

27. **The correct answer is (E).** Because we need to consider the relationship of sentence 13 to the rest of the passage, we see that this sentence deals with a new type of clock (the digital clock), yet it is currently located between sentences 12 and 14, which both deal with traditional clocks. Since we want to keep like topics together, the best place for this sentence is at the end of the second paragraph, following sentence 15.

28. **The correct answer is (B).** Because both sentence 14 and 15 deal with the different ways traditional clocks mark the hours, they can be easily combined into one sentence using a comma and the conjunction "and." Choice (A) can be eliminated because it changes the verb "have" to "are having," which is not correct, given that the rest of the verbs in the sentence are in the simple present tense. Choice (C) is incorrect: the conjunction "but" should not be used to join two sentences that discuss the same topic. Choice (D) incorrectly states that the chimes of traditional clocks are a result of a few having birds or figurines. Choice (E) uses the proper conjunction, but, as in choice (A), incorrectly changes the verb tense.

MATH

WORKING BACKWARDS

1. If $\frac{(x+4)}{(5+1)} = 2$, then $x =$

   A. 2
   B. 4
   C. 6
   D. 8
   E. 10

   $\frac{(8+4)}{6} = \frac{12}{6} = 2$

2. If $8x + 7 = 55$, then $x =$

   A. −4
   B. −2
   C. 4
   D. 5
   E. 6

   $8x + 7 = 55$
   $-7 - 7$
   $\frac{8x}{8} = \frac{48}{8}$
   $x = 6$

3. If $8a + 3a - 4a = 28$, $a =$

   A. 2
   B. 4
   C. 5
   D. 5.5
   E. 6.5

   $8a + 3a - 4a = 28$
   $\frac{7a}{7} = \frac{28}{7}$
   $a = 4$

4. A furniture upholsterer charges $20.00 a yard for premium fabric for the first 30 yards and $15.00 a yard for every yard used beyond 30 yards. A project that Rae commissioned required $1,875.00 worth of premium fabric. How many yards of premium fabric were used?

   A. 115
   B. 120
   C. 125
   D. 130
   E. 140

5. At the end of a 30-day month, Karim had worked out at the gym 20 more days than he had not worked out at the gym. How many days did Karim work out at the gym during that month?

   A. 25
   B. 26
   C. 27
   D. 28
   E. 29

   20

6. If the product of 3 consecutive odd integers is 315, what is the middle integer?

   A. 3
   B. 5
   C. 7
   D. 9
   E. 11

   1 3 5

7. If a number is tripled, then increased by 6 and then decreased by 3, the number yielded is 12. What is the number?

   A. 2
   B. 3
   C. 4
   D. 5
   E. 7

Note: Photocopying any part of this book is prohibited by law.

8. The tens digit of a two-digit number is five less than twice the units digit. If the digits are reversed, the resulting number is 9 more than the original number. What is the original number?

A. 13

B. 27

C. 34

D. 55

E. 97

9. The sum of the smaller of two numbers and 7 is equal to three times the larger number minus 2. The larger of the two numbers is 1 more than the smaller. What is the smaller of the two numbers?

A. −3

B. −2

C. 2

D. 3

E. 4

ADDITIONAL PRACTICE QUESTIONS

1. If $\frac{(2x+4)}{(6-3)} = 4$, what is the value of x?

   A. 2

   B. 4

   C. 6

   D. 8

   E. 10

2. Steve's telephone company charges him $0.25 per minute for the first 150 minutes and $0.45 for each additional minute. Last month Steve paid $60.00 for his telephone calls. How many minutes did Steve spend talking on the phone?

   A. 50

   B. 150

   C. 175

   D. 200

   E. 250

3. The sum of three consecutive integers is 27. What is the smallest number?

   A. 7

   B. 8

   C. 9

   D. 10

   E. 11

4. If $3x + 5 = 14$, what is the value of x?

   A. 3

   B. 6

   C. 7

   D. 12

   E. 27

5. The junior class at a certain high school has 16 more girls than boys. If there are 152 students in the class, how many of them are boys?

   A. 65

   B. 68

   C. 72

   D. 76

   E. 84

Note: Photocopying any part of this book is prohibited by law.

ANSWERS AND EXPLANATIONS

1. The correct answer is (D).

You have to solve an equation; there are numbers as answer choices—this is a great Working Backwards question.

Plug the answer choices into the equation and see which one gives you 2. That'll be the correct answer.

Step 1: Start with Answer Choice (C).

Start with choice (C). If $x = 6$, then $\frac{(x+4)}{(5+1)} = \frac{(6+4)}{(5+1)} = \frac{10}{6}$. Choice (C) doesn't work.

Step 2: Eliminate Answers that are Too Big or Too Small.

Since choice (C) is too small, you can eliminate it along with answer choices (A) and (B).

Step 3: Run the Remaining Answers through the Question Stem Until You Find the Right One.

Now, try choice (D), $x = 8$. Then $\frac{(x+4)}{(5+1)} = \frac{(8+4)}{(5+1)} = \frac{12}{6} = 2$. The equation works so choice (D) is the answer. If you had tried (E) first, you would have found that (E) was too big, and you could have chosen (D) without doing any more work.

2. The correct answer is (E).

Go through the answer choices, looking for the value of x for which $8x + 7$ is equal to 55.

Step 1: Start with Answer Choice (C).

If you were to use 4 for x, then:

$$\begin{aligned} \text{If } 8x + 7 &= 55 \\ 8(4) + 7 &= 55 \\ 32 + 7 &= 55 \\ 39 &\neq 55 \end{aligned}$$

Well, this doesn't work. Cancel choice (C) and move on.

Step 2: Eliminate Answers that are Too Big or Too Small.

Which way do you go in this case? Well, if you choose choice (A) and choice (B), you'll see that you arrive at negative numbers rather than the +55 that the equation specifies.

$$\begin{aligned} 8(-4) + 7 &\neq 55 \\ 8(-2) + 7 &\neq 55 \end{aligned}$$

These choices won't work. Cancel them.

Step 3: Run the Remaining Answers through the Question Stem Until You Find the Right One.

Try answer Choice (D):

If $x = 5$ then

$$\begin{aligned} \text{If } 8x + 7 &= 55 \\ 8(5) + 7 &= 55 \\ 40 + 7 &= 55 \\ 47 &\neq 55 \end{aligned}$$

This doesn't work either—only answer Choice (E) is left so it must be correct. Here's how:

If $x = 6$ then $8x + 7 = 55$ is equal to $8(6) + 7 = 55$. That is $48 + 7 = 55$. This works!

3. The correct answer is (B). Run the answer choices through the equation, looking for the one that will make the equation work.

Step 1: Start with Answer Choice (C). If $a = 5$, then:

$$\begin{aligned} 8a + 3a - 4a &= 28 \\ 8(5) + 3(5) - 4(5) &= 28 \\ 40 + 15 - 20 &= 28 \\ 35 &\neq 28 \end{aligned}$$

This doesn't work. Cancel answer choice (C).

Note: Photocopying any part of this book is prohibited by law.

Step 2: Eliminate Answers that are Too Big or Too Small.

If you're not sure in which direction to move—that is, if you're not sure whether bigger or smaller numbers will get you closer to the answer—don't waste time thinking about it too much. Just pick either choice (B) or choice (D) and keep going.

Here, going for something larger for *a* will only make the left-hand side of the equation even bigger. You need something smaller. Eliminate choices (D) and (E).

Step 3: Run the Remaining Answer through the question stem Until you Find the Right One.

Try answer choice (B):

If *a* = 4, then

$$8a + 3a - 4a = 28$$
$$8(4) + 3(4) - 4(4) = 28$$
$$32 + 12 - 16 = 28$$
$$28 = 28$$

This works.

4. The correct answer is (A).

Step 1: Start with Answer Choice (C).

You're Working Backwards into the following equation, which represents the situation described in the question:

$20(first 30 yards) + $15(every yard thereafter) = $1,875

For answer choice (C), 125:

$$\$20(\text{first 30 yards}) = \$600$$
$$\$15 \text{ (remaining 95 yards)} = \$1,425$$
$$\$600 + \$1,425 = \$2,025$$

Too much.

Eliminate Answer Choice (C).

Step 2: Eliminate Answers that are Too Big or Too Small. If answer choice (C) gave you too many yards, can answer choices (D) and (E) be correct? No. They only increase the amount. Eliminate them.

Step 3: Run the Remaining Answers through the Question Stem Until You Find the Right One.

Try choice (B), 120:

$$\$20(\text{first 30 yards}) = \$600$$
$$\$15 \text{ (remaining 90 yards)} = \$1,350$$
$$\$600 + \$1,350 = \$1,950$$

Still too much.

Eliminate answer choice (B). That leaves (A), which must be correct since it is the only answer left. If you feel you must, check answer choice (A). You'll find that the equation works when 115 yards of fabric are used:

$$\$20(\text{first 30 yards}) = \$600$$
$$\$15 \text{ (remaining 85 yards)} = \$1,275$$
$$\$600 + \$1,275 = \$1,875$$

5. The correct answer is (A).

Step 1: Start with Answer Choice (C).

Begin with what you know: there are 30 total days.

If Karim worked out 27 days, there had to be 30 – 27 = 3 days when he did not work out.

You are also told that Karim worked out 20 more days than he didn't work out. Is 27 equal to 3 + 20? No. So, you can scratch choice (C).

Step 2: Eliminate Answers that are Too Big or Too Small.

When the number of days that Karim worked out was 27, there were only 3 days when he didn't work out. This makes the difference between days he worked out and days he didn't work out greater than the 20 that the question stipulates (27 – 3 = 24). So, you need more days that Karim didn't work out, which means you need fewer days that he did. Eliminate (D) and (E).

Step 3: Run the Remaining Answers through the Question Stem Until You Find the Right One.

Try choice (B), 26 days. If Karim worked out 26 days, there had to be 30 – 26 = 4 days when he did not work out.

Note: Photocopying any part of this book is prohibited by law.

You are also told that Karim worked out 20 more days than he didn't work out. Is 26 equal to 4 + 20? No. So, you can scratch this answer choice as well.

That leaves choice (A), 25 days. You can just select choice (A) automatically at this point, but here's how it works out: If Karim worked out 25 days, there had to be 30 - 25 = 5 days when he did not work out.

You are also told that Karim worked out 20 more days than he didn't work out. Is 25 equal to 5 + 20? Yes, it is.

6. **The correct answer is (C).**

Step 1: Start with Answer Choice (C). If each of the answer choices represents the middle of three consecutive odd integers, then answer choice (C) represents the consecutive integers 5, 7, and 9. Multiply:

$$5 \times 7 \times 9 = 315.$$

Sometimes you get lucky when Working Backwards— answer choice (C) works right off the bat, and you don't have to go any further.

7. **The correct answer is (B).** The correct answer choice when tripled, increased by 6 and then decreased by 3, will equal 12.

Step 1: Start with Answer Choice (C). If your number is 4, then tripling 4, increasing it by 6 and then decreasing it by 3 gives you 3(4) + 6 - 3 = 15.

This is too big, you are looking for 12, so eliminate answer choice (C).

Step 2: Eliminate Answers that are Too Big or Too Small. If you can't tell if (C) is too big or too small, just proceed to another answer choice. If you have to check each answer choice, so be it. Better to go slowly and get the question right than to move too quickly and get the question wrong. In this case though, you might see that increasing the number will only increase the outcome, so move on to the smaller values.

Step 3: Run the Remaining Answers through the Question Stem Until You Find the Right One.

Try choice (B). If your number is 3 then tripling 3, increasing it by 6 and then decreasing it by 3 gives you 3(3) + 6 - 3 = 12.

This is right on the money.

8. **The correct answer is (C).**

Step 1: Start with Answer Choice (C).

Work slowly through this question; there's a lot of information here. Test choice (C) against the two conditions stated in the question stem:

Original number: 34.

Is the tens digit five less than twice the units digit?

3 = 2(4) - 5. Yes.

When the digits are reversed, is the resulting number (43) 9 more than the original number?

$$43 = 34 + 9$$
$$43 = 43$$

Sometimes you get lucky when Working Backwards — choice (C) works right off the bat, and you don't have to go any further.

9. **The correct answer is (D).**

Step 1: Start with Answer Choice (C).

You really have to go slowly here. You have two numbers that you're considering; your ultimate job is to find the smaller of the two. You know that:

1) The sum of the smaller of two numbers and 7 is equal to three times the larger number minus 2.

2) The larger of the two numbers is 1 more than the smaller.

The larger of the two numbers is 1 more than the smaller —since the smaller number is 2, the larger number is 3.

Note: Photocopying any part of this book is prohibited by law.

Now, check the 2,3 number pair against the first rule:

The sum of the smaller of two numbers and 7 is equal to three times the larger number minus 2.

$$2 + 7 = 3(3) - 2$$
$$9 = 9 - 2$$
$$9 = 7$$

That one doesn't work.

Cancel answer choice (C).

Step 2: Eliminate Answers that are Too Big or Too Small.

In this case, it's hard to tell which direction to go. Since it is easier to work with positive rather than negative numbers, try choice (D) next.

Step 3: Run the Remaining Answers through the Question Stem Until You Find the Right One.

When you check choice (D), you'll find that it fits perfectly.

The larger of the two numbers is 1 more than the smaller — since the smaller number is 3, the larger number is 4.

Now, check the 3,4 number pair against the first rule:

The sum of the smaller of two numbers and 7 is equal to three times the larger number minus 2.

$$3 + 7 = 3(4) - 2$$
$$10 = 12 - 2$$
$$10 = 10$$

Yes, it is.

This works, so choice (D) is the answer. If you had tried the choices in a different order, you might have taken a little longer, but trying out the choices is still the fastest way to go in questions like this one.

ADDITIONAL PRACTICE QUESTIONS

1. **The correct answer is choice (B).** If you are going to solve this problem by working backwards, you have to plug in each of the answer choices until you find the one that correctly solves the equation. Start with choice (C):

    $$\frac{2(6)+4}{(6-3)} = \frac{12+4}{3}$$
    $$= \frac{16}{3}.$$

    Since $\frac{16}{3} = 5.\overline{3}$, it is too large. Eliminate choice (C) and also choices (D) and (E) since they will also be too large. Now try choice (A):

    $$\frac{2(2)+4}{(6-3)} = \frac{4+4}{3}$$
    $$= \frac{8}{3}.$$

    This is also incorrect. Therefore, choice (B) must be correct. Check it to make sure:

    $$\frac{2(4)+4}{(6-3)} = \frac{8+4}{3}$$
    $$= \frac{12}{3}$$
    $$= 4.$$

    This is, in fact, correct. Choice (B) is correct.

2. **The correct answer is choice (D).** First write an equation representing the situation that you can use to work backwards from. Let x represent the number of minutes over 150 that Steve used:

$$\$0.25(150) + \$0.45x = \$60$$
$$\$37.50 + \$0.45x = \$60.$$

Now plug the answer choices into the equation until you get the correct answer. Start with choice (C). Since x represents the number of minutes after 150, you need to use 175 – 150 = 25

$$\$37.50 + \$0.45(25) = \$37.5 + \$11.25$$
$$= \$48.75$$

This answer is too small, so you can eliminate choice (C), along with choices (A) and (B). Now try choice (D), plugging 200 – 150 = 50 in for x:

$$\$37.50 + \$0.45(50) = \$37.5 + \$22.5$$
$$= \$60.$$

3. **The correct answer is choice (B).** Start with choice (C). Since you are looking for the smallest of three consecutive integers, choice (C) represents the integers 9, 10 and 11. The sum 9 + 10 + 11 = 30 is greater than 27. Therefore, you can eliminate choice (C), as well as choices (D) and (E). Now check choice (A), which represents integers 7, 8, and 9. The sum 7 + 8 + 9 = 24 is too small. Choice (B) must then be correct. You can check this by verifying that the sum 8 + 9 + 10 = 27. Choice (B) is correct.

4. **The correct answer is choice (A).** Plug each of the answer choices in for x until you find the correct answer. Start with choice (C):

$$3x + 5 = 14$$
$$3(7) + 5 = 14$$
$$21 + 5 = 14$$
$$26 \neq 14$$

This answer is too large so you can eliminate choice (C), along with choices (D) and (E) which will also be too large. Now try choice (A):

$$3x + 5 = 14$$
$$3(3) + 5 = 14$$
$$9 + 5 = 14$$
$$14 = 14$$

This statement is true; therefore $x = 3$. Choice (A) is correct.

5. **The correct answer is choice (B).** First, try choice (C). If there are 72 boys then there must be 152 – 72 = 80 girls. But we also know that there are 16 more girls than boys, which means that 16 + 72 must be equal to 80. However, 16 + 72 = 88, which is too large. Eliminate choice (C), along with choices (D) and (E), as these will also be too large. Now try choice (B). If there are 68 boys, then there must be 152 – 68 = 84 girls. Now check to make sure that 68 + 16 = 84. It does, so choice (B) is correct.

PLUGGING IN NUMBERS

1. Gianni has two children, Lily and Umberto. If Lily were 5 years older than she is now, she would be twice as old as Umberto is now. If Lily is Y years old, how old is Umberto?

   A. Y

   B. $Y + 5$

   C. $Y + 7$

   D. $\dfrac{Y + 2}{5}$

   E. $\dfrac{Y + 5}{2}$

2. Deborah bought a house for h dollars and resold it two years later at a 20 percent profit. Which of the following gives the amount of Deborah's profit?

   A. $\$0.20h$

   B. $\$0.02h$

   C. $\$0.80h$

   D. $\$0.08h$

   E. $\$0.98h$

3. Which of the following expressions is equivalent to $2(x - 7)^2$?

   A. $2x - 49$

   B. $2x + 98$

   C. $2x^2 - 98$

   D. $2x^2 + 28x + 49$

   E. $2x^2 - 28x + 98$

4. A clothing manufacturer sews b buttons equally divided among j jackets. The company wants to order enough buttons so that each jacket can have one spare button sewn on its inside lining. How many buttons does the company need to order?

   A. $\dfrac{b}{j} + 1$

   B. $b + 1$

   C. $b + j$

   D. $bj + 1$

   E. $b(j + 1)$

5. Miles invested in a theatre production on January 1. The value of his investment increased by 50% by the end of January. By the end of February his investment lost 20% of the value it had at the beginning of February. The value of his investment at the end of February was what percent of the original amount he invested on January 1?

   A. 50%

   B. 70%

   C. 90%

   D. 110%

   E. 120%

6. Todd's boss started him off with a very low salary, but made an agreement with him that he would increase his salary by 20% every six months for the next two years. If Todd began working for his boss with a salary of S, what was his salary after two years?

   A. $.2S$

   B. $1.2\,S$

   C. $1.44\,S$

   D. $207.36S$

   E. $444.2S$

7. If b is 10 less than c, then the sum of six times c and four times b is equivalent to which of the following?

   A. $10(b + 6)$

   B. $10(b - 6)$

   C. $\dfrac{(b+6)}{10}$

   D. $10(c + 4)$

   E. $\dfrac{(c-4)}{10}$

ADDITIONAL PRACTICE QUESTIONS

1. If Josh was 3 years older than he is now, he would be half as old as Mike is now. If Josh is Y years old now, how old is Mike?

   A. $2(Y - 3)$

   B. $\dfrac{Y - 3}{2}$

   C. $Y + 6$

   D. $2(Y + 3)$

   E. $3(Y + 2)$

2. Which of the following expression is equivalent to $(2x + 3)^2$?

   A. $2x^2 + 6x + 9$

   B. $4x + 6$

   C. $4x^2 + 12x + 9$

   D. $4x^2 + 9$

   E. $4x^2 + 9x + 6$

3. Shawn works at a restaurant and makes s dollars per hour. If Shawn receives a 3% raise, what is his new salary?

   A. $\$0.03s$

   B. $\$0.30s$

   C. $\$0.97s$

   D. $\$1.03s$

   E. $\$1.30s$

4. On January 1st, Nick invested in a certain stock. By the end of January, the value of the stock had decreased by 15%. By the end of February, the value of the stock had increased by 20%. The value of his investment at the end of February was what percent of his original investment?

   A. 30%

   B. 35%

   C. 95%

   D. 102%

   E. 300%

5. If x is four more than y, then the sum of three times x and five times y is equivalent to which of the following?

   A. $4(2x - 3)$

   B. $4(2x + 3)$

   C. $\dfrac{(2y + 3)}{4}$

   D. $4(2y - 3)$

   E. $4(2y + 3)$

Note: Photocopying any part of this book is prohibited by law.

ANSWERS AND EXPLANATIONS

1. The correct answer is (E).

Step 1: Pick a Simple Number to Replace the Variables.

Let Y equal some number that's easy to work with, say, $Y = 7$. So, Lily is now 7 years old.

Step 2: Plug that number into the equations in the question.

"If Lily were 5 years older than she is now. . ."

So, if Lily were $7 + 5 = 12$ years old. . . .

". . . she would be twice as old as Umberto is now."

If 12 years old is twice as old as Umberto, then Umberto is 6 years old.

6 is your target number.

Step 3: Plug the Numbers into the Answer Choices. Eliminate Those that Give a Different Result than the Target Number.

A. $Y = 7$ Eliminate.

B. $Y + 5 = 7 + 5 = 12$ Eliminate.

C. $Y + 7 = 7 + 7 = 14$ Eliminate.

D. $\dfrac{Y+2}{5} = \dfrac{7+2}{5} = \dfrac{9}{5}$ Eliminate.

E. $\dfrac{Y+5}{2} = \dfrac{7+5}{2} = \dfrac{12}{2}$ Keep this.

2. The correct answer is (A). Remember that since a percent means "per hundred," 20% is represented as .20 "twenty hundredths," or as .2 "two tenths." So, in order to determine what 20% of a number is, you must multiply it by .20 or by .2.

You can select a value for h if you find that to be helpful. Pick a number that is easy to work with, and remember that the number does not necessarily have to be realistic for the given situation. The easiest number to pick for percent questions is 100.

So, if $h = 100$, then $0.20h = 20$ since when you multiply a number by 100, you move the deci-

mal point 2 places to the right. So, when you plug in 100 for h in each of the answer choices, the correct answer will yield 20 as an answer:

A. $\$0.20h$ $\$0.20(100) = 20$ Keep this.

B. $\$0.02h$ $\$0.02(100) = 2$ Eliminate.

C. $\$0.80h$ $\$0.80(100) = 80$ Eliminate.

D. $\$0.08h$ $\$0.08(100) = 8$ Eliminate.

E. $\$0.98h$ $\$0.98(100) = 98$ Eliminate.

Only choice (A), $\$0.20h$, works.

3. The correct answer is (E).

Step 1: Pick a Simple Number to Replace the Variables.

This is a great plugging in numbers question since expanding this expression using FOIL could lead to an error, but plugging in numbers is very easy. Since you are subtracting 7 from x, pick a value for x that is bigger than 7, say $x = 10$.

Step 2: Plug that number into the equations or expressions in the question.

$2(x - 7)^2 = 2(10 - 7)^2 = 2(3)^2 = 2(9) = 18$.

18 is your target number.

Step 3: Plug the Number into the Answer Choices. Eliminate Those that Give a Different Result than the Target Number.

A. $2x - 49 = 2(10) - 49 = 20 - 49 = -29$. Eliminate

B. $2x + 98 = 2(10) + 98 = 20 + 98 = 118$. Eliminate

C. $2x^2 - 98 = 2(10)^2 - 98 = 200 - 98 = 102$. Eliminate.

D. $2x^2 + 28x + 49 = 2(10)^2 + 28(10) + 49 = 200 + 280 + 49 = 529$. Eliminate

E. $2x^2 - 28x + 98 = 2(10)^2 - 28(10) + 98 = 200 - 280 + 98 = 18$. This is the only answer choice that works, so it is correct.

4. **The correct answer is (C).** The best way to tackle this question is to pick numbers for b and j. Remember that you want to pick numbers that are easy to work with and that the numbers do not necessarily have to be realistic for the situation given. Say, for instance, that $b = 100$ and $j = 5$. If you are going to distribute 100 buttons equally among 5 jackets, there will be 20 buttons on each jacket. Now, each of the five jackets will need to have one extra button, so that's five extra buttons. So, 20 buttons on each of 5 jackets plus the 5 extra buttons totals 105 buttons.

    Now, plug the values that you selected for b and j in the answer choices and see which one yields 105:

    A. $\dfrac{b}{j} + 1$: $\dfrac{100}{5} + 1$, $20 + 1 = 21$ Eliminate.

    B. $b + 1$: $100 + 1 = 101$ Eliminate.

    C. $b + j$: $100 + 5 = 105$ Keep this.

    D. $bj + 1$: $(100)(5) + 1 = 500 + 1 = 501$ Eliminate.

    E. $b(j + 1)$: $100 (5 + 1) = 100 (6) = 600$ Eliminate.

    Only choice (C), $b + j$, works.

5. **The correct answer is (E).**

    Step 1: Pick a Simple Number to Replace the Variables. This is a potentially sneaky Plug In question because it never comes right out and offers a variable like P or x or y. But a variable, or unknown quantity, is implied. You don't know how much money Miles initially invested, so make up a number to represent it. Since you're working with percents, say Miles started off by investing $100 in the theatre production.

    Step 2: Plug that number into the equations in the question. If Miles started off with $100 in the theatre production, you know that:

    "... the value of his investment increases by 50% during the month of January..."

    $$100 \times .50 = 50$$

    By the end of January, Miles has earned $50 on his initial $100 investment. He now has $150.

    "... decreases by 20% in February."

    $$\$150 \times .20 = \$30$$
    $$\$150 - \$30 = \$120$$

    So, if Miles started with $100, he wound up with $120.

    Step 3: Plug the Numbers into the Answer Choices. Eliminate Those that Give a Different Result than the Target Number.

    "The value of his investment at the end of February was what percent of the original amount he invested on January 1?"

    or

    $120 is what percent of $100? It's 120%, or answer choice (E).

6. **The correct answer is (D).**

    Step 1: Pick a Simple Number to Replace the Variables. Whenever you deal with percents and you have the opportunity to Plug In, make your life easier and Plug In 100.

    Step 2: Plug that number into the equations or expressions in the question. If Todd's salary starts out at $S = 100$ and increases by 20% every 6 months for a total of 2 years, or 24 months (2×12 months) Todd will see 4 cycles of increase ($4 \times 6 = 24$).

    $S = 100$

    First 6 months = $.2S + S = 20 + 100 = 120$

    Second 6 months = $.2(120) + 120 = 24 + 120 = 144$

    Third 6 months = $.2(144) + 144 = 28.8 + 144 = 172.8$

    Fourth 6 months = $.2(172.8) + 172.8 = 34.56 + 172.8 = 207.36$

    Step 3: Plug the Numbers into the Answer Choices. Eliminate Those that Give a Different Result than the Target Number. The only answer choice equivalent to 207.36 when $S = 100$ is answer choice (D).

7. **The correct answer (A).**

Step 1: Pick a Simple Number to Replace the Variables.

First translate:"If b is 10 less than c": $b = c - 10$
"the sum of six times c and four times b": $6c + 4b$

Let $c = 25$. If $c = 25$, then $b = c - 10 = 15$.

Step 2: Plug that number into the equations in the question.

Knowing the value of b and of c, you can say that:
$6c + 4b = 6(25) + 4(15) = 150 + 60 = 210$

210 becomes your target number.

Step 3: Plug the Numbers into the Answers Choices. Eliminate Those that Give a Different Result than the Target Number.

A. $10(b + 6) = 10(15 + 6) = 10(21) = 210$
Keep this.

B. $10(b - 6) = 10(15 - 6) = 10(9) = 90$
Eliminate.

C. $\frac{(b+6)}{10} = \frac{(15+6)}{10} = \frac{21}{10}$ Eliminate.

D. $10(c + 4) = 10(25 + 4) = 10(29) = 290$
Eliminate.

E. $\frac{(c-4)}{10} = \frac{(25-4)}{10} = \frac{21}{10}$ Eliminate.

Only choice (A) yields 210 when $c = 25$ and $b = 15$.

ADDITIONAL PRACTICE QUESTIONS

1. **The correct answer is (A).** Let's pick a number for Y, for example, 17. So Josh is 17 years old. If he were three years older, he would be $17 + 3 = 20$ years old. If this is half of Mike's age, then Mike is $2 \times 20 = 40$ years old. Now, plug 17 in for Y in each of the equations in the answer choices and eliminate the choices that do not give you 40:

A. $2(17 - 3) = 2(14) = 28$ Eliminate.
B. $\frac{17-3}{2} = \frac{14}{2} = 7$ Eliminate.
C. $17 + 6 = 23$ Eliminate.
D. $2(17 + 3) = 2(20) = 40$ Keep this.
E. $3(17 + 2) = 3(19) = 57$ Eliminate.

2. **The correct answer is (C).** Choose a value for x, for example 2. Plugging this value into the equation given in the question gives you:

$$(2x + 3)^2 = (2(2) + 3)^2 = (4 + 3)^2$$
$$= 7^2$$
$$= 49.$$

Now plug $x = 2$ into each of the answer choices to find the one that gives you 49:

A. $2x^2 + 6x + 9$
$= 2(2)^2 + 6(2) + 9$
$= 2(4) + 6(2) + 9$
$= 8 + 12 + 9$
$= 29$. Eliminate.

B. $4x + 6$
$= 4(2) + 6$
$= 8 + 6$
$= 14$. Eliminate.

C. $4x^2 + 12x + 9$
$= 4(2)^2 + 12(2) + 9$
$= 4(4) + 12(2) + 9$
$= 16 + 24 + 9$
$= 49$. Keep this.

D. $4x^2 + 9$
    $= 4(2)^2 + 9$
    $= 4(4) + 9$
    $= 16 + 9$
    $= 25.$ Eliminate.

E. $4x^2 + 9x + 6$
    $= 4(2)^2 + 9(2) + 6$
    $= 4(4) + 9(2) + 6$
    $= 16 + 18 + 6$
    $= 40.$ Eliminate.

3. **The correct answer is (D).** Choose a value for s, for example $10. If Shawn earns $10 per hour and receives a 3% raise, his salary will increase by $0.03 \times $10 = 0.30, which means that his new salary will be $10 + $0.30 = $10.30. Now plug $s = $10 into each answer choice to determine which one is correct:

A. $\$0.03s = \$0.03(\$10)$
    $= \$0.30.$ Eliminate.

B. $\$0.30s = \$0.30(\$10)$
    $= \$3.00.$ Eliminate.

C. $\$0.97s = \$0.97(\$10)$
    $= \$9.70.$ Eliminate.

D. $\$1.03s = \$1.03(\$10)$
    $= \$10.30.$ Keep this.

E. $\$1.30s = \$1.30(\$10)$
    $= \$13.00.$ Eliminate.

4. **The correct answer is (D).** Suppose Nick invested $100. If the value of the stock decreased by 15%, then the value of his investment will decrease by $100 \times 0.15 = $15. His investment is now worth $100 - $15 = $85. If the value of the stock increases by 20%, Nick's investment will increase by $85 \times 0.20 = $17, which means that his investment is now worth $85 + $17 - $102. $102 is 102% of 100. Choice (D) is correct.

5. **The correct answer is (E).** Since x is four more than y, then $x = y + 4$. We are trying to determine the value of the sum of three times x and five times y, or $3x + 5y$. Now choose a number for y, for example 6. Then x must be equal to $6 + 4 = 10$ and $3x + 5y = 3(10) + 5(6) = 30 + 30 = 60$. Now substitute 10 and 6 for x and y in each of the answer choices. Eliminate the choices that do not give 60 as the answer:

A. $4(2x - 3) = 4(2(10) - 3)$
    $= 4(20 - 3)$
    $= 4(17)$
    $= 68.$ Eliminate.

B. $4(2x + 3) = 4(2(10) + 3)$
    $= 4(20 + 3)$
    $= 4(23)$
    $= 92.$ Eliminate.

C. $\dfrac{(2y+3)}{4} = \dfrac{2(6)+3}{4}$
    $= \dfrac{12+3}{4}$
    $= \dfrac{15}{4}.$ Eliminate.

D. $4(2y - 3) = 4(2(6) - 3)$
    $= 4(12 - 3)$
    $= 4(9)$
    $= 36.$ Eliminate.

E. $4(2y + 3) = 4(2(6) + 3)$
    $= 4(12 + 3)$
    $= 4(15)$
    $= 60.$ Keep this.

Note: Photocopying any part of this book is prohibited by law.

NUMBER PROPERTIES

1. The sum of three consecutive even integers is 48. What is the largest of these three integers?
   A. 12
   B. 14
   C. 16
   D. 18
   E. 20

2. What is the value of $7 + (6 \times 3^2) \div (4 - 1)$?
   A. 13
   B. $20\frac{1}{3}$
   C. 25
   D. 39
   E. 115

3. If c and d are both odd integers, which of the following must be odd?
   A. $c + d$
   B. $2c$
   C. $2d$
   D. $2c + d$
   E. $3d + c$

4. What is the value of $6 - (-7)$?
   A. -13
   B. -1
   C. $\frac{6}{7}$
   D. 1
   E. 13

5. What is the value of $-27 \div (-9)$?
   A. -36
   B. -18
   C. -3
   D. $\frac{1}{3}$
   E. 3

6. The sum of 5 distinct prime numbers is an even number. Which of the following is one of the five numbers in the sum?
   A. 2
   B. 3
   C. 5
   D. 7
   E. 11

7. The photos on display in a gallery can each be displayed in a group of 4, 5, or 6 depending upon how the photographer wants to feature them. If the photographer wants the flexibility to display a set of photos in a group of any of the three sizes, which of the following could represent how many photos the photographer has on display?
   A. 20
   B. 24
   C. 30
   D. 60
   E. 80

8. A jewelry designer strings colored beads for a necklace in the following pattern: white, black, and brown. If she strings 86 beads for the necklace, how many black beads will be on the necklace?

ADDITIONAL PRACTICE QUESTIONS

1. What is the length of the line segment shown on the number line below?

    A. –4

    B. 2

    C. 3

    D. 4

    E. 5

2. The sum of four consecutive integers is 42. What is the smallest of these integers?

    A. 8

    B. 9

    C. 10

    D. 11

    E. 12

3. If *a* and *b* are both odd integers, which of the following must be odd?

    A. $2ab$

    B. $a + b$

    C. $2a + 2b$

    D. $b - a$

    E. ab

4. What is the value of $6 + (6 - 4)^2 \times (2 + 1)$?

    A. 18

    B. 20

    C. 30

    D. 52

    E. 78

5. What is the value of $-2 - (-6)$?

    A. –8

    B. –4

    C. 4

    D. 8

    E. 12

Note: Photocopying any part of this book is prohibited by law.

ANSWERS AND EXPLANATIONS

1. **The correct answer is (D).** You can either do this question algebraically, or by Working Backwards.

   Algebraically:

   Remember that consecutive even numbers skip by 2's.

   Let:

   n = the first even integer
   $n + 2$ = the second even integer
   $n + 4$ = the third even integer

   The sum of the three numbers is:

   $$\begin{array}{r} n \\ n + 2 \\ \underline{n + 4} \\ 3n + 6 \end{array}$$

   This sum is equal to 48:

   $3n + 6 = 48$

   Proceed to solve:

   $$\begin{array}{r} 3n + 6 = 48 \\ \underline{-6 \quad -6} \\ \dfrac{3n}{3} = \dfrac{42}{3} \end{array}$$

   Now, you can find the largest of the three numbers:

   $n = 14$
   $n + 2 = 16$
   $n + 4 = 18$

   18 is the largest of the three numbers.

   Choice (D) is correct. Check by simply adding the numbers. $14 + 16 + 18 = 48$.

   By Working Backward:

   Start with the middle choice (C), so that you can go higher or lower in the choices depending upon the answer that you get.

   In this case, choice (C) is 16, and the two consecutive even integers before it are 14 and 12.

   $16 + 14 + 12 = 42$

   Choice (C) is too small; try choice (D) next. The largest number is 18, so the sum of the three numbers is

   $18 + 16 + 14 = 48$

2. **The correct answer is (C).** Go through and evaluate the expression according to the Order of Operations. Begin by doing the operations that are contained in the parentheses. Be sure to follow the Order of Operations within the parentheses as well: Exponents first, followed by multiplication and division in order from left to right, and finally, addition and subtraction in order from left to right:

   $7 + (6 \times 3^2) \div (4 - 1)$

   $7 + (6 \times 9) \div (3)$

   $7 + (54) \div (3)$

   Now, do the division.

   $7 + (54) \div (3)$

   $7 + 18$

   Conclude by doing the addition.

   $7 + 18 = 25$

3. **The correct answer is (D).** The easiest way to tackle this question is to select two simple odd integer values for c and d and plug them into the answer choices. Whichever choice yields an odd result will be your answer:

   Let $c = 3$ and $d = 5$.

   A. $c + d$: $3 + 5 = 8$.   Eliminate.

   B. $2c$: $2(3) = 6$.   Eliminate.

   C. $2d$: $2(5) = 10$.   Eliminate.

   D. $2c + d$: $2(3) + 5 = 11$.   Keep this one.

   E. $3d + c$: $3(5) + 3 = 18$.   Eliminate.

Note: Photocopying any part of this book is prohibited by law.

4. The correct answer is (E). When you are asked to calculate 6 – (–7), you are really being asked what the difference is between 6 and –7. You can see on a number line that this difference is 13:

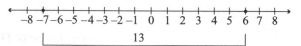

It is possible to answer this question without drawing a number line. Since addition and subtraction are inverse operations of each other, you can subtract –7 from 6 by adding its opposite, which is 7.

$$6 + (7) = 13$$

5. The correct answer is (E). When dividing integers, do the operation and follow these rules for signs:

If the signs are the same, the answer is positive.

If the signs are different, the answers are negative.

Therefore, the value of $-27 \div (-9)$ is 3.

Choice (E) is correct.

6. The correct answer is (A). All prime numbers other than 2 are odd numbers. Therefore, at least four of the five numbers in this sum would have to be odd numbers.

Since any two odd numbers will add up to an even number, the sum of these 4 odd numbers will be even. (For instance, if the numbers were 3, 5, 7 and 11, the sum would be 26, an even number.)

Since the sum of an odd and even number is odd, the fifth prime number will have to be even to maintain the even sum. It will have to be the only even prime number, 2.

7. The correct answer is (D). The correct answer has to be evenly divisible by 4, 5 and 6. Only 60 is a multiple of all three numbers:

$$60 \div 4 = 15$$
$$60 \div 5 = 12$$
$$60 \div 6 = 10$$

8. The correct answer is 29. Since there are three different beads, you want to first determine how many full cycles of three beads there will be by dividing 86 by 3:

$$3\overline{)86} \quad 28 \text{ r.2}$$

Since there are 2 beads left over, there will be an additional white bead and an additional black bead on the necklace. So there will be 29 black beads on the necklace.

ADDITIONAL PRACTICE QUESTIONS

1. **The correct answer is (D).** In order to find the distance of a line segment on a number line, you can subtract the beginning point from the end point. In this case, the segment goes from –1 to 3, which means that the length of the line segment is $3 - (-1) = 3 + 1 = 4$. Choice (D) is correct.

2. **The correct answer is (B).** Let the smallest integer be x. Then each of the next three consecutive integers can be written as $x + 1, x + 2$, and $x + 3$. Now, find the four integers in terms of x, set it equal to 42 and solve:

$$x + (x + 1) + (x + 2) + (x + 3) = 42$$
$$4x + 6 = 42$$
$$4x + 6 - 6 = 42 + 6 - 6$$
$$4x = 36$$
$$x = 9$$

The smallest of the four integers is 9. Choice (B) is correct.

3. **The correct answer is (E).** Choose two odd integers to represent a and b, for example $a = 3$ and $b = 5$. Now, plug these values into the answer choices to find the one that is odd:

$2ab = 2(3)(5) = 30$
$a + b = 3 + 5 = 8$
$2a + 2b = 2(3) + 2(5) = 16$
$b - a = 5 - 3 = 2$
$ab = (3)(5) = 15$

Choice (E) is the only one that is odd, therefore it must be correct.

4. **The correct answer is (A).** In order to compute this equation, you must use PEMDAS. First calculate everything inside the parentheses: $6 + 2^2 \times 3$. Now apply any exponents: $6 + 4 \times 3$. Now do the multiplication: $6 + 12$. Finally, complete the addition: $6 + 12 = 18$. Choice (A) is correct.

5. **The correct answer is (C).** Rewrite the expression as $-2 + 6$, which is equivalent to $6 - 2$, which is equal to 4. Choice (C) is correct.

WORD PROBLEMS

1. Elliot goes to the college bookstore and spends $3.50 on a notebook. He spends five times that amount on a textbook, and half the amount he spent on the textbook on a workbook. How much did Elliot spend at the college bookstore?

    A. $17.50

    B. $21.00

    C. $22.75

    D. $29.75

    E. $31.50

2. Ken has 4 fewer vacation days than Jim does. Ken then uses half his vacation days on a trip to the shore. How many vacation days does Ken use to take his trip to the shore if Jim has 18 vacation days?

3. If the ratio of Liza's annual income to David's annual income is $\frac{4}{5}$, and David's annual income is $40,000, what is Liza's annual income?

    A. $10,000

    B. $30,000

    C. $32,000

    D. $45,000

    E. $50,000

4. According to the graph below, which of the following is the closest approximation to the average increase per year in the weight, in pounds, of Person X between 1994 and 1999?

    WEIGHT OF PERSON X, IN POUNDS

    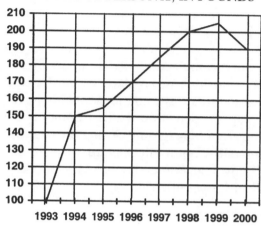

    A. 9

    B. 11

    C. 25

    D. 45

    E. 55

5. A marina that rents motorboats charges $50 per hour per boat plus an additional $10 per occupant per boat per hour. If these charges include tax, what is the total cost of a family of 4 renting a single boat for 3 hours?

    A. $90

    B. $170

    C. $180

    D. $270

    E. $720

Note: Photocopying any part of this book is prohibited by law.

6. If $3y$ is 8 more than y, then y^2 is how many times greater than $\sqrt{y}$?

   A. $2\sqrt{2}$

   B.   8

   C.   16

   D. $24 - \sqrt{2}$

   E. $64\sqrt{2}$

7. A video game is designed around a player hitting a moving target. A player is awarded 5 points for each successful connection with the target. A player is penalized with a 1 point deduction if an attempt results in missing the target. If the sum of the point values given to 20 attempts is 82, how many times did the player successfully hit the target in 20 attempts?

   A.   14

   B.   15

   C.   16

   D.   17

   E.   18

8. The local garden store sells mulch in 10-pound and 25-pound bags. If Don buys 30 bags, and the total weight of the bags is less than 400 pounds, what is the greatest possible number of 25-pound bags Don could have bought?

   A.   10

   B.   9

   C.   8

   D.   7

   E.   6

9. The table below shows the distances between four cities. What is the greatest possible value of m?

Distances in MILES between Four Cities

	Burke	Clinton	Delta	Evans
Burke		8	15	20
Clinton	8		10	m
Delta	15	10		n
Evans	20	m	n	

Note: Photocopying any part of this book is prohibited by law.

ADDITIONAL PRACTICE QUESTIONS

1. Tracy went to the mall and spent $40 on a pair of shoes. She spent three times that amount on a new coat and a quarter of the amount she spent on the coat on a shirt. How much money did Tracy spend on these three items?

   A. $80

   B. $130

   C. $160

   D. $170

   E. $190

2. If the ratio of Erin's weight to Brett's weight is $\frac{3}{5}$ and Brett weighs 180 pounds, how much does Erin weigh?

   A. 90

   B. 108

   C. 120

   D. 144

   E. 300

3. Allison has 14 more dollars than Erica. Allison spent two-thirds of her money at the arcade. If Erica has $13, how much did Allison spend at the arcade?

   A. $8.67

   B. $9.00

   C. $9.30

   D. $18.00

   E. $27.00

4. A fabric store charges $0.60 per yard for the first 50 yards of fabric and $0.40 for each additional yard. How much would it cost to purchase 80 yards of fabric?

   A. $24

   B. $30

   C. $42

   D. $68

   E. $80

5. If $3x$ is eight more than x, then x^2 is how many times greater than $\sqrt{x}$?

   A. 2

   B. 4

   C. 6

   D. 8

   E. 14

ANSWERS AND EXPLANATIONS

1. **The correct answer is (D).** Go through the Three Steps for Word Problems.

    Step 1: Read Through the Question. Okay, you've got Elliot making a trip to the college bookstore and buying three items. You need to know how much he spent in total.

    Step 2: Reread the Question and Translate the English into Math. Let's see what you've got:

    "Elliot spends $3.50 on a notebook" $3.50

    "He spends five times that amount on a textbook" $(5 \times \$3.50) = \$17.50$

    "He spends half the amount he spent on the textbook on a workbook $(\frac{1}{2} \times \$17.50) = \$8.75$

    Step 3: Solve the Math.

    $3.50 (for a notebook) + $17.50 (for the textbook) + $8.75 (for the workbook) = $29.75

2. **The correct answer is (7).** Follow the Three Steps for Word Problems.

    Step 1: Read Through the Question. You've got two people, Ken and Jim. Each person has a number of vacation days. You know that you can figure out the number of vacation days Ken has based on the amount that Jim has. Then, you need to figure out how many vacation days Ken uses to take his trip to the shore.

    Step 2: Reread the Question and Translate the English into Math.

    Ken has 4 fewer vacation days than Jim, so $K = J - 4$

    Jim has 18 vacation days, so $J = 18$

    Thus, Ken has 14 vacation days $(18 - 4 = 14)$

    Ken then used half his vacation days on his trip to the shore. Which leads you to Step 3...

    Step 3: Solve the Math.

    $$\frac{14}{2} = 7$$

    Grid in 7.

3. **The correct answer is (C).** This question is based on a straightforward ratio.

    Step 1: Read Through the Question. You have two people, Liza and David. You have David's annual income plus the ratio of Liza's annual income to David's annual income. You need to solve for Liza's annual income.

    Step 2: Reread the Question and Translate the English into Math. Remember that a ratio is a three-part equation:

    Ratio $= \frac{\text{Part}}{\text{Part}}$. Here the ratio is $\frac{4}{5}$, and the parts are Liza's and David's annual incomes.

    In this case, your ratio is $\frac{4}{5} = \frac{\text{Liza}}{\text{David}}$, or $\frac{4}{5} = \frac{\text{Liza}}{\$40,000}$

    Step 3: Solve the Math.

    $$\frac{4}{5} = \frac{\text{Liza}}{\$40,000}$$

    $$\frac{4}{5} \times \$40,000 = \text{Liza}$$

    $32,000 = Liza

    Liza's annual income is $32,000.

4. **The correct answer is (B).**

    Step 1: Read through the question.

    You need to find the average increase in weight between 1994 and 1999 *per year*. To do this, subtract the weight of Person X in 1994 from his or her weight in 1999 and divide by the number of years.

    Step 2: Examine the Chart or Graph.

    The chart provides a list of years, and the weight of Person X during that year.

Note: Photocopying any part of this book is prohibited by law.

Step 3: Locate the Numbers You Need and Do the Math.

The weight of Person X in 1999 is about 205 pounds. The weight of Person X in 1994 is about 150 pounds. Therefore, between these years, Person X's weight increased by 55 pounds: 205 – 150 = 55. That is an increase of $\frac{55}{5}$ = 11 pounds per year—choice (B).

5. **The correct answer is (D).** Read the question carefully, and calculate the charges one step at a time.

First, calculate the basic charge for the motorboat for 3 hours:

$$3 \times 50 = 150.$$

Then, figure out what the additional charge would be for 4 occupants being on the motorboat for 3 hours:

$$4 \times 3 \times 10 = 120.$$

Finally, combine the two products:

$$150 + 120 = 270.$$

The family could rent the boat for $270.

6. **The correct answer is (B).** Begin by using the information provided in the first part of the sentence to solve for y:

$$3y = y + 8$$
$$3y - y = 8$$
$$\frac{2y}{2} = \frac{8}{2}$$
$$y = 4$$

Then, determine the value of 4^2 and the value of $\sqrt{4}$:

$$4^2 = 16$$
$$\sqrt{4} = 2$$

So, the question becomes: "16 is how many times greater than 2?"

16 is 8 times greater than 2. $2 \times 8 = 16$.

7. **The correct answer is (D).** The best way to answer this question is by Working Backwards. Start with choice (C).

If 16 out of 20 attempts resulted in the target being hit, then 16×5, or 80 points would be awarded for successful hits.

If there were 16 hits, then there were 4 (20 – 16) misses. 1 point is lost for each of these 4 misses, so 4 points were lost in all.

80 – 4 = 76. So, choice (C), 16 is too small. You can actually tell that 16 is too small at the point at which you determined that 16 hits only awarded 80 points, since the question stipulates 82 points.

At this point, you can eliminate choices (A) and (B) as they are even smaller. Move on to choice (D).

If 17 out of 20 attempts resulted in the target being hit, then 17×5, or 85 points would be awarded for successful hits.

If there were 17 hits, then there were 3 (20 – 17) misses. 1 point is lost for each of these 3 misses, so 3 points were lost in all.

$$85 - 3 = 82.$$

8. **The correct answer is (E).** Follow the Three Steps for solving Word Problems.

Step 1: Read Through the Question. Don has the opportunity to buy mulch in two different bag weights. But the question specifically asks for the greatest possible number of 25-pound bags Don could have bought, given that the total weight of bags purchased was under 400 pounds and that the total number of bags purchased was 30.

Step 2: Reread the Question and Translate the English into Math. You want to stockpile Don with as many 25-pound bags of mulch as possible without going over the 400-pound limit.

Now, if all 30 bags were 25-pounders, that would be a combined weight of 750 pounds—way over the 400-pound limit. Some of the bags are 10-pounders. Therefore, you need to make sure that the combined weight of the number of 10-pound bags that makes up part of the total of 30 bags doesn't push the combined weight of all bags beyond the 400-pound limit.

The quickest way to handle this is to Work Backwards from answer choices until you find a number that works.

Begin with choice (C). If Don purchases 8 of the 25-pound bags ...

$$8 \times 25 = 200$$

You're under the 400 pounds limit, so you're off to a good start.

But the problem also stipulates that 30 total bags were purchased. So, if Don bought 8 25-pound bags, then he must have also bought 22 10-pound bags:

$$22 \times 10 = 220$$

That's not going to work—200 pounds + 220 pounds = 420 pounds. That's too much; cancel choice (C).

Since (C) was too large, (A) and (B) must also be too large. Eliminate them as well.

Now, try choice (D), 7 bags:

$$7 \times 25 = 175$$
$$23 \times 10 = 230$$
$$175 + 230 = 405$$

Really close, but still too much.

Choice (E) has to be the answer. You can just select choice (E) automatically at this point, but here's how it works out:

$$6 \times 25 \text{ pounds} = 150$$
$$24 \times 10 \text{ pounds} = 240$$
$$150 + 240 = 390$$

That's under 400, so (E) works.

9. **The correct answer is (28).**

Step 1: Read through the question.

The question is pretty straightforward—what is the greatest possible value of m?

Step 2: Examine the Chart or Graph.

The chart has four rows and four columns, each labeled with the name of a city. At the intersection of a row and a column is a distance—the distance between those two cities in miles.

For instance, the intersection of the Burke row and the Clinton column is 8, so it is 8 miles from Clinton to Burke. The number you are interested in is m—which you can see from the chart is the distance between Clinton and Evans.

Step 3: Locate the Numbers you Need and Do the Math

Try sketching a map, putting Clinton as far as possible from Evans.

You know the distances from Burke to Clinton (8 miles) and from Burke to Evans (20 miles), so use Burke as a starting point:

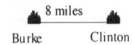

In order for Clinton as far as possible from Evans, Burke needs to be between Clinton and Evans:

So, the greatest possible distance from Evans to Clinton is 20 miles + 8 miles = 28 miles. That is, the greatest possible value of m is 28.

Grid in 28.

Note: Photocopying any part of this book is prohibited by law.

ADDITIONAL PRACTICE QUESTIONS

1. **The correct answer is (E).** We know that Tracy went to the mall and bought three items. We need to determine how much money she spent on the three items. We know that she spent $40 on shoes, $3 \times \$40 = \$120$ on a coat, and $\frac{1}{4} \times \$120 = \$30$ on a shirt. In total, she spent $\$40 + \$120 + \$30 = \$190$. Choice (E) is correct.

2. **The correct answer is (B).** We know Brett's weight and the ratio of Erin's weight to Brett's weight. We are trying to determine Erin's weight:

    $$\frac{3}{5} = \frac{\text{Erin}}{\text{Brett}}$$
    $$\frac{3}{5} = \frac{E}{180}$$
    $$5E = 180 \times 3$$
    $$5E = 540$$
    $$\frac{5E}{5} = \frac{540}{5}$$
    $$E = 108.$$

3. **The correct answer is (D).** We know that Allison has 14 more dollars than Erica, and since Erica has $13, Allison must have $13 + \$14 = \$27$. If Allison spent two thirds of her money at the arcade, then she spent $\$27 \times \frac{2}{3} = \$18$ at the arcade. Choice (D) is correct.

4. **The correct answer is (C).** First calculate how much it would cost to purchase the first 50 yards, $\$0.60 \times 50 = \$30$. In order to purchase 80 yards, you would have to buy $80 - 50 = 30$ additional yards. The cost of the 30 additional yards is $\$0.40 \times 30 = \$12$. Therefore, purchasing 80 yards of fabric would cost $\$30 + \$12 = \$42$. Choice (C) is correct.

5. **The correct answer is (D).** Use the information given in the first part of the question to determine the value of x:

    $$3x = x + 8$$
    $$3x - x = x - x + 8$$
    $$2x = 8$$
    $$\frac{2x}{2} = \frac{8}{2}$$
    $$x = 4$$

    Since we know that $x = 4$ we also know that $x^2 = 16$ and $\sqrt{4} = 2$. Since $\frac{16}{2} = 8$, x^2 is eight times greater than $\sqrt{x}$. Choice (D) is correct.

Note: Photocopying any part of this book is prohibited by law.

DATA INTERPRETATION

Refer to the following graph to answer questions 1–2:

STUDENTS ENROLLED AT CITY HIGH SCHOOL

FRESHMAN	☗ ☗ ☗ ⸱
SOPHOMORES	☗ ☗ ☗
JUNIORS	☗ ☗ ☗
SENIORS	☗ ☗ ⸱

☗ = 100 Students

1. According to the picture graph above, what is the best approximation of the total number of students at City High?

    A. 1,400

    B. 1,200

    C. 1,100

    D. 650

    E. 550

2. According to the picture graph above, what is the best approximation for the percentage of total students at City High who are juniors?

    A. 3%

    B. 20%

    C. 25%

    D. 30%

    E. 35%

3. The chart below shows the number of degrees by which the noontime temperature had risen or fallen over the course of seven days. According to the chart, the total change in temperature for all seven days is equal to the change in the temperature for which single day?

CHANGES IN NOONTIME TEMPERATURES IN ALANDALE	
Days	**Change in Noontime Temperature (in degrees)**
Sunday	+4
Monday	−2
Tuesday	+8
Wednesday	−1
Thursday	+2
Friday	−7
Saturday	−5

    A. Sunday

    B. Tuesday

    C. Wednesday

    D. Friday

    E. Saturday

Note: Photocopying any part of this book is prohibited by law.

4. The pie chart below shows the number of sales of each of four specials in a school cafeteria on a given day. There were 360 sales that day. If $\frac{1}{6}$ of the total number of sales was from pizza, $\frac{1}{3}$ was from tuna melts, and $\frac{5}{12}$ was from meat loaf, what is the value of y?

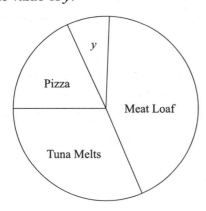

A. 20

B. 30

C. 40

D. 50

E. 60

Refer to the following graph to answer questions 5–7:

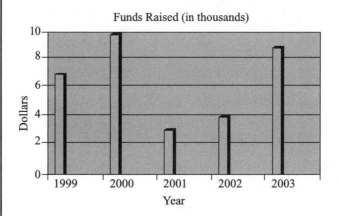

5. Walter runs an annual fundraiser for a worthy cause. Based on the graph above, how much money did Walter raise in the year 2002? (Ignore the dollar sign when gridding.)

6. Walter runs an annual fundraiser for a worthy cause. Based on the graph above, in the year 2000, Walter raised as much money as was raised at the fundraisers of which two years combined?

A. 1999 and 2001

B. 1999 and 2002

C. 1999 and 2003

D. 2001 and 2003

E. 2001 and 2002

7. According to the graph above, the greatest change in the amount of funds raised occurred between which two consecutive years?

   A. 1999 and 2000

   B. 2000 and 2001

   C. 2001 and 2002

   D. 2002 and 2003

   E. It cannot be determined from the information given.

Refer to the following graph to answer questions 8–10:

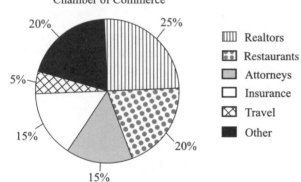

Businesses of the Bentown
Chamber of Commerce

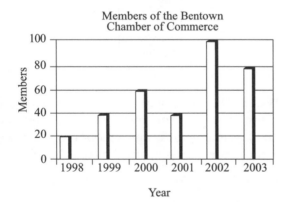

Members of the Bentown
Chamber of Commerce

8. How many realtors were in the Bentown Chamber of Commerce in the year 2000?

   A. 10

   B. 15

   C. 25

   D. 40

   E. 60

9. During what year were there 16 restaurants belonging to the Bentown Chamber of Commerce?

   A. 1999

   B. 2000

   C. 2001

   D. 2002

   E. 2003

10. How many more attorneys were there in the year 2003 than in the year 1998?

   A. 3

   B. 6

   C. 9

   D. 12

   E. 15

Refer to the following graph to answer questions 11–14:

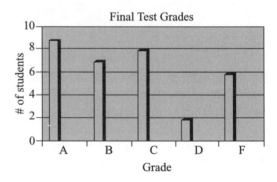

Final Test Grades

11. How many students received a C on the final exam?

   A. 2

   B. 4

   C. 6

   D. 8

   E. 10

12. How many students received a grade above a D?

    A. 2

    B. 6

    C. 12

    D. 24

    E. 26

13. What percentage of students received an A or a B?

    A. 16

    B. 24

    C. 32

    D. 50

    E. 75

14. Which of the following statements is best supported by the given data?

    A. The majority of students failed the final exam.

    B. Four times as many students received a C as received a D.

    C. Most students received a C grade on the final exam.

    D. More A's were received than C's and D's combined.

    E. The fewest number of students received an F.

15. A gym keeps a record of its clients' current weights alongside their membership numbers. Which of the following scatter plots would most likely be representative of the correlation between weights and membership numbers?

A.
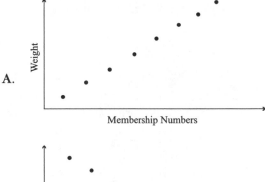

B.

C.

D.
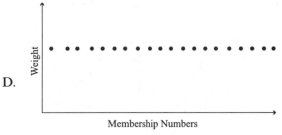

E.

ADDITIONAL PRACTICE QUESTIONS

1. If there are 2,500 students at the university, how many of those are business majors?

Distribution of Majors at a Local University

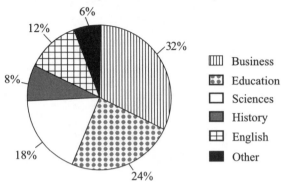

A. 320

B. 400

C. 600

D. 800

E. 1,700

2. If an ice cream cone costs $1.25, how many chocolate cones did the store sell?

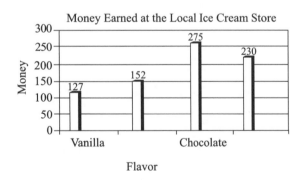

A. 200

B. 220

C. 240

D. 250

E. 275

3. All of the students at the area high school were polled to determine the most popular type of movie. If there are 800 students in the high school, how many more students chose comedy than action?

Favorite Type of Movie

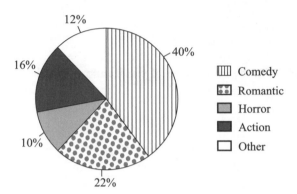

A. 96

B. 128

C. 192

D. 240

E. 320

4. According to the chart above, how many inches of rain fell in Town X in the months of March, April, and May?

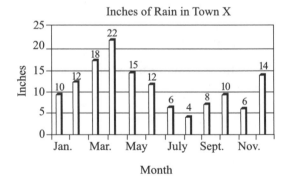

A. 15

B. 18

C. 22

D. 49

E. 55

Note: Photocopying any part of this book is prohibited by law.

5. If the school's budget is $150,000, how much money is used to buy books?

Budget at School X

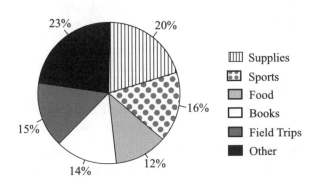

A. $14,000

B. $18,000

C. $21,000

D. $24,000

E. $30,000

ANSWERS AND EXPLANATIONS

1. **The correct answer is (B).** Examine the picture graph and list the number of students in each grade. Assume that each partial student is exactly half of a student and therefore represents 50 students.

   Freshmen: 350
   Sophomores: 300
   Juniors: 300
   Seniors: 250

   Total the students in each grade:
   $$350 + 300 + 300 + 250 = 1,200$$

2. **The correct answer is (C).** Use the percent formula to answer this question. The number of juniors will be the part and the total number of students will be the whole.

   Find the total number of students by adding up the number of students in each grade:

   Freshmen: 350
   Sophomores: 300
   Juniors: 300
   Seniors: 250
   $$350 + 300 + 300 + 250 = 1,200$$

   $$\frac{\text{part}}{\text{whole}} = \frac{\%}{100}$$
   $$\frac{300}{1,200} = \frac{x}{100}$$
   $$\frac{1}{4} = \frac{x}{100}$$
   $$\frac{4x}{4} = \frac{100}{4}$$
   $$x = 25$$

   25% of students at City High are juniors.

3. **The correct answer is (C).** Begin by combining the integers representing the degree changes for the seven days:

   First, combine the positive integers:
   $$4 + 8 + 2 = 14$$

   Then, combine the negative integers by adding the numbers and keeping their negative signs:
   $$(-2) + (-1) + (-7) + (-5) = -15$$

   Finally, combine the positive total with the negative total by subtracting the numbers and taking the sign of the larger number:
   $$14 + (-15) = -1$$

   The total change in temperature for all seven days is –1, which is equal to the change in the temperature for Wednesday.

4. **The correct answer is (B).** First, find the sum of the given fractional values:
   $$\frac{1}{6} + \frac{1}{3} + \frac{5}{12}$$

   The Least Common Denominator for the three fractions is 12 since 12 is the smallest number that 6, 3 and 12 divide into evenly.

   $$\frac{1}{6} = \frac{2}{12} \qquad \frac{1}{3} = \frac{4}{12}$$
   $$\frac{2}{12} + \frac{4}{12} + \frac{5}{12} = \frac{11}{12}$$

   So, the remaining section is $\frac{1}{12}$ of the pie. The question tells you that the total number of sales is 360, so the correct answer is $360 \div 12 = 30$.

   So, $y = 30$.

5. **The correct answer is 4000.** Look along the horizontal axis and find the year 2002. Notice that the bar representing the year 2002 goes up to 4. Note that the title of the graph indicates that the bars on the graph indicate the funds raised *in thousands*. So, $4,000 would have been raised in the year 2002.

   Grid in 4000.

Note: Photocopying any part of this book is prohibited by law.

6. **The correct answer is (A).** Look along the horizontal axis and find the year 2000. Notice that the bar representing the year 2000 goes up to 10. Look for two other years whose bars go as high as a pair of numbers that would add up to 10. 1999 and 2001 have bars that go as high as 7 and 3 respectively.

7. **The correct answer is (B).** Examine the vertical bars in comparison to one another. Just upon visual examination, it is evident that the greatest change in the amount of funds raised occurred between 2000 and 2001. When you examine the numbers, you see that the funds raised dropped from $10,000 in 2000 to $3,000 in 2001. This change is the most significant one between any two consecutive years represented on the graph.

8. **The correct answer is (B).** Examine the bar graph titled "Members of the Bentown Chamber of Commerce" first. Look along the horizontal axis and find the year 2000. Notice that the bar representing the year 2000 goes up to 60. So during the year 2000, there were a total of 60 members of the Bentown Chamber of Commerce."

Now, examine the pie graph titled "Businesses of the Bentown Chamber of Commerce." Notice that the striped portion of the pie representing realtors constitutes 25% of the pie.

Now, you have all of the information that you need to answer the question. Determine what 25% of 60 is:

$$\frac{is}{of} = \frac{\%}{100}$$

$$\frac{x}{60} = \frac{25}{100}$$

$$\frac{x}{60} = \frac{1}{4}$$

$$4x = 1(60)$$

$$4x = 60$$

$$\frac{4x}{4} = \frac{60}{4}$$

$$x = 15$$

15 realtors were in business in Bentown in the year 2000.

9. **The correct answer is (E).** Begin by examining the pie graph entitled "Businesses of the Bentown Chamber of Commerce." Notice that the dotted portion of the pie representing restaurants constitutes 20% of the pie.

Now, you have all of the information that you need to answer the question. Determine what number 16 is 25% of, and match it to one of the bars on the graph titled "Members of the Bentown Chamber of Commerce:"

$$\frac{is}{of} = \frac{\%}{100}$$

$$\frac{16}{x} = \frac{20}{100}$$

$$\frac{16}{x} = \frac{1}{5}$$

$$1x = 5(16)$$

$$x = 80$$

Finally, look at the graph titled "Members of the Bentown Chamber of Commerce" to see which year has a bar extending to 80. The year 2003 does.

Note: Photocopying any part of this book is prohibited by law.

10. **The correct answer is (C).** Begin by examining the pie graph entitled "Businesses of the Bentown Chamber of Commerce." Notice that the gray portion of the pie representing attorneys constitutes 15% of the pie. Now, look at the graph titled "Members of the Bentown Chamber of Commerce" to see what the total number of members was for the years 1998 and 2003. Notice that the bar representing the year 1998 goes up to 20, and the bar representing the year 2003 goes up to 80.

If you determine what 15% of 20 is and 15% of 80 is and take the difference between these two amounts, you'll have your answer.

First determine what 15% of 20 is:

$$\frac{is}{of} = \frac{\%}{100}$$

$$\frac{x}{20} = \frac{15}{100}$$

$$\frac{x}{20} = \frac{3}{20}$$

$$x = 3$$

Then, determine what 15% of 80 is:

$$\frac{is}{of} = \frac{\%}{100}$$

$$\frac{x}{80} = \frac{15}{100}$$

$$\frac{x}{80} = \frac{3}{20}$$

$$20x = 3(80)$$

$$20x = 240$$

$$\frac{20x}{20} = \frac{240}{20}$$

$$x = 12$$

So, if there were 12 attorneys in 2003 and 3 attorneys in 1998, there were 12 – 3 = 9 more attorneys in the year 2003 than in the year 1998.

11. **The correct answer is (D).** Look for the bar representing a C grade on the horizontal axis. Then, find the corresponding value on the vertical axis, which is 8.

12. **The correct answer is (D).** The three grades that are above a D are an A, a B, and a C. Since 9 students received an A, 7 students received a B, and 8 students received a C, then 9 + 7 + 8 = 24 students received a grade above a D.

13. **The correct answer is (D).** The total number of students can be found by adding up how many students received each grade: 9 + 7 + 8 + 2 + 6 = 32 students in the class. 9 + 7 = 16 out of 32 students received an A or a B, and $\frac{16}{32} = \frac{1}{2} = 50\%$. So, 50% of the students received an A or a B.

14. **The correct answer is (B).** A total of 8 students received C's. A total of 2 students received D's. Since $\frac{8}{4} = 2$, the statement given in choice (B) is correct.

15. **The correct answer is (E).** You would not expect there to be any correlation whatsoever between clients' weights and their membership numbers since membership numbers are assigned arbitrarily. When there is very low or zero correlation, the points will appear randomly scattered throughout the graph. Only choice (E) displays a graph with the scattered points indicating that there would be no correlation between weights and membership numbers.

The scatterplot in choice (A) indicates a direct correlation, that as the clients' membership numbers increase, their reported weights do as well. The scatterplot in choice (B) indicates an inverse relationship between these variables, that as the clients' membership numbers increase, their reported weights decrease. The points in the scatterplot in choice (C) resemble half a parabola, representing exponential growth. The scatterplot in choice (D) would indicate that each client has the exact same weight.

ADDITIONAL PRACTICE QUESTIONS

1. **The correct answer is (D).** According to the chart, 32% of the students are business majors. If there are 2,500 total students then:

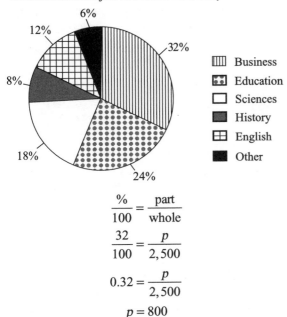

Distribution of Majors at a Local University

- Business
- Education
- Sciences
- History
- English
- Other

$$\frac{\%}{100} = \frac{\text{part}}{\text{whole}}$$

$$\frac{32}{100} = \frac{p}{2,500}$$

$$0.32 = \frac{p}{2,500}$$

$$p = 800$$

There are 800 business majors at the university.

2. **The correct answer is (B).** According to the chart, the store made $275 from selling chocolate ice cream cones. Since each cone cost $1.25, the store must have sold $\frac{\$275}{\$1.25}$ = 220 chocolate cones.

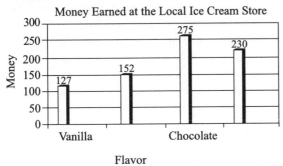

Money Earned at the Local Ice Cream Store

3. **The correct answer is (C).** According to the chart, 40% of the students chose comedy and 16% of the students chose action. This means that 0.40 × 800 = 320 students chose comedy and 0.16 × 800 = 128 students chose action. Therefore, 320 – 128 = 192 more students chose comedy than action.

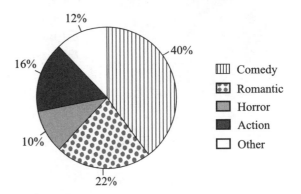

Favorite Type of Movie

- Comedy
- Romantic
- Horror
- Action
- Other

4. **The correct answer is (E).** In March, 18 inches of rain fell. In April, 22 inches of rain fell, and in May, 15 inches of rain fell. In total, 18 + 22 + 15 = 55 inches of rain fell in March, April, and May. Choice (E) is correct.

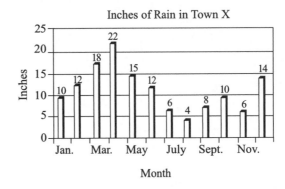

Inches of Rain in Town X

Note: Photocopying any part of this book is prohibited by law.

5. The correct answer is (C). Since 14% of the $150,000 budget is used to buy books, then:

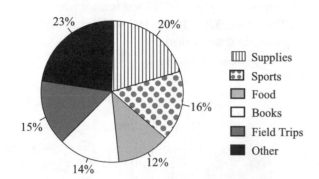

Budget at School X

23%   20%

16%

15%

14%   12%

Supplies
Sports
Food
Books
Field Trips
Other

$$\frac{\%}{100} = \frac{\text{part}}{\text{whole}}$$

$$\frac{14}{100} = \frac{p}{150,000}$$

$$0.14 = \frac{p}{150,000}$$

$$p = 21,000.$$

Note: Photocopying any part of this book is prohibited by law.

POWERS

1. What is the value of $(-7x^5)^2$?

   A. $-14x^7$

   B. $-7x^{10}$

   C. $49x^7$

   D. $49x^{10}$

   E. $49x^{25}$

2. $m^5 \div m^5 =$

   A. 0

   B. 1

   C. m^1

   D. m^{10}

   E. m^{25}

3. If $p = 2$, what is the value of $(p^4)\,p^3$?

4. The number 60,223 could be written as which of the following?

   A. $6(10^5) + 2(10^2) + 2(10) + 3$

   B. $6(10^4) + 0(10^3) + 2(10^2) + 2(10)$

   C. $6(10^4) + 0(10^3) + 2(10^2) + 2(10) + 3$

   D. $6(10^4) + 2(10^2) + 2(10) + 3(10)$

   E. $6(10^4) + 0(10^3) + 2(10^2) + 3(10)$

5. $4^5 \times 4^3 =$

   A. 4^2

   B. $4^2 \times 15$

   C. 4^8

   D. 16^8

   E. 4^{15}

6. $9^{27} - 9^{26}$ is equivalent to which of the following values?

   A. 9

   B. 9^2

   C. 81

   D. $8(9^{26})$

   E. $9 \times (9^{26})$

7. $\dfrac{\left(d^5\right)^2}{d^8} =$

   A. $\dfrac{1}{d^2}$

   B. $\dfrac{1}{d}$

   C. d

   D. d^2

   E. d^{18}

8. $\left(\dfrac{1}{2}x^4\right)^{-2} =$

   A. $\dfrac{1}{x^4}$

   B. $\dfrac{1}{4}x^2$

   C. $-\dfrac{4}{x^8}$

   D. $\dfrac{4}{x^8}$

   E. $4x^2$

Note: Photocopying any part of this book is prohibited by law.

ADDITIONAL PRACTICE QUESTIONS

1. Which of the following is equivalent to $x^3y^2 \times x^4y$?

    A. xy^9

    B. x^6y^4

    C. x^7y^2

    D. x^7y^3

    E. $x^{12}y^2$

2. Which of the following is equivalent to $(a^2b^3)^4$?

    A. ab^9

    B. a^2b^{12}

    C. a^6b^7

    D. a^8b^3

    E. a^8b^{12}

3. Which of the following is equivalent to $\frac{x^4y^2}{x^2y}$?

    A. xy^2

    B. x^2y

    C. x^2y^2

    D. x^6y^3

    E. x^8y^2

4. Which of the following is equivalent to $(xy^2)^3$?

    A. xy^6

    B. x^2y

    C. x^3y^5

    D. x^3y^6

    E. x^4y^5

5. Which of the following is equivalent to $\frac{ab^3}{a^3b}$?

    A. a^2b^2

    B. $\frac{b^2}{a^2}$

    C. a^3b^3

    D. $\frac{a^2}{b^2}$

    E. a^4b^4

Note: Photocopying any part of this book is prohibited by law.

ANSWERS AND EXPLANATIONS

1. **The correct answer is (D).** Simplify one step at a time. First, raise the coefficient to the power:
$$(-7)^2 = 49$$

   Raise the variable to the power by keeping the base and multiplying the exponents:
$$(x^5)^2 = x^{10}$$
$$(-7x^5)^2 = 49x^{10}$$

2. **The correct answer is (B).** There are a couple of different ways to approach this question. The easiest rule to apply to it is that any number divided by itself is equal to 1.

   If you approach this question according to the rules governing operations with exponents, you know that you are supposed to subtract the exponents when you are dividing variables with a common base: $m^5 \div m^5 = m^0$. Since any number raised to the zero power equals 1, $m^5 \div m^5 = 1$.

   Finally, you could always plug in a value for m, perform the operations and solve and see which answer choice matches. Since you're going to be raising m to the fifth power, you'll want to select a relatively small value for m, like 2:
$$m^5 \div m^5 = (2)^5 \div (2)^5$$
$$= 32 \div 32$$
$$= 1$$

   No matter which method you select, 1 is your answer.

3. **The correct answer is 128.** Remember, to multiply exponents with the same bases, add the exponents. This is easier to understand if you recall what exponent notation actually means:

   p^4 is a quicker way of writing: $p \times p \times p \times p$.

   p^3 is a quicker way of writing: $p \times p \times p$.

   So, $(p^4) p^3$ can be rewritten as $p\,p\,p\,p\,p\,p\,p$. There are 7 ps, so $(p^4) p^3 = p^7$.

   Since you know that $p = 2$, the value of $(p^4) p^3 = p^7$ becomes:
$$2^7 = 2 \times 2 \times 2 \times 2 \times 2 \times 2 \times 2$$
$$= 128$$

4. **The correct answer is (C).** Remember, when 10 is raised to a power, the exponent tells you how many zeroes are in the number.

   For example: 10^4 is a quick way of writing 10,000—the digit 1 followed by 4 zeros. Thus, $6 \times 10^4 = 60,000$. Given this pattern, 60,223 is equal to:
$$6 \times 10^4 = 60,000$$
$$0 \times 10^3 = 0,000$$
$$2 \times 10^2 = 200$$
$$2 \times 10 = 20$$
$$3 = 3$$

   $6(10^4) + 0(10^3) + 2(10^2) + 3 = 60,223$.

   (The "0,000" $= 0 \times 10^3$ step is included to follow the required pattern exactly. "0×10^3" is another way of saying "there is a value of 0 in the thousands place.")

5. **The correct answer is (C).** Remember, to multiply exponents with the same bases, keep the base and add the exponents—even when the base is a number. For $4^5 \times 4^3$, keep the base, 4, and add the exponents: $5 + 3 = 8$. Therefore, $4^5 \times 4^3 = 4^8$.

6. **The correct answer is (D).** Don't panic when you see large exponents. You should never calculate something like this. The test-makers are actually trying to determine whether you understand how to add and subtract exponents. If you do, this problem becomes pretty basic. Remember that you can't simply add or subtract powers. That is, $9^{27} - 9^{26}$ is NOT equal to $9^{(27-26)} = 9^1$. That's what you would do for $9^{27} \div 9^{26}$.

   If you factor out 9^{26} from $9^{27} - 9^{26}$, you're left with $9^{26}(9 - 1)$, which simplifies to $9^{26}(8)$.

Note: Photocopying any part of this book is prohibited by law.

7. **The correct answer is (D).** To answer this question, you need to know the rules governing operations with exponents.

Specifically, when you raise a power to a power, you multiply the exponents. In this case:

$$(d^5)^2 = d^{(5 \times 2)}$$
$$= d^{10}$$

Specifically, when you divide a power by a power, you subtract the exponents. In this case:

$$\frac{\left(d^5\right)^2}{d^8} = \frac{d^{10}}{d^8}$$
$$= d^{10-8}$$
$$= d^2.$$

Alternatively, since the answers are variables, you could try Plugging-in numbers. Let $d = 2$. Then:

$$\frac{\left(d^5\right)^2}{d^8} = \frac{\left(2^5\right)^2}{d^8}$$
$$= \frac{(32)^2}{256}$$
$$= \frac{1024}{256}$$
$$= 4.$$

This is your target number. Now, run through all the answer choices to see which yields 4 when $d = 2$:

A. $\frac{1}{d^2} = \frac{1}{(2)^2} = \frac{1}{4}$.   Eliminate.

B. $\frac{1}{d} = \frac{1}{2}$.   Eliminate.

C. $d = 2$.   Eliminate.

D. $d^2 = (2)^2 = 4$.   Keep this.

E. $d^{18} = (2)^{18} = 262,144$.   Eliminate.

8. **The correct answer is (D).** This question tests your knowledge about raising a fraction coefficient to a negative power and about raising a power to a negative power.

Simplify one step at a time, starting with raising the coefficient, $\frac{1}{2}$, to the –2 power.

Remember that the rule for raising a coefficient to a negative power is to take the inverse of what that value would be raised to the positive version of that power. It does NOT have anything to do with making the number a negative number. So, $\left(\frac{1}{2}\right)^2 = \frac{1}{4}$ and the inverse of $\frac{1}{4}$ is 4. So, the coefficient of your answer is 4. Knowing this much narrows your choices down to choices (D) and (E).

Finish up by raising x^4 to the –2 power. The rule for raising a power of a variable to a negative power is to take the inverse of what that value would be raised to the positive version of that power. Since $(x^4)^2 = x^8$, so $(x^4)^{-2} = \frac{1}{x^8}$. Multiply this variable result with the coefficient result to get your final answer:

$$\left(\frac{1}{2}x^4\right)^{-2} = (4)\left(\frac{1}{x^8}\right) = \frac{4}{x^8}$$

ADDITIONAL PRACTICE QUESTIONS

1. **The correct answer is (D).** Remember, when multiplying terms with the same base, add the exponents together. Therefore, $x^3y^2 \times x^4y = x^{(3+4)}y^{(2+1)} = x^7y^3$.

2. **The correct answer is (E).** When a power is raised to another power, the exponents are multiplied. Therefore, $(a^2b^3)^4 = a^{(2 \times 4)}b^{(3 \times 4)} = a^8b^{12}$.

3. **The correct answer is (B).** When dividing terms with the same base, their exponents can be subtracted from each other. Therefore, $\frac{x^4y^2}{x^2y}$ $= x^{(4-2)}y^{(2-1)} = x^2y$. Choice (B) is correct.

4. **The correct answer is (D).** When a power is raised to another power, the exponents are multiplied together. Therefore, $(xy^2)^3 = x^{(1 \times 3)}y^{(2 \times 3)} = x^3y^6$.

5. **The correct answer is (B).** When terms with the same base are being divided, the exponents are subtracted from each other. Therefore, $\frac{ab^3}{a^3b} = a^{(1-3)}b^{(3-1)} = a^{-2}b^2 = \frac{b^2}{a^2}$.

Note: Photocopying any part of this book is prohibited by law.

ROOTS

1. What two whole numbers does $\sqrt{77}$ lie between?

    A. 76 and 78

    B. $\sqrt{77}$ and $\sqrt{78}$

    C. 8 and 9

    D. 7 and 8

    E. 6 and 7

2. If a square has an area of 72 square centimeters, what is the length of one side of that square in centimeters?

    A. $3\sqrt{2}$

    B. $4\sqrt{3}$

    C. 8

    D. $6\sqrt{2}$

    E. 18

3. The expression $\sqrt{300}$ is equivalent to:

    A. $50\sqrt{6}$

    B. $12\sqrt{5}$

    C. $3\sqrt{10}$

    D. $10\sqrt{3}$

    E. $100\sqrt{3}$

4. The expression $\sqrt{27} + \sqrt{12}$ is equivalent to:

    A. $\sqrt{39}$

    B. $5\sqrt{3}$

    C. $5\sqrt{6}$

    D. $10\sqrt{3}$

    E. $13\sqrt{3}$

5. What is the difference between $5\sqrt{5}$ and $\sqrt{45}$?

    A. $\sqrt{5}$

    B. $2\sqrt{5}$

    C. 5

    D. 15

    E. $8\sqrt{5}$

6. The expression $\sqrt{50} + 3\sqrt{2}$ can be written in the form of $x\sqrt{2}$. Find the value of x.

7. Which of the following is equivalent to $\sqrt{\frac{81}{121}}$?

    A. $\sqrt{\frac{9}{11}}$

    B. $\frac{3}{11}$

    C. $\frac{9}{11}$

    D. $3\sqrt{\frac{3}{11}}$

    E. 33

8. Which of the following values is equivalent to $(\frac{3}{4}\sqrt{18})(8\sqrt{8})$?

    A. $12\sqrt{3}$

    B. $22\frac{3}{4}\sqrt{2}$

    C. $8\frac{3}{4}\sqrt{26}$

    D. 72

    E. 96

Note: Photocopying any part of this book is prohibited by law.

ADDITIONAL PRACTICE QUESTIONS

1. Which of the following is equivalent to $\sqrt{x^6 y^8}$?

   A. $\sqrt{x^3 y^4}$

   B. $x^3 y^4$

   C. $x^4 y^6 \sqrt{xy}$

   D. $x^4 y^6$

   E. $\sqrt{x^4 y^6}$

2. Which of the following is $\sqrt{72}$ in simplest terms?

   A. $2\sqrt{36}$

   B. $3\sqrt{8}$

   C. $6\sqrt{2}$

   D. $9\sqrt{8}$

   E. $36\sqrt{2}$

3. Which of the following is the simplest form of $\frac{\sqrt{126}}{\sqrt{18}}$?

   A. $\sqrt{7}$

   B. $\frac{\sqrt{14}}{\sqrt{2}}$

   C. $7\sqrt{3}$

   D. 7

   E. $3\sqrt{7}$

4. What is the value of $\sqrt{5} + \sqrt{3} - \sqrt{27}$?

   A. $-\sqrt{19}$

   B. $\sqrt{5} + 4\sqrt{3}$

   C. $\sqrt{5} + 2\sqrt{3}$

   D. $\sqrt{5} - 2\sqrt{3}$

   E. $\sqrt{8} - 3\sqrt{3}$

5. Which of the following is the simplest form of $\sqrt{14} \times \sqrt{18}$?

   A. $\sqrt{252}$

   B. $\sqrt{63}$

   C. $7\sqrt{6}$

   D. $3\sqrt{28}$

   E. $6\sqrt{7}$

Note: Photocopying any part of this book is prohibited by law.

ANSWERS AND EXPLANATIONS

1. **The correct answer is (C).** You can eliminate choice (B) right away since $\sqrt{77}$ and $\sqrt{78}$ are not whole numbers. Think of your perfect squares to help you to answer the question. The number 77 is between the two perfect squares 64 and 81. Since $8^2 = 64$ and $9^2 = 81$, $\sqrt{77}$ lies between 8 and 9.

2. **The correct answer is (D).** The area of a square is equal to the length of a side squared. So, the length of a side of the square is equal to the square root of the area.

   In this case, the length of a side of the square is $\sqrt{72}$.

   Now, that's not an answer choice, so you must be expected to simplify it. To do this, look for the largest perfect square that is a factor of 72, which is 36:

   $$\sqrt{72} = \sqrt{36} \times \sqrt{2}$$
   $$= 6\sqrt{2}$$

   If you didn't come up with 36 as the largest perfect square factor of 72, but instead came up with 9, you could still simplify it, however it will involve an extra step:

   $$\sqrt{72} = \sqrt{9} \times \sqrt{8}$$

   Now, the key here is not to just simplify to $3\sqrt{8}$ because $\sqrt{8}$ can be simplified further since it has the perfect square, 4, as a factor:

   $$\sqrt{9} \times \sqrt{8} = \sqrt{9} \times \sqrt{4} \times \sqrt{2}$$
   $$= 3 \times 2 \times \sqrt{2}$$
   $$= 6\sqrt{2}.$$

   Alternatively, you could have Worked Backwards by squaring each of the answer choices to see which gave you an area of 72.

   Start with (C). If the length is 8, then the area is $8^2 = 64$. That's less than 72, so choice (C) can be eliminated, as well as the smaller answers, choices (A) and (B).

   Now try (D). If the length is $6\sqrt{2}$ then the area is:

   $$(6\sqrt{2})^2 = (6)^2 \times (\sqrt{2})^2$$
   $$= 36 \times 2$$
   $$= 72.$$

3. **The correct answer is (D).** To simplify a radical, break down the number under the radical sign into two factors, one of which is the largest perfect square by which it is divisible. Each factor is now under its own radical sign, one multiplying the other:

   $$\sqrt{300} = \sqrt{100} \times \sqrt{3}$$

   Next, convert the radical that is a perfect square to its square root:

   $$\sqrt{100} = 10$$

   Your simplified radical is this square root multiplying the non-perfect square still under the radical:

   $$10\sqrt{3}$$

4. **The correct answer is (B).** Only like radicals can be combined. So, before you can combine these radicals, you have to simplify them.

   To simplify a radical, break down the number under the radical sign into two factors, one of which is the largest perfect square by which it is divisible. Each factor is now under its own radical sign, one multiplying the other:

   $$\sqrt{27} = \sqrt{9} \times \sqrt{3}.$$

   Next, convert the radical that is a perfect square to its square root:

   $$\sqrt{9} = 3.$$

   Your simplified radical is this square root multiplying the non-perfect square still under the radical:

   $$3\sqrt{3}.$$

   Now, simplify $\sqrt{12}$ in the same manner.

Break down 12 into two factors, one of which is the largest perfect square by which it is divisible. (Since the question is asking you to combine $\sqrt{12}$ with $\sqrt{27}$, which you've already simplified to $3\sqrt{3}$, you're expecting one of the factors of 12 to be 3). $12 \div 3$ is equal to 4, which is a perfect square. Put each factor under its own radical sign, one multiplying the other:

$$\sqrt{12} = \sqrt{4} \times \sqrt{3}$$

Next, convert the radical that is a perfect square, 4, to its square root, 2:

$$\sqrt{4} = 2$$

Your simplified radical is this square root multiplying the non-perfect square still under the radical:

$$2\sqrt{3}.$$

Finally, you're ready to add these radicals. Add the coefficients and carry the radical along:

$$3\sqrt{3} + 2\sqrt{3} = 5\sqrt{3}.$$

5. **The correct answer is (B).** Only like radicals can be subtracted. So, before you can take the difference between these radicals, you have to simplify them. $5\sqrt{5}$ is already in simplest form, so you want to begin by putting $\sqrt{45}$ into simplified form.

Break down 45 into two factors, one of which is the largest perfect square by which it is divisible. (Since the question is asking you to combine $\sqrt{45}$ with the already simplified $5\sqrt{5}$ you're expecting one of the factors of 45 to be 5). $45 \div 5$ is equal to 9, which is a perfect square. Put each factor under its own radical sign, one multiplying the other:

$$\sqrt{45} = \sqrt{9} \times \sqrt{5}.$$

Next, convert the radical that is a perfect square, 9, to its square root, 3:

$$\sqrt{9} = 3.$$

Your simplified radical is this square root multiplying the non-perfect square still under the radical:

$$3\sqrt{5}.$$

Finally, you're ready to subtract these radicals:

$$5\sqrt{5} - 3\sqrt{5} = 2\sqrt{5}.$$

6. **The correct answer is 8.** This question appears to be more complicated than it actually is. It is essentially just a combining radicals question, but instead of calculating the entire answer, you are just going to be calculating the coefficient.

Only like radicals can be combined, so before you can combine these radicals, you have to simplify them. $3\sqrt{2}$ is already in simplest form, so you want to begin by putting $\sqrt{50}$ into simplified form.

Break down 50 into two factors, one of which is the largest perfect square by which it is divisible. (Since the question is asking you to combine $\sqrt{50}$ with the already simplified $3\sqrt{2}$ you're expecting one of the factors of 50 to be 2). $50 \div 2 = 25$, which is a perfect square. Put each factor under its own radical sign, one multiplying the other:

$$\sqrt{50} = \sqrt{25} \times \sqrt{2}$$

Next, convert the radical that is a perfect square, 25, to its square root, 5:

$$\sqrt{25} = 5.$$

Your simplified radical is this square root multiplying the non-perfect square still under the radical:

$$5\sqrt{2}.$$

Finally, you're ready to add these radicals:

$$3\sqrt{2} + 5\sqrt{2} = 8\sqrt{2}.$$

Remember that the question stipulates that the answer can be written in the form of $x\sqrt{2}$ and asks you to find the value of x. Since you now know that $x\sqrt{2}$ is $8\sqrt{2}$ you know that $x = 8$.

7. **The correct answer is (C).** To take the square root of a fraction such as $\frac{81}{121}$, take the square root of the numerator and the square root of the denominator. Both 81 and 121 are perfect squares since $\sqrt{81} = 9$ and $\sqrt{121} = 11$. So, $\sqrt{\frac{81}{121}}$ is equal to $\frac{9}{11}$.

8. **The correct answer is (D).** Begin by doing the multiplication, coefficient by coefficient, radical by radical:

$$\left(\frac{3}{4}\sqrt{18}\right)(8\sqrt{8}) = \left(\frac{3}{4} \times 8\right)\left(\sqrt{18} \times \sqrt{8}\right)$$
$$= 6 \times \sqrt{144}$$
$$= 6 \times 12$$
$$= 72.$$

ADDITIONAL PRACTICE QUESTIONS

1. **The correct answer is (B).** Taking the square root of a number is the same as raising the number to the $\frac{1}{2}$ power, which means that $\sqrt{x^6 y^8} = \left(x^6 y^8\right)^{\frac{1}{2}}$. Now use the rule for multiplying exponents:

$$\sqrt{x^6 y^8} = \left(x^6 y^8\right)^{\frac{1}{2}}$$
$$= \left(x^{6 \times \frac{1}{2}}\right)\left(y^{8 \times \frac{1}{2}}\right)$$
$$= x^3 y^4.$$

2. **The correct answer is (C).** Look for factors of 72 that are perfect squares:

$$\sqrt{72} = \sqrt{9 \times 8}$$
$$= \sqrt{9 \times 4 \times 2}$$
$$= \sqrt{9} \times \sqrt{4} \times \sqrt{2}$$
$$= 3 \times 2 \times \sqrt{2}$$
$$= 6\sqrt{2}.$$

Since 2 is prime and cannot be factored any more, $\sqrt{72}$ in simplest terms is $6\sqrt{2}$.

3. **The correct answer is (A).** Look for factors that are perfect squares:

$$\frac{\sqrt{126}}{\sqrt{18}} = \frac{\sqrt{9 \times 14}}{\sqrt{9 \times 2}}$$
$$= \frac{\sqrt{9} \times \sqrt{14}}{\sqrt{9} \times \sqrt{2}}$$
$$= \frac{3\sqrt{14}}{3\sqrt{2}}$$
$$= \sqrt{\frac{14}{2}}$$
$$= \sqrt{7}.$$

Since 7 is prime and cannot be factored anymore, the simplest form of $\frac{\sqrt{126}}{\sqrt{18}}$ is $\sqrt{7}$.

Note: Photocopying any part of this book is prohibited by law.

4. **The correct answer is (D).**

$$\sqrt{5} + \sqrt{3} - \sqrt{27} = \sqrt{5} + \sqrt{3} - \sqrt{9 \times 3}$$
$$= \sqrt{5} + \sqrt{3} - (\sqrt{9} \times \sqrt{3})$$
$$= \sqrt{5} + \sqrt{3} - 3\sqrt{3}$$
$$= \sqrt{5} - 2\sqrt{3}.$$

5. **The correct answer is (E).** Look for factors that are perfect squares:

$$\sqrt{14} \times \sqrt{18} = \sqrt{7 \times 2} \times \sqrt{9 \times 2}$$
$$= \sqrt{7 \times 9 \times 4}$$
$$= \sqrt{7} \times \sqrt{9} \times \sqrt{4}$$
$$= 3 \times 2 \times \sqrt{7}$$
$$= 6\sqrt{7}.$$

Since 7 is prime and cannot be factored any more, the simplest form of $\sqrt{14} \times \sqrt{18}$ is $6\sqrt{7}$.

AVERAGES

1. Eight amusement park attractions had a total of 1,056 riders during a particular session. What was the average number of riders per attraction during the session?

   A. 8

   B. 13

   C. 116

   D. 132

   E. 160

2. A tour company is responsible for assigning 650 tourists to tour buses. If each bus accommodates on average 50 passengers, how many buses were filled with passengers?

   A. 13

   B. 15

   C. 50

   D. 130

   E. 32,500

3. Kwame has taken four math exams so far this quarter, and has received scores of 89, 85, 96, and 87. What is the minimum score that Kwame needs to receive in order to attain an average math test score of at least 90 to make honor roll?

   A. 88

   B. 89

   C. 90

   D. 92

   E. 93

4. What is the average (arithmetic mean) of 3.2, 4.7, 8.8, and 9.3?

5. A telemarketer made 67 phone calls on Monday, 72 phone calls on Tuesday, 65 phone calls on Wednesday, and 79 phone calls on Thursday. How many calls must he make on Friday to meet his 5-day average quota of 75 calls?

   A. 71

   B. 75

   C. 80

   D. 92

   E. 95

6. Maury does community service for 2 hours each day from Sunday through Friday. How many hours of community service must he do on Saturday in order to raise his daily average by an hour for the 7-day week?

7. Each student in a class of 30 is asked how many e-mails he or she received the day before. The table shows the possible number of e-mails and the number of students who received each amount. What is the average number of e-mails received per student?

E-MAILS RECEIVED YESTERDAY	
Number of E-Mails	Number of Students
0	1
1	6
2	3
3	7
4	9
5	3
6	1

A. 1.0

B. 1.5

C. 3.0

D. 3.5

E. 4.5

8. If the average (arithmetic mean) of x, $2x - 3$, $x + 2$, $2x - 1$ and $2x + 2$ is 8, what is the value of x?

ADDITIONAL PRACTICE QUESTIONS

1. At the public library, 8 shelves of books contain a total of 128 books. What is the average number of books per shelf?

   A. 8

   B. 16

   C. 24

   D. 32

   E. 136

2. Volunteers at a food drive pack 1,500 cans of soup into boxes. If each box holds an average of 30 cans, how many boxes are full?

   A. 30

   B. 50

   C. 150

   D. 300

   E. 45,000

3. An elementary school has 5 first-grade classes. The first four classes have 22, 25, 20, and 23 students respectively. If the average number of first-grade students per class is 22, how many students are in the fifth class?

   A. 20

   B. 21

   C. 22

   D. 23

   E. 24

4. Melissa went to a book store and bought 8 books. If the average cost of each book was $5.50, what was the total amount of money that Melissa spent on books?

   A. $4.40

   B. $5.50

   C. $14.50

   D. $44.00

   E. $49.50

5. Jeff scored a 74, 94, 86, 78, 92, and 80 on his math tests. What was his average score?

   A. 80

   B. 83

   C. 84

   D. 85

   E. 86

ANSWERS AND EXPLANATIONS

1. **The correct answer is (D).** To determine the average number of riders per attraction during the session, divide the number of riders, 1,056, by the number of attractions, 8:

$$8\overline{)1{,}056} \quad 132$$

The average number of riders per attraction during the session was 132.

2. **The correct answer is (A).** To determine how many buses were filled with passengers, divide the number of tourists, 650, by the average number of passengers each bus holds, 50:

$$50\overline{)650} \quad 13$$

13 buses were filled with passengers.

3. **The correct answer is (E).** First, plug all of the values that you are given into the average equation. Select a variable to represent the missing value (make sure that you include the missing value when you are counting the number of values):

$$\text{Average} = \frac{\text{The sum of the values}}{\text{The number of values}}$$

$$90 = \frac{89 + 85 + 96 + 87 + x}{5}.$$

Then, total the values in the numerator:

$$90 = \frac{357 + x}{5}.$$

Next, multiply both sides by the denominator of the fraction.

$$90 \times 5 = \frac{357 + x}{5} \times 5$$

$$450 = 357 + x.$$

Finally, solve for the missing value by subtracting from both sides.

$$450 = 357 + x$$
$$450 - 357 = 357 - 357 + x$$
$$93 = x$$

Kwame needs a minimum score of 93 to attain an average math test score of at least 90 to make honor roll. Choice (E) is correct.

4. **The correct answer is 6.5.** Determine the average of 3.2, 4.7, 8.8, and 9.3:

First, write out the equation for determining an average:

$$\text{Average} = \frac{\text{The sum of the values}}{\text{The number of values}}.$$

Next, add up the values to determine the total to put in the numerator of the fraction:

$$3.2 + 4.7 + 8.8 + 9.3 = 26$$

Then, count the total number of values to put in the denominator of the fraction.

There are 4 values in this set, so, the fraction is $\frac{26}{4}$.

Finally, reduce the fraction:

$$\frac{26}{4} = 6.5.$$

The average of the numbers is 6.5.

5. **The correct answer is (D).** First, plug all of the values that you are given into the average equation. Select a variable to represent the missing value:

$$75 = \frac{67 + 72 + 65 + 79 + x}{5}.$$

Make sure that you include the missing value when you are counting the number of values.

Then, total the values in the numerator:

$$75 = \frac{283 + x}{5}.$$

Note: Photocopying any part of this book is prohibited by law.

Next, multiply both sides by the denominator of the fraction.

$$75 \times 5 = \frac{283 + x}{5} \times 5$$
$$375 = 283 + x.$$

Finally, solve for the missing value by subtracting from both sides.

$375 = 283 + x$
$375 - 283 = 283 - 283 + x$
$92 = x$

6. **The correct answer is 9.** First, plug all of the values that you are given into the average equation. Select a variable to represent the missing value. Sunday through Friday constitutes 6 days. Since Maury's current average is 2 hours, if he wants to boost his weekly average by an hour, he'll want to raise his average to 3 hours:

$$3 = \frac{6(2) + x}{7}.$$

Make sure that you include the missing value when you are counting the number of values.

Then, simplify the values in the numerator:

$$3 = \frac{12 + x}{7}.$$

Next, multiply both sides by the denominator of the fraction.

$$3 \times 7 = \frac{12 + x}{7} \times 7$$
$$21 = 12 + x.$$

Finally, solve for the missing value by subtracting from both sides.

$21 = 12 + x$
$21 - 12 = 12 - 12 + x$
$9 = x$

Maury will have to work 9 hours on Sunday.

7. **The correct answer is (C).** To find the average (arithmetic mean), you need to know the total number of e-mails received by the 30 students. To find the total number of e-mails, you need to multiply the "Number of E-Mails" by the "Number of Students," and then total these amounts:

$$
\begin{aligned}
0 \times 1 &= 0 \\
1 \times 6 &= 6 \\
2 \times 3 &= 6 \\
3 \times 7 &= 21 \\
4 \times 9 &= 36 \\
5 \times 3 &= 15 \\
6 \times 1 &= \underline{6} \\
&\ 90
\end{aligned}
$$

Next, find the total number of students.

$$
\begin{aligned}
&1 \\
&6 \\
&3 \\
&7 \\
&9 \\
&3 \\
&\underline{+1} \\
&30
\end{aligned}
$$

Finally, calculate the average by dividing the total number of e-mails, 90, by the total number of students:

$$90 \div 30 = 3.$$

8. **The correct answer is 5.** Write out the equation for determining an average:

$$\text{Average} = \frac{\text{The sum of the values}}{\text{The number of values}}.$$

First, add up the values to determine the total to put in the numerator of the fraction:

$$
\begin{array}{r}
x \\
2x - 3 \\
x + 2 \\
2x - 1 \\
+\ 2x + 2 \\
\hline
8x
\end{array}
$$

Then, count the total number of values to put in the denominator of the fraction.

There are 5 values in this set, so the fraction is:

$$\frac{8x}{5}.$$

Finally, set the fraction equal to the average:

$$\frac{8x}{5} = 8.$$

Solve for x:

$$\frac{8x}{5} = \frac{8}{1}$$
$$8x(1) = 8(5)$$
$$\frac{8x}{8} = \frac{40}{8}$$
$$x = 5.$$

Grid in 5 as your answer.

ADDITIONAL PRACTICE QUESTIONS

1. **The correct answer is (B).** In order to find the average number of books per shelf, we must use the average formula:

$$\text{Average} = \frac{\text{sum of the values in a given set}}{\text{\# of values in a given set}}.$$

In this situation, the set that we are dealing with is the shelves of books. Since we know that there are 128 books, the sum of the values in this set must be 128. We also know that there are 8 shelves. Plugging these values into the equation yields:

$$A = \frac{128}{8}$$
$$= 16.$$

2. **The correct answer is (B).** Remember the average formula:

$$\text{Average} = \frac{\text{sum of values in a given set}}{\text{\# of values in a given set}}.$$

Let x represent the number of boxes that are full. We know that the total number of cans is 1,500 and we know that the average number of cans per box is 30. Substituting these values into the average formula gives you:

$$30 = \frac{1,500}{x}$$
$$30x = 1,500$$
$$x = 50.$$

Note: Photocopying any part of this book is prohibited by law.

3. **The correct answer is (A).** Remember the average formula:

$$\text{Average} = \frac{\text{sum of values in a given set}}{\text{\# of values in a given set}}.$$

Let x represent the number of students in the fifth class. We can now write the sum of the number of students as $22 + 25 + 20 + 23 + x = 90 + x$. We also know that the average number of students per class is 22 and there are 5 classes. Now substitute these values into the average formula and solve for x:

$$22 = \frac{90 + x}{5}$$
$$110 = 90 + x$$
$$110 - 90 = 90 - 90 + x$$
$$x = 20.$$

4. **The correct answer is (D).** Remember the average formula:

$$\text{Average} = \frac{\text{sum of values in a given set}}{\text{\# of values in a given set}}.$$

Let x be the total amount of money that Melissa spent on books. We know that she bought 8 books and the average cost was $5.50. Now, plug these values into the average formula and solve for x:

$$\$5.50 = \frac{x}{8}$$
$$x = \$44.00.$$

5. **The correct answer is (C).** Remember the average formula:

$$\text{Average} = \frac{\text{sum of values in a given set}}{\text{\# of values in a given set}}.$$

First, find the sum of Jeff's test scores, which is $74 + 94 + 86 + 78 + 92 + 80 = 504$. Since we know that there were a total of 6 tests, we can now compute the average:

$$A = \frac{504}{6}$$
$$= 84.$$

MEAN, MEDIAN, AND MODE

1. The weights of five newborns, in pounds were recorded as follows: 5.1, 6.3, 7.6, 8.0, and 8.5. What was the median weight?

A. 3.4

B. 5

C. 5.1

D. 7.1

E. 7.6

2. What is the median of 3, 4, 8, and 9?

Questions 3 and 4 are based on the following:
10 members of an organization owe the following amounts in past dues: $86, $91, $80, $98, $85, $93, $86, $71, $89, $91.

3. What is the median amount of back dues owed?

A. 27

B. 86

C. 86.5

D. 87

E. 87.5

4. What is the mode of amount of back dues owed?

A. 2

B. 10

C. 86

D. 87

E. 87.5

5. If in a class of 35 students, the median grade on an exam is 80, which of the following must be true?

A. The mode grade is also 80.

B. 50% of the students got a grade higher than 80.

C. 50% of the students got a grade lower than 80.

D. At least one student scored an 80.

E. 50% of the students got a grade of 80.

6. For which of the following sets of data is the median and mode the same?

A. 3,4,5,6,7

B. 1,2,3,3,4,4,4

C. 3,4,6,6

D. 2,2,2,3,3,4

E. 3,4,7,8,8,9,10

7. How many scores in the set of data below are less than the median?
87, 90, 60, 82

8. What is the median of the following set of data if the only mode is 14?
14, x, 18, 14, 18, 20, 17, 13, 22

A. 9

B. 14

C. 17

D. 17.5

E. 18

Note: Photocopying any part of this book is prohibited by law.

ADDITIONAL PRACTICE QUESTIONS

1. The 8 students in Mr. Thompson's class were all measured. Their heights were, in inches, 50, 45, 48, 52, 46, 54, 47, and 51. What is the median height?

   A. 48

   B. 49.125

   C. 49

   D. 49.5

   E. 50

2. After grading her student's tests, Mrs. Johnson finds that three students received a 90, four students received an 85, two students received an 80, and three students received a 70. What is the mode of the student's test scores?

   A. 70

   B. 80

   C. 82

   D. 85

   E. 90

3. In its first four games, a basketball team scored 56, 68, 42, and 50 points. What is the mean of the points scored in the first four games?

   A. 50

   B. 53

   C. 54

   D. 55

   E. 56

4. The chart below shows the earnings for a clothing store over a given week. What is the median?

Day	Earnings
Sunday	$500
Monday	$250
Tuesday	$120
Wednesday	$100
Thursday	$200
Friday	$285
Saturday	$800

   A. $242.50

   B. $250.00

   C. $310.00

   D. $320.00

   E. $450.00

5. At the end of the high school soccer season, three teams had won 13 games, four teams had won 8 games, one team had won 5 games, and two teams had won 0 games. What is the mode?

   A. 0

   B. 6.5

   C. 7.6

   D. 8

   E. 13

Note: Photocopying any part of this book is prohibited by law.

ANSWERS AND EXPLANATIONS

1. **The correct answer is (E).** In order for you to determine the median, the weights have to be lined up in order; this question already provides you with the weights in order. The median is always the middle term or the average of the two middle terms. Since there are 5 pieces of data in this question, there is a middle term, 7.6, and that is your median.

2. **The correct answer is 6.** The median is the middle value among a group of values that are arranged in ascending or descending order.

    To find the median, first arrange the values in order:
    $$3, 4, 8, 9.$$

    Since there is an even number of values, find the median by taking the average (arithmetic mean) of the two middle values:
    $$\frac{4+8}{2} = \frac{12}{2}$$
    $$= 6.$$

    The median value is 6.

3. **The correct answer is (E).** In order to determine the median, you have to line up the terms in order and take the middle term. The terms are in order, as follows:

    $71, $80, $85, $86, $86, $89, $91, $91, $93, $98.

    The median is always the middle term or the average of the two middle terms. Since there are 10 pieces of data in this question, there will not be a middle term, and you will have to average the two middle terms, 86 and 89:

    $$\text{Average} = \frac{\text{The sum of the values}}{\text{The number of values}}.$$

    Add up the values to determine the total to put in the numerator of the fraction:

    $86 + 89 = 175.$

    Since there are 2 values being considered here, the fraction is $\frac{175}{2}$.

    Finally, reduce the fraction:
    $$\frac{175}{2} = 87.5.$$

    The average of the numbers is 87.5, and the median is, therefore, 87.5.

4. **The correct answer is (C).** In order to determine the mode, you need to see which value in the set of data appears most frequently. In this set of data, the value 86 appears twice, while none of the other values repeat at all. Therefore, 86 is the mode.

5. **The correct answer is (D).** The median is always the middle term or the average of the two middle terms. Since there are 35 pieces of data in this question, there is a middle term, and since 80 is the median, at least one student had to have actually scored an 80. Note that this wouldn't necessarily be the case had there been an even number of students in the class, since the median would have been attained by averaging two middle values. While each of the remaining choices could possibly be true, they do not have to necessarily be true.

6. **The correct answer is (E).** Choice (E) contains the only set of data where the median and mode are the same:

    3, 4, 7, **8**, **8**, 9, 10.

    The mode, the value in the set of data that appears most frequently, is 8. The number 8 appears twice, while none of the other values in the set repeat at all. The median, or middle value, is also 8.

7. **The correct answer is 2.** The median is the middle value among a group of values that are arranged in ascending or descending order.

To find the median, first arrange the values in order:

$$60, 82, 87, 90.$$

Since there is an even number of values, find the median by taking the average (arithmetic mean) of the two middle values:

$$\frac{82+87}{2} = \frac{169}{2}$$
$$= 84.5.$$

Both 60 and 82 are less than 84.5, so 2 values are less than the median.

8. **The correct answer is (C).** In order to determine the mode, you need to see which value in the set of data appears most frequently. In this set of data, the value 17 appears twice, and the value 14 appears twice. None of the other values repeat at all. Since the question stipulates that the only mode is 14, the missing value, x, must be 14:

$$14, 14, 18, 14, 18, 20, 17, 13, 22.$$

Now that you know all of the values, put all of the values in order to determine which value is the median or middle value:

$$13, 14, 14, 14, \mathbf{17}, 18, 18, 20, 22.$$

The value 17 is the median.

Note: Photocopying any part of this book is prohibited by law.

ADDITIONAL PRACTICE QUESTIONS

1. **The correct answer is (C).** First list the heights in order from smallest to largest:

$$45$$
$$46$$
$$47$$
$$48$$
$$50$$
$$51$$
$$52$$
$$54$$

The median is the value that is in the middle. Since 48 and 50 are both in the middle, the median is the average of the two, which is $\frac{48+50}{2} = \frac{98}{2} = 49$. Choice (C) is correct.

2. **The correct answer is (D).** The mode of a set is the number that appears most often in the set. Since four students scored an 85, more than any other score, 85 is the mode. Choice (D) is correct.

3. **The correct answer is (C).** To find the mean, use the same formula that you would to find the average:

$$\text{Average} = \frac{\text{sum of the values in a given set}}{\text{\# of values in a given set}}.$$

First, find the sum of points scored in the first four games, which is $56 + 68 + 42 + 50 = 216$. Now plug these values into the formula to find the mean:

$$A = \frac{216}{4}$$
$$= 54.$$

4. **The correct answer is (B).** First order the numbers from smallest to largest:

$$\$100$$
$$\$120$$
$$\$200$$
$$\$250$$
$$\$285$$
$$\$500$$
$$\$800$$

The median is the number in the middle, which is $250. Choice (B) is correct.

5. **The correct answer is (D).** The mode is the number that shows up most frequently in a set. In this case, 8 shows up 4 times, which is more than any other number, so 8 is the mode. Choice (D) is correct.

RATIOS

1. Marcos can type at a rate of 3,300 words per hour. What is the ratio of words typed to minutes spent typing?

   A. 1 : 3,300

   B. 1 : 1,650

   C. 1 : 55

   D. 55 : 1

   E. 3,300 : 1

2. Salvatore contributed $150.00 at a fundraiser, and his partner, Samantha, contributed $100.00. What is the ratio of Salvatore's contribution to Samantha's contribution?

   A. $\dfrac{1}{3}$

   B. $\dfrac{2}{3}$

   C. $\dfrac{3}{2}$

   D. $\dfrac{5}{3}$

   E. $\dfrac{1}{10}$

3. Which of the following ratios are equal to one another?
$$\frac{3}{12}, \frac{9}{21}, \frac{4}{24}, \frac{2}{16}, \frac{6}{30}, \frac{5}{20}, \frac{12}{48}$$

   A. $\dfrac{3}{12}, \dfrac{5}{20}, \dfrac{12}{48}$

   B. $\dfrac{9}{21}, \dfrac{6}{30}, \dfrac{5}{20}$

   C. $\dfrac{3}{12}, \dfrac{4}{24}, \dfrac{6}{30}$

   D. $\dfrac{6}{30}, \dfrac{5}{20}, \dfrac{12}{48}$

   E. $\dfrac{4}{24}, \dfrac{2}{16}, \dfrac{12}{48}$

4. Fortunato spent $15 of his money on a CD and $25 of his money on a DVD. What is the ratio of what he spent on the DVD to what he spent on the CD?

   A. $\dfrac{3}{5}$

   B. $\dfrac{3}{8}$

   C. $\dfrac{2}{5}$

   D. $\dfrac{5}{3}$

   E. $\dfrac{8}{3}$

5. Shannon ran 8 miles in the morning and 5 miles in the evening, while training for a race. What is the ratio of the miles she ran in the morning to the miles she ran for the entire day?

   A. $\dfrac{5}{8}$

   B. $\dfrac{5}{3}$

   C. $\dfrac{8}{13}$

   D. $\dfrac{8}{5}$

   E. $\dfrac{5}{13}$

6. A high school soccer team contains 7 juniors and 17 seniors. What is the ratio of the total number of players on the team to the number of senior players?

   A. 7 : 17

   B. 17 : 7

   C. 17 : 24

   D. 7 : 24

   E. 24 : 17

7. At a certain high school, there are 54 teachers in total. There are 6 more male teachers than female teachers. What is the ratio of female teachers to male teachers at the school?

   A. 3 : 5

   B. 4 : 5

   C. 5 : 4

   D. 5 : 9

   E. 8 : 5

8. In a pet store that sells only dogs and cats, the ratio of dogs to cats is 4 to 3. If 4 dogs are sold, the ratio of dogs to cats becomes 1 to 1. How many pets did the store have originally?

   A. 7

   B. 12

   C. 16

   D. 24

   E. 28

9. The ratio of wins for the Cougars during season A to wins during season B was 7 to 3. If the ratio of wins during season B to wins during season C was 3 to 5, what was the ratio of wins during season A to wins during season C?

   A. 7 to 5

   B. 5 to 3

   C. 3 to 7

   D. 3 to 2

   E. 3 to 1

Note: Photocopying any part of this book is prohibited by law.

ADDITIONAL PRACTICE QUESTIONS

1. On a co-ed soccer team, there are 14 boys and 6 girls. What is the ratio of boys to girls?

    A. 3:7

    B. 4:7

    C. 7:3

    D. 7:4

    E. 7:10

2. In a certain pet store, the ratio of cats to dogs is 2:3. If there are 12 cats, how many dogs are in the store?

    A. 12

    B. 18

    C. 27

    D. 36

    E. 54

3. A certain candy store sells lollipops, chocolate bars, and bubble gum. The ratio of lollipops to chocolate bars is 2:3 and the ratio of chocolate bars to bubble gum is 4:5. What is the ratio of lollipops to bubble gum?

    A. 2:5

    B. 3:4

    C. 5:4

    D. 8:15

    E. 15:8

4. In the drama club at a certain high school, there are 32 boys and 68 girls. What is the ratio of the number of boys to the total number of students in the drama club?

    A. 8:17

    B. 8:25

    C. 17:8

    D. 17:25

    E. 25:8

5. A certain video rental store has a total of 650 videos. The ratio of comedy to action videos is 3:2. If there are 150 action videos, how many videos are neither comedy nor action?

    A. 225

    B. 275

    C. 375

    D. 425

    E. 500

ANSWERS AND EXPLANATIONS

1. **The correct answer is (D).** When you're working with ratios, it's important to pay attention to both order and to uniformity of units. Be sure that the order of your answer is *words typed* to *minutes spent*. Notice also that you're told that Marcos can type at a rate of 3,300 words *per hour*, but the question asks you to find the ratio of words typed to *minutes* spent typing. So, you need to convert hours to minutes: 3,300 words *per hour* is equal to 3,300 words *per 60 minutes*:

$$\frac{words}{minutes} = \frac{3,300}{60}$$
$$= \frac{55 \text{ words}}{1 \text{ minute}}.$$

So, the ratio of words typed to minutes spent typing is 55:1.

2. **The correct answer is (C).** The question asks for the ratio of Salvatore's contribution to Samantha's contribution.

Set up the ratio, paying careful attention to order, and reduce:

$$\frac{\text{Salvatore's contribution}}{\text{Samantha's contribution}} = \frac{150}{100}$$
$$= \frac{3}{2}.$$

Since ratios must have two parts, $\frac{3}{2}$ is the reduced form of the ratio.

3. **The correct answer is (A).** Reduce each of the fractions to its simplest form, and see which reduce to the same fraction.
$$\frac{3}{12} = \frac{1}{4}, \frac{9}{21} = \frac{3}{7}, \frac{4}{24} = \frac{1}{6}, \frac{2}{16} = \frac{1}{8}, \frac{6}{30} = \frac{1}{5}, \frac{5}{20} = \frac{1}{4}, \frac{12}{48} = \frac{1}{4}.$$
$\frac{3}{12}, \frac{5}{20}$ and $\frac{12}{48}$ each reduce to $\frac{1}{4}$.

4. **The correct answer is (D).** The question asks for the ratio of what Fortunato spent on the DVD to what he spent on the CD. Be sure to watch your order.

Set up the ratio, and reduce:

$$\frac{DVD}{CD} = \frac{25}{15}$$
$$= \frac{5}{3}.$$

Since ratios must have two parts, $\frac{5}{3}$ is the reduced form of the ratio.

5. **The correct answer is (C).** You are looking for the ratio of morning miles to total miles:

$$\frac{\text{morning miles}}{\text{total miles}} = \frac{8}{8+5}$$
$$= \frac{8}{13}.$$

6. **The correct answer is (E).** Remember that order is very important when working with ratios:

$$\frac{\text{total players on team}}{\text{senior players}} = \frac{7+17}{17}$$
$$= \frac{24}{17}.$$

7. **The correct answer is (B).** Before you set up the ratio, you need to determine how many male teachers and how many female teachers the school has by doing a little algebra.

Since the male teachers are being described in terms of the female teachers (there are 6 more male teachers than female teachers), let x equal the number of female teachers and $x + 6$ equal the number of male teachers. Combine these together, set them equal to the total number of teachers, 54, and solve for x:

$$x + (x + 6) = 54$$
$$2x + 6 = 54$$
$$2x + 6 - 6 = 54 - 6$$
$$2x = 48$$
$$\frac{2x}{2} = \frac{48}{2}$$
$$x = 24.$$

So, there are 24 female teachers and 30 male teachers.

Now, set up your ratio of female teachers to male teachers at the school, paying careful attention to order, and reduce:

$$\frac{\text{female teachers}}{\text{male teachers}} = \frac{24}{30}$$
$$= \frac{4}{5}.$$

Since ratios must have two parts, $\frac{4}{5}$, or $4:5$ is the reduced form of the ratio.

8. **The correct answer is (E).** The best approach to this question is to Work Backwards, starting with choice (C).

    The fact that the dog-to-cat ratio is $4:3$ means that there could be 4 dogs and 3 cats, or 8 dogs and 6 cats, or 12 dogs and 9 cats, and so on. The ratio only tells you that the number of dogs is 4 times some value, and the number of cats is 3 times the same value. If there were 4 dogs and 3 cats, that value would be 1; for 8 dogs and 6 cats, that value would be 2; for 12 dogs and 9 cats, that value would be 3, and so on.

    First, let x be the value of which 4 and 3 are multiples. So, the number of dogs will be $4x$. Likewise, the number of cats will be $3x$. Next, set up your equation indicating that the sum of these two numbers is 16, as in choice (C):

    $$4x + 3x = 16$$
    $$\frac{7x}{7} = \frac{16}{7}$$
    $$x = 2\frac{2}{7}$$
    $$4x = 4\left(2\frac{2}{7}\right) = 9\frac{1}{7}.$$

    You can stop right there. You know that the number of dogs has to be a whole number. (You can't sell *part* of a dog.)

    You know that the total number of animals should be a multiple of 7, so that when you set $7x$ equal to it, x will end up being a whole number.

The only choices here that are multiples of 7 are choice (A), 7 and choice (E), 28.

If there were a total of 7 pets, then there would be 4 dogs and 3 cats. If 4 dogs were then sold, there would be no dogs and 3 cats, which is not the 1:1 ratio the question requires.

If there were 28 pets in total, then there would be 16 dogs and 12 cats:

$$4x + 3x = 28$$
$$\frac{7x}{7} = \frac{28}{7}$$
$$x = 4$$
$$4x = 4(4) = 16$$
$$3x = 3(4) = 12.$$

If 4 dogs were then sold, then there would be 12 dogs and 12 cats, a 1:1 ratio.

9. **The correct answer is (A).** Season B is the constant in this situation. You are able to compare wins in season A and season C because the question compares each of them to season B.

    $$\frac{\text{Season } A}{\text{Season } B} = \frac{7}{3}.$$

    $$\frac{\text{Season } B}{\text{Season } C} = \frac{3}{5}.$$

    $$\frac{\text{Season } A}{\text{Season } C} = \frac{7}{5}.$$

    The ratio of wins during season A to wins during season C was 7 to 5.

ADDITIONAL PRACTICE QUESTIONS

1. The correct answer is (C). First, set up the ratio as a fraction, paying attention to order, which is $\frac{14}{6}$. Now, express the fraction is lowest terms by dividing both the numerator and the denominator by the greatest common factor, 2:

$$\frac{14}{6} = \frac{7}{3}.$$

The ratio is 7 to 3.

2. The correct answer is (B). Let x represent the number of dogs in the store. Since the ratio of cats to dogs is 2:3 and there are 12 cats, you need to find x such that $\frac{3}{2} = \frac{x}{12}$. Cross-multiply so that you have a linear equation that you can solve for x:

$$\frac{3}{2} = \frac{x}{12}$$
$$2x = 36$$
$$x = 18.$$

3. The correct answer is (D). According to the given information, we have $\frac{2 \text{ lollipops}}{3 \text{ chocolate bars}}$ and $\frac{4 \text{ chocolate bars}}{5 \text{ bubble gums}}$. Notice that if you multiply the two ratios together, the chocolate bars will cancel out, leaving you with a fraction in terms of lollipops per chocolate bars, which is what we are looking for:

$$\frac{2 \text{ lollipops}}{3 \text{ chocolate bars}} \times \frac{4 \text{ chocolate bars}}{5 \text{ bubble gums}} = \frac{8 \text{ lollipops}}{15 \text{ bubble gums}}.$$

The ratio of lollipops to bubble gum is 8 to 15.

4. The correct answer is (B). Since there are 32 boys and 68 girls in the drama club, there are a total of $32 + 68 = 100$ students in the club. Now write the ratio of boys to total students in a fraction, paying close attention to the order, which is $\frac{32}{100}$. Finally, put the fraction in lowest terms by dividing both the numerator and the denominator by the greatest common factor, 4. So, $\frac{32}{100} = \frac{8}{25}$. The ratio of boys to the total number of students is 8 to 25. Choice (B) is correct.

5. The correct answer is (B). Let x represent the number of comedy videos. We first need to determine the number of comedy videos by finding x such that $\frac{3}{2} = \frac{x}{150}$. Cross-multiplying and solving for x gives us:

$$\frac{3}{2} = \frac{x}{150}$$
$$2x = 450$$
$$x = 225.$$

We now know that there are $225 + 150 = 375$ comedy and action videos. Therefore, there are $650 - 375 = 275$ videos that are neither action nor comedy. Choice (B) is correct.

Note: Photocopying any part of this book is prohibited by law.

PROPORTION AND RATES

1. A deli served 300 customers during a 12-hour day. At what rate did the deli serve customers?

   A. 12 customers per hour

   B. 25 customers per hour

   C. 30 customers per hour

   D. 50 customers per hour

   E. 3,600 customers per hour

2. A car drove at 70 miles per hour for 3.5 hours. How far did it travel in total?

   A. 20 miles

   B. 35 miles

   C. 140 miles

   D. 245miles

   E. 350 miles

3. If 3 cars can park all day in the parking lot for a cost of $83.94, how many cars can park all day in the parking lot at the same rate for $195.86?

4. Samson can peel potatoes at the rate of 55 potatoes per half hour and Horace can peel potatoes at the rate of 72 per half hour. How many potatoes can the boys peel if they work together for 2.5 hours?

5. If Kyle bikes at a constant speed of 15 miles per hour, how many <u>minutes</u> will it take for him to bike half a mile?

   A. 0.5

   B. 1

   C. 1.5

   D. 2

   E. 4

6. Pamela prepared 54 coffee drinks over the course of a 3-hour shift at her weekend job at the cafe. If she prepared 90 coffee drinks during another shift working at the same rate, how many hours did that shift last?

Note: Photocopying any part of this book is prohibited by law.

7. It is estimated that the construction of a new mini-mall will take 20,000 person-days to complete. If a team of 80 workers is working on this project, how long should it take to complete?

A. 80 days

B. 160 days

C. 200 days

D. 250 days

E. 1,600,000 days

8. A car took 9 hours to travel between two cities that are 600 miles apart. If the return trip took 11 hours, what was the average speed of the car, in miles per hour, for the round trip?

A. 30

B. 50

C. 55

D. 60

E. 67

ADDITIONAL PRACTICE QUESTIONS

1. A boat traveled at 24 miles per hour for 3 hours. How many total miles did the boat travel?

    A. 8

    B. 24

    C. 27

    D. 72

    E. 144

2. A factory worker made 224 boxes in a 7-hour workday. At what rate did the worker produce boxes?

    A. 7 boxes per hour

    B. 30 boxes per hour

    C. 32 boxes per hour

    D. 224 boxes per hour

    E. 1,568 boxes per hour

3. On a road trip, Jim drove at a constant rate of 65 miles per hour. How many hours did it take him to drive 520 miles?

    A. 8

    B. 9

    C. 13

    D. 16

    E. 260

4. Ryan can run one lap around the track, $\frac{1}{4}$ mile, in 1 minute and 30 seconds. At this rate, how many miles could Ryan run in an hour?

    A. 5

    B. 6

    C. 9

    D. 10

    E. 12

5. Tim can type 80 words per minute and Tom can type 60 words per minute. If they each type for 3 hours, how many total words can they type?

    A. 4,200

    B. 4,800

    C. 10,800

    D. 14,400

    E. 25,200

Note: Photocopying any part of this book is prohibited by law.

ANSWERS AND EXPLANATIONS

1. **The correct answer is (B).** Set up a proportion paying careful attention to order:

    $$\frac{\text{customers served}}{\text{hours}} = \frac{300}{12}$$

    $$= 25 \text{ customers served per hour.}$$

    The deli served 25 customers per hour.

2. **The correct answer is (D).** Plug the information that the question gives you into the appropriate places in the equation to determine the rate:

    $$\text{rate} = \frac{\text{distance}}{\text{time}}$$

    $$70 \text{ mph} = \frac{x}{3.5 \text{ hours}}$$

    $$70 \text{ mph} \times (3.5 \text{ hours}) = \frac{x}{3.5 \text{ hours}} \times (3.5 \text{ hours})$$

    $$x = 245 \text{ miles.}$$

3. **The correct answer is 7.** Set up your proportion and get out your calculator.

    $$\frac{\text{number of cars}}{\text{cost}} = \frac{3}{\$83.94} = \frac{x}{\$195.86}$$

    $$\$83.94x = 3(\$195.86)$$

    $$\frac{\$83.94x}{\$83.94} = \frac{\$587.58}{\$83.94}$$

    $$x = 7.$$

    Alternatively, you could have calculated the cost per car and divided that cost into $195.86.

    $$\frac{\text{cost}}{\text{number of cars}} = \frac{\$83.94}{3}$$

    $$= \$27.98 \text{ per car}$$

    $$\frac{\$195.86}{\$27.98} = 7.$$

    7 cars can park all day in the parking lot at the same rate for $195.86.

4. **The correct answer is 635.** If Samson can peel 55 potatoes in a half hour, then he can peel 275 in 2.5 hours:

    $$\frac{\text{number of potatoes}}{\text{number of hours}} = \frac{55}{0.5} = \frac{x}{2.5}$$

    $$0.5x = 2.5(55)$$

    $$\frac{0.5x}{0.5} = \frac{137.5}{0.5}$$

    $$x = 275.$$

    If Horace can peel 72 potatoes in a half hour, then he can peel 360 in 2.5 hours:

    $$\frac{\text{number of potatoes}}{\text{number of hours}} = \frac{72}{0.5} = \frac{x}{2.5}$$

    $$0.5x = 2.5(72)$$

    $$\frac{0.5x}{0.5} = \frac{180}{0.5}$$

    $$x = 360.$$

    So, together the boys can peel $275 + 360 = 635$ potatoes in 2.5 hours.

5. **The correct answer is (D).** You will be using the standard rate formula to answer this question:

    $$\text{rate} = \frac{\text{distance}}{\text{time}}.$$

    Since the question is asking you to report the time *in minutes*, the first thing that you want to do is convert the given rate into miles *per minute*:

    $$\frac{15 \text{ miles}}{60 \text{ minutes}} = \frac{x \text{ miles}}{1 \text{ minute}}$$

    $$\frac{15}{60} = \frac{x}{1}$$

    $$\frac{60x}{60} = \frac{15}{60}$$

    $$x = \frac{1}{4}.$$

    So, if it takes Kyle a minute to bike a quarter-mile, it will take him 2 minutes to bike half a mile.

Note: Photocopying any part of this book is prohibited by law.

6. The correct answer is 5. Set up a proportion paying careful attention to order:

$$\frac{\text{number of coffee drinks prepared}}{\text{length of shift}} = \frac{54}{3} = \frac{90}{x}$$

$$54x = 3(90)$$

$$\frac{54x}{54} = \frac{270}{54}$$

$$x = 5.$$

Alternatively, you could have calculated the coffees prepared per hour and divided that into 90:

$$\frac{\text{number of coffee drinks prepared}}{\text{length of shift}} = \frac{54}{3}$$

$$= 18 \text{ per hour}$$

$$\frac{90}{18} = 5.$$

The shift lasted 5 hours.

7. The correct answer is (D). Consider what the concept of person-days means. If a project is estimated to take 20,000 person-days to complete, it would take one person 20,000 days. But, big projects, such as the construction of a mini-mall, wouldn't be taken on by just one person. In the case of this question, 80 people are working on the project. You can eliminate choice (E) right away as it is way too big; it should take 80 people *less* time than it would take one person, not more.

The total number of days that the project will take to complete, 20,000 days, is being shared by 80 workers, so divide 20,000 by 80:

$$\frac{\text{person-days}}{\text{people}} = \frac{20,000}{80}$$

$$= 250.$$

It should take a team of 80 workers 250 days to complete this project.

8. The correct answer is (D). You will be using the standard rate formula to answer this question:

$$\text{rate} = \frac{\text{distance}}{\text{time}}.$$

Since you are being asked to find the average speed for the round trip, you need to double the distance between the two cities: 600 miles × 2 = 1,200 miles:

$$x = \frac{1,200 \text{ miles}}{20 \text{ hours}}$$

$$= 60 \text{ miles per hour.}$$

Note: Photocopying any part of this book is prohibited by law.

ADDITIONAL PRACTICE QUESTIONS

1. **The correct answer is (D).**

    $$\frac{24 \text{ miles}}{\text{hour}} \times 3 \text{ hours} = 72 \text{ miles}.$$

2. **The correct answer is (C).** If the worker made 224 boxes in 7 hours, then he made $\frac{224 \text{ boxes}}{7 \text{ hours}} = \frac{32 \text{ boxes}}{\text{hour}}$. Choice (C) is correct.

3. **The correct answer is (A).** Plug the given values into the rate equation and solve for the missing value:

    $$\text{rate} = \frac{\text{distance}}{\text{time}}$$
    $$65 \frac{\text{miles}}{\text{hour}} = \frac{520 \text{ miles}}{t \text{ hours}}$$
    $$65t = 520$$
    $$t = 8 \text{ hours}.$$

4. **The correct answer is (D).** If it takes Ryan 1.5 minutes to run $\frac{1}{4}$ mile, then it takes him $1.5 \times 4 = 6$ minutes to run 1 mile. Now use the rate formula to determine how many miles Ryan can run in 1 hour, or 60 minutes:

    $$\text{rate} = \frac{\text{distance}}{\text{time}}$$
    $$\frac{1 \text{ mile}}{6 \text{ minutes}} = \frac{d}{60 \text{ minutes}}$$
    $$d = 10 \text{ miles}.$$

5. **The correct answer is (E).** Since there are 3 hours $\times \frac{60 \text{ minutes}}{1 \text{ hour}} = 180$ minutes in 3 hours we need to determine how many words Tim and Tom can each type in 180 minutes and then add them together. Tim can type 180 minutes $\times \frac{80 \text{ words}}{1 \text{ minute}} = 14,400$ words in 3 hours. Tom can type 180 minutes $\times \frac{60 \text{ words}}{1 \text{ minute}} = 10,800$ words in 3 hours. Together, they can type $14,400 + 10,800 = 25,200$ words in 3 hours. Choice (E) is correct.

PERCENTAGES

1. 32 is 80% of what number?

 A. 25.6

 B. 36

 C. 40

 D. 48

 E. 80

2. What is 45% of 45% of 120?

 A. 4.5

 B. 20.5

 C. 24.3

 D. 60.0

 E. 120.0

3. What is 0.4% of 60?

 A. 0.2

 B. 0.24

 C. 2.4

 D. 24.0

 E. 150.0

4. Which of the following percents is equal to $\frac{13}{20}$?

 A. 13%

 B. 20%

 C. 52%

 D. 65%

 E. 70%

5. Which of the following is the representation of $\frac{22}{5}$ as a percent?

 A. 0.440%

 B. 4.40%

 C. 44%

 D. 440%

 E. 44.04%

6. Which fraction is equivalent to 85%?

 A. $\frac{3}{4}$

 B. $\frac{4}{5}$

 C. $\frac{5}{6}$

 D. $\frac{21}{25}$

 E. $\frac{17}{20}$

Note: Photocopying any part of this book is prohibited by law.

7. According to the table below, what percent of team members scored fewer than 90 points for the season?

POINTS SCORED BY BASKETBALL TEAM PLAYERS FOR SEASON

Points Scored	Number of Players
60-69	7
70-79	5
80-89	6
90-99	3
100-109	1
110-1192	

A. 18%

B. 24%

C. 65%

D. 75%

E. 80%

8. 25 percent of 56 is what percent of 70?

A. 7%

B. 10%

C. 15%

D. 20%

E. 40%

ADDITIONAL PRACTICE QUESTIONS

1. 6 is 15% of what number?

    A. 4

    B. 20

    C. 40

    D. 80

    E. 90

2. What is 60% of 20% of 140?

    A. 11.67

    B. 16.80

    C. 28

    D. 32

    E. 84

3. What is 0.45% of 160?

    A. 0.72

    B. 3.56

    C. 7.2

    D. 35.56

    E. 72

4. What is 62% of 80?

    A. 4.96

    B. 12.9

    C. 49.6

    D. 50.4

    E. 129

5. What fraction is equivalent to 64%?

    A. $\dfrac{4}{6}$

    B. $\dfrac{6}{4}$

    C. $\dfrac{6.4}{100}$

    D. $\dfrac{8}{25}$

    E. $\dfrac{16}{25}$

Note: Photocopying any part of this book is prohibited by law.

ANSWERS AND EXPLANATIONS

1. **The correct answer is (C).** Set up your equation, plugging the numbers into the appropriate positions. In this case, 32 is the "part" and x is the "whole":

$$\frac{\text{part}}{\text{whole}} = \frac{\%}{100}$$

$$\frac{32}{x} = \frac{80}{100}$$

$$\frac{32}{x} = \frac{4}{5}$$

$$4x = 5(32)$$

$$4x = 160$$

$$\frac{4x}{4} = \frac{160}{4}$$

$$x = 40.$$

32 is 80% of 40.

2. **The correct answer is (C).** First, determine what 45% of 120 is:

$$\frac{\text{part}}{\text{whole}} = \frac{\%}{100}$$

$$\frac{x}{120} = \frac{45}{100}$$

$$\frac{x}{120} = \frac{9}{20}$$

$$20x = 9(120)$$

$$\frac{20x}{20} = \frac{1,080}{20}$$

$$x = 54.$$

Now, you're asking the question, "What is 45% of 54?"

$$\frac{\text{part}}{\text{whole}} = \frac{\%}{100}$$

$$\frac{x}{54} = \frac{45}{100}$$

$$\frac{x}{54} = \frac{9}{20}$$

$$20x = 9(54)$$

$$20x = 486$$

$$\frac{20x}{20} = \frac{486}{20}$$

$$x = 24.3.$$

45% of 45% of 120 is 24.3. Choice (C) is correct.

3. **The correct answer is (B).** You calculate decimal percents the same way that you calculate whole number percents. Just plug the numbers into their appropriate positions in the equation and proceed to solve:

$$\frac{\text{part}}{\text{whole}} = \frac{\%}{100}$$

$$\frac{x}{60} = \frac{0.4}{100}$$

$$100x = 0.4(60)$$

$$100x = 24$$

$$\frac{100x}{100} = \frac{24}{100}$$

$$x = 0.24.$$

0.4% of 60 is 0.24.

4. **The correct answer is (D).** First, convert $\frac{13}{20}$ to a decimal:

$$20\overline{)13.00}^{0.65}$$

The decimal 0.65 reads as "sixty-five hundredths" and can be converted to a percent by moving the decimal point two places to the right, which is multiplying it by 100; $0.65 \times 100 = 65\%$.

5. **The correct answer is (D).** If you know that any fraction greater than 1 will convert to a percent greater than 100, you can just select choice (D), 440%, right away here, since it is the only percent greater than 100 among the choices.

The mathematical procedure for converting $\frac{22}{5}$ to 440% involves two steps. First, convert $\frac{22}{5}$ to a decimal by dividing 22 by 5:

$$5\overline{)22.0}^{4.4}$$

Then, change the decimal to a percent by moving the decimal point 2 places to the right, which multiplies it by 100, and makes it a percent; $4.4 \times 100 = 440$. Therefore, $\frac{22}{5} = 440\%$ Choice (D) is correct.

6. **The correct answer is (E).** Since a percent means "per one hundred," convert 85% to a fraction by putting it over 100: $\frac{85}{100}$. Reduce the fraction $\frac{85}{100}$ by dividing 85 and 100 by their Greatest Common Factor, which is 5:

$$\frac{85 \div 5}{100 \div 5} = \frac{17}{20}.$$

The fraction $\frac{17}{20}$ is equivalent to 85%.

7. **The correct answer is (D).** Compute how many players are on the team by totalling the second column:
$$7 + 5 + 6 + 3 + 1 + 2 = 24$$

Next, determine the number of team members that scored fewer than 90 points for the season. You need to add the number of players in the first three rows to arrive at the number of team members that scored fewer than 90 points for the season:
$$7 + 5 + 6 = 18$$

Now you have all of the information that you need to set up an equation to determine the percent of players scoring fewer than 90 points:

$$\frac{\text{part}}{\text{whole}} = \frac{\%}{100}$$
$$\frac{18}{24} = \frac{x}{100}$$
$$\frac{3}{4} = \frac{x}{100}$$
$$\frac{4x}{4} = \frac{300}{4}$$
$$x = 75.$$

75% of the players scored fewer than 90 points for the season.

8. **The correct answer is (D).** First, determine what 25% of 56 is:

$$\frac{\text{part}}{\text{whole}} = \frac{\%}{100}$$
$$\frac{x}{56} = \frac{25}{100}$$
$$\frac{x}{56} = \frac{1}{4}$$
$$\frac{4x}{4} = \frac{56}{4}$$
$$x = 14.$$

Now the question asks, "14 is what percent of 70?"

$$\frac{\text{part}}{\text{whole}} = \frac{\%}{100}$$
$$\frac{14}{70} = \frac{x}{100}$$
$$\frac{1}{5} = \frac{x}{100}$$
$$\frac{5x}{5} = \frac{100}{5}$$
$$x = 20.$$

14 is 20% of 70.

ADDITIONAL PRACTICE QUESTIONS

1. **The correct answer is (C).** Let x represent the missing value. Plug the given values into the percent formula and solve for x:

$$\frac{\%}{100} = \frac{\text{part}}{\text{whole}}$$

$$\frac{15}{100} = \frac{6}{x}$$

$$0.15 = \frac{6}{x}$$

$$0.15x = 6$$

$$x = 40.$$

2. **The correct answer is (B).** First use the percent formula to find 20% of 140:

$$\frac{\%}{100} = \frac{\text{part}}{\text{whole}}$$

$$0.20 = \frac{p}{140}$$

$$p = 28.$$

Now use the percent formula to find 60% of 28:

$$\frac{\%}{100} = \frac{\text{part}}{\text{whole}}$$

$$0.60 = \frac{p}{28}$$

$$p = 16.8.$$

3. **The correct answer is (A).** Use the percent formula to find the missing value:

$$\frac{\%}{100} = \frac{\text{part}}{\text{whole}}$$

$$0.0045 = \frac{p}{160}$$

$$p = 0.72.$$

4. **The correct answer is (C).**

Use the percent formula to find the missing value:

$$\frac{\%}{100} = \frac{\text{part}}{\text{whole}}$$

$$0.62 = \frac{p}{80}$$

$$p = 49.6.$$

5. **The correct answer is (E).** In order to find the equivalent fraction, use the percentage as the numerator and 100 as the denominator: $\frac{64}{100}$. Then, put the fraction in lowest terms by dividing both the numerator and denominator by the greatest common factor, 4: $\frac{64}{100} = \frac{16}{25}$. Choice (E) is correct.

PERCENTAGES WORD PROBLEMS

1. In a collection of 250 coins, 30% of the coins were minted prior to 1910. How many coins were minted prior to 1910?

   A. 35

   B. 75

   C. 80

   D. 100

   E. 130

2. The Lions won 16 of their last 20 games. Which of the following percentages represents the games that they lost if there were no ties?

   A. 20%

   B. 25%

   C. 40%

   D. 60%

   E. 75%

3. Jill bought a school yearbook for $51.00. She got a 15% discount on it since she was on the yearbook staff. What was the original price of the yearbook?

   A. $7.65

   B. $43.35

   C. $52.50

   D. $60.00

   E. $66.00

4. Shirley set a goal for herself to increase her math average by 20% as compared with last quarter. If she had an 80 average last quarter, what will her goal average be for this quarter?

5. Kai had to pay an 18% service charge for ordering a concert ticket from a ticket broker. If the original cost of the ticket is $90, how much would Kai have to pay the ticket broker for a ticket?

   A. $16.20

   B. $73.80

   C. $91.80

   D. $106.20

   E. $162.00

6. An airline has fares for off-peak flights that are 30 percent less than the fares for their peak flights. If the fare for a peak flight from New York to Atlanta is $350.00, how much would this flight cost during an off-peak time?

   A. $105.00

   B. $220.00

   C. $245.00

   D. $308.00

   E. $320.00

Note: Photocopying any part of this book is prohibited by law.

7. A total of 800 calls for contributions were made during a school's annual alumni fund drive. If 95 percent of the first 300 alumni called contributed, 80 percent of the next 400 called contributed, and 75 percent of the last 100 called contributed, what percent of the alumni called contributed?

   A. 70%

   B. $83\frac{1}{3}\%$

   C. 85%

   D. $87\frac{1}{2}\%$

   E. 89%

8. A salesman sold 75 percent of his first shipment of 800 units. How many of his next shipment of 600 units must he sell in order to have sold 80 percent of all of the units?

ADDITIONAL PRACTICE QUESTIONS

1. A certain used car lot has 250 cars. If 30% of them are blue, how many cars are not blue?

   A. 75

   B. 83

   C. 167

   D. 175

   E. 220

2. Ed's job pays $75,000 per year. If he receives a 4% raise, what will Ed's new salary be?

   A. $3,000

   B. $78,000

   C. $79,000

   D. $105,000

   E. $300,000

3. Amanda scored 72 points out of a possible 80 on her math test. What percentage of the points did she score?

   A. 57.6

   B. 70

   C. 72

   D. 80

   E. 90

4. Alex read 70% of the books that his sister owns. If he read 14 books, how many books does she own?

   A. 10

   B. 19

   C. 20

   D. 21

   E. 24

5. Allison baked 40 brownies. If she ate 15% of the brownies, how many did she eat?

   A. 3

   B. 6

   C. 13

   D. 15

   E. 25

ANSWERS AND EXPLANATIONS

1. The correct answer is (B). Let x represent the number of coins minted prior to 1910. Plug the given values into the percentage formula and solve for x:

$$\frac{\text{part}}{\text{whole}} = \frac{\%}{100}$$

$$\frac{x}{250} = \frac{30}{100}$$

$$\frac{x}{250} = \frac{3}{10}$$

$$10x = (3)250$$

$$\frac{10x}{10} = \frac{750}{10}$$

$$x = 75.$$

75 coins were minted prior to 1910.

2. The correct answer is (A). Notice that the question asks you to find the percentage of games *lost*, but provides you with how many games were *won*. If the Lions won 16 of their last 20 games, they must have lost 4 of their last 20 games. Convert $\frac{4}{20}$ to a percent:

$$\frac{\text{part}}{\text{whole}} = \frac{\%}{100}$$

$$\frac{4}{20} = \frac{x}{100}$$

$$\frac{1}{5} = \frac{x}{100}$$

$$5x = (1)100$$

$$\frac{5x}{5} = \frac{100}{5}$$

$$x = 20.$$

The Lions lost 20% of their games.

3. The correct answer is (D). $51.00 is the price *after* the reduction. The question asks you to find the original price, which has to be higher than $51.00. So, you can eliminate choices (A) and (B) right away.

So, how do you calculate a 15% discount from an unknown number to arrive at a given number? Just use the $\frac{\text{part}}{\text{whole}} = \frac{\%}{100}$ equation. $51.00 is the new price that has been discounted by 15%, so it represents 85% (100% – 15%) of the original whole price, which is what you're looking for:

$$\frac{\text{part}}{\text{whole}} = \frac{\%}{100}$$

$$\frac{51}{x} = \frac{85}{100}$$

$$\frac{51}{x} = \frac{17}{20}$$

$$17x = (51)20$$

$$\frac{17x}{17} = \frac{1{,}020}{17}$$

$$x = 60.$$

The original price of the yearbook was $60.00.

4. The correct answer is 96. First, determine what 20% of 80 is:

$$\frac{\text{part}}{\text{whole}} = \frac{\%}{100}$$

$$\frac{x}{80} = \frac{20}{100}$$

$$\frac{x}{80} = \frac{1}{5}$$

$$\frac{5x}{5} = \frac{80}{5}$$

$$x = 16.$$

20% of 80 is 16.

Then, add 16 on to Shirley's existing average, 80, to determine her goal average: $80 + 16 = 96$.

Shirley's goal average for this quarter is 96.

5. The correct answer is (D). First, determine what the service charge for the ticket would be.

$$\frac{\text{part}}{\text{whole}} = \frac{\%}{100}$$

$$\frac{x}{90} = \frac{18}{100}$$

$$100x = 18(90)$$

$$100x = 1,620$$

$$\frac{100x}{100} = \frac{1,620}{100}$$

$$x = 16.20.$$

An 18% service charge would be $16.20. Add this service charge of $16.20 to the original cost of the ticket, $90.00 to determine the total that Kai had to pay: $90.00 + $16.20 = $106.20.

Kai would have to pay the ticket broker $106.20 for a ticket.

6. The correct answer is (C). First, calculate the discount, 30% of $350.00:

$$\frac{\text{part}}{\text{whole}} = \frac{\%}{100}$$

$$\frac{x}{350} = \frac{30}{100}$$

$$\frac{x}{350} = \frac{3}{10}$$

$$10x = 3(350)$$

$$\frac{10x}{10} = \frac{1,050}{10}$$

$$x = 105.$$

Then, subtract $105.00 from $350.00 to get the off-peak fare:
$$\$350.00 - \$105.00 = \$245.00.$$

7. The correct answer is (C). First, determine the individual percentages:

95% of the first 300:

$$\frac{\text{part}}{\text{whole}} = \frac{\%}{100}$$

$$\frac{x}{300} = \frac{95}{100}$$

$$\frac{x}{300} = \frac{19}{20}$$

$$\frac{20x}{4} = \frac{(19)300}{4}$$

$$\frac{20x}{20} = \frac{5,700}{20}$$

$$x = 285.$$

80% of 400:

$$\frac{\text{part}}{\text{whole}} = \frac{\%}{100}$$

$$\frac{x}{400} = \frac{80}{100}$$

$$\frac{x}{400} = \frac{4}{5}$$

$$\frac{5x}{4} = \frac{(4)400}{4}$$

$$\frac{5x}{5} = \frac{1,600}{5}$$

$$x = 320.$$

You do not need to set up the equation for the final amount: 75% of 100 is 75.

Now, add up the number of contributors:
$$285 + 320 + 75 = 680.$$

Finally, you have all of the information that you need to set up an equation to determine the percent of alumni called who are contributors:

$$\frac{\text{part}}{\text{whole}} = \frac{\%}{100}$$

$$\frac{680}{800} = \frac{x}{100}$$

$$\frac{800x}{800} = \frac{68,000}{800}$$

$$x = 85.$$

Note: Photocopying any part of this book is prohibited by law.

8. **The correct answer is 520.** First, determine how many units were sold in the first shipment, 75% of 800:

$$\frac{part}{whole} = \frac{\%}{100}$$

$$\frac{x}{800} = \frac{75}{100}$$

$$\frac{x}{800} = \frac{3}{4}$$

$$\frac{4x}{4} = \frac{(3)800}{4}$$

$$\frac{4x}{4} = \frac{2,400}{4}$$

$$x = 600.$$

Gather what information you have so far: 600 out of the first shipment of 800 units were sold. There are 1,400 units altogether, 800 from the first shipment and 600 from the next shipment. You are looking for what portion of the remaining number of units must be sold to achieve an 80% sale rate. If you let x equal this amount, you have enough information to set up the percent equation:

$$\frac{part}{whole} = \frac{\%}{100}$$

$$\frac{600 + x}{1,400} = \frac{80}{100}$$

$$\frac{600 + x}{1,400} = \frac{4}{5}$$

$$5(600 + x) = 4(1,400)$$

$$3,000 + 5x = 5,600$$

$$3,000 - 3,000 + 5x = 5,600 - 3,000$$

$$5x = 2,600$$

$$\frac{5x}{5} = \frac{2,600}{5}$$

$$x = 520.$$

You can check this answer:

$$\frac{600 + 520}{1,400} = \frac{1,120}{1,400}$$

$$= 0.8$$

$$= 80\%.$$

Grid in 520 as your answer.

ADDITIONAL PRACTICE QUESTIONS

1. **The correct answer is (D).** Let x represent the number of cars on the lot that are blue. Use the percent formula to determine the value of x:

$$\frac{\%}{100} = \frac{part}{whole}$$

$$\frac{30}{100} = \frac{x}{250}$$

$$0.30 = \frac{x}{250}$$

$$x = 75.$$

Since 75 of the cars are blue, then $250 - 75 = 175$ cars are not blue. Choice (D) is correct.

2. **The correct answer is (B).** First use the percent formula to determine the amount that Ed's salary will increase:

$$\frac{\%}{100} = \frac{part}{whole}$$

$$0.04 = \frac{p}{75,000}$$

$$p = 3,000.$$

This means that Ed's new salary will be $75,000 + $3,000 = $78,000. Choice (B) is correct.

3. **The correct answer is (E).** Use the percent formula to determine the missing value:

$$\frac{\%}{100} = \frac{part}{whole}$$

$$\frac{\%}{100} = \frac{72}{80}$$

$$\% = \left(\frac{72}{80}\right) \times 100$$

$$= 0.90 \times 100$$

$$= 90\%.$$

Note: Photocopying any part of this book is prohibited by law.

4. **The correct answer is (C).** Plug the given values into the percent formula and solve for the missing value:

$$\frac{\%}{100} = \frac{\text{part}}{\text{whole}}$$

$$\frac{70}{100} = \frac{14}{w}$$

$$0.70 = \frac{14}{w}$$

$$0.70w = 14$$

$$w = 20.$$

5. **The correct answer is (B).** Plug the given values into the percent formula and solve for the missing value:

$$\frac{\%}{100} = \frac{\text{part}}{\text{whole}}$$

$$\frac{15}{100} = \frac{p}{40}$$

$$0.15 = \frac{p}{40}$$

$$p = 6.$$

LINES

1. Line segment XY has length 2.8. Line segment XZ has length 4.0. What is the length of segment YZ?

A. 1.2

B. 2.1

C. 3.5

D. 4.9

E. 7.7

2. If BC measures $2\frac{1}{2}$ times what AB measures and AC measures 14, what does AB measure?

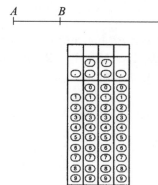

3. On a number line, if point S has coordinate 16 and point R has coordinate –4, what is the coordinate of the point that is located $\frac{3}{5}$ of the way from S to R?

A. 13

B. 11

C. 8

D. 4

E. –1

4. If line segment XY has a midpoint labeled point M, and if line segment XY has a total length of 7, what is the length of segment XM?

A. 3

B. 3.5

C. 4

D. 4.5

E. 14

5. Each of the following statements is true for the example drawn EXCEPT:

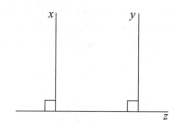

A. lines x and y are parallel.

B. line x is perpendicular to line z.

C. line x is equal in measure to line y.

D. lines x and y will never meet, no matter how far they extend in either direction.

E. line x intersects line z.

ADDITIONAL PRACTICE QUESTIONS

1. Line segment *AB* has a length of 2.3 cm. Line segment *AC* has a length of 4.2 cm. What is the length of line segment *BC*?

    A. 1.9
    B. 2.1
    C. 2.3
    D. 4.2
    E. 6.5

2. In the diagram below, lines *PQ* and *RS* are parallel. Line *TW* intersects *PQ* and *RS* at points *V* and *U*, respectively. If angle *RUT* has a measure of 36°, what is the measure of angle *UVQ*?

    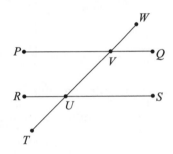

    A. 36°
    B. 42°
    C. 54°
    D. 138°
    E. 144°

3. Line segment *XY* has length 4.6 cm. Line segment *YZ* has length 6.2 cm. What is the length of *XZ*?

    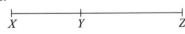

    A. 1.6 cm
    B. 4.6 cm
    C. 6.2 cm
    D. 10.8 cm
    E. 12.1 cm

4. In the diagram below, lines *AB* and *CD* are parallel. Line *EH* intersects *AB* and *CD* at points *G* and *F*, respectively. If angle *EFD* has measure 124°, what is the measure of angle *AGH*?

    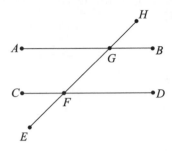

    A. 56°
    B. 62°
    C. 118°
    D. 124°
    E. 134°

5. If line segment *PR* has length 12.6 cm and line segment *QR* has length 5.2 cm, what is the length of line segment *PQ*?

    A. 3.7 cm
    B. 5.2 cm
    C. 7.4 cm
    D. 12.6 cm
    E. 17.8 cm

Note: Photocopying any part of this book is prohibited by law.

ANSWERS AND EXPLANATIONS

1. **The correct answer is (A).** You can see the following relationship among the line segments from the diagram:

$$XY + YZ = XZ.$$

The question provides you with the measures of XY (2.8) and XZ (4.0), so substitute these values into the equation and solve:

$$XY + YZ = XZ$$
$$2.8 + YZ = 4.0$$
$$2.8 - 2.8 + YZ = 4.0 - 2.8$$
$$YZ = 1.2$$

2. **The correct answer is 4.** This problem can be solved fairly easily by employing some basic algebra. Since the question is asking you to find the measure of AB, and the measure of BC is being described in terms of the measure of AB, let x equal the measure of AB. Since the measure of BC is described as being $2\frac{1}{2}$ times the measure of AB, let $2\frac{1}{2}x$, or $2.5x$, equal the measure of BC.

You can see the following relationship among the line segments from the diagram:

$$AB + BC = AC$$
$$x + 2.5x = 14$$
$$1x + 2.5x = 14$$
$$3.5x = 14$$
$$\frac{3.5x}{3.5} = \frac{14}{3.5}$$
$$x = 4$$

AB measures 4.

3. **The correct answer is (D).** First, determine the distance from 16 to –4. You can do that by taking the difference between the two values: $16 - (-4) = 20$.

Then determine what $\frac{3}{5}$ of this 20-unit distance would be:

$$\frac{3}{5} \times 20 = 12.$$

The question asks you for the coordinate of the point that is located $\frac{3}{5}$ of the way from S to R so, you'll want to count down 12 spaces from 16, which will leave you at 4.

Draw a sketch if it helps you to visualize the question—just don't get too bogged down in detail:

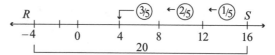

4. **The correct answer is (B).** By definition, the midpoint of a line segment divides it into two equal parts. If point M is the midpoint of line XY, then it must mark the absolute middle of XY's measure. Segment XM would therefore be half the length of XY, with a measure of 3.5.

5. **The correct answer is (C).** Each answer choice except for (C) is true according to the rules governing parallel lines. The measure of lines x and y is never addressed in the given information, so it cannot be assumed.

ADDITIONAL PRACTICE QUESTIONS

1. **The correct answer is (A).** Since the length of the entire line segment *AC* is 4.2 cm and the length of the segment *AB* is 2.3, then the length of the remaining line segment *BC* is equal to the difference of *AC* and *AB*: 4.3 – 2.3 = 1.9. Choice (A) is correct.

2. **The correct answer is (E).** Since lines *PQ* and lines *RS* are parallel, angles *RUT* and *WVQ* are equal. Also, angles *WVQ* and *UVQ* are supplementary, which means that the sum of their measures must equal 180°. Therefore, the measure of angle *UVQ* is equal to 180° – 36° = 144°.

3. **The correct answer is (D).** The length of *XZ* is the sum of the segments *XY* and *YX*, which is 4.2 + 6.2 = 10.8.

4. **The correct answer is (D).** Since lines *AB* and *CD* are parallel, then the measures of angles *AGH* and *EFD* are equal. Therefore, the measure of angle *AGH* is 124°. Choice (D) is correct.

5. **The correct answer is (C).** Since the length of the entire line segment *PR* is 12.6 cm and the length of segment *QR* is 5.2 cm, then the length of segment *PQ* is equal to the difference of the lengths of *PR* and *QR*, or 12.6 – 5.2 = 7.4. Choice (C) is correct.

ANGLES

1. Lines *RS* and *TU* intersect at point *V*. If angle *RVT* has a measure of 35°, what is the measure of angle *SVU*?

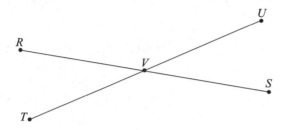

A. 35°

B. 45°

C. 70°

D. 145°

E. 215°

2. If angle *FGP* measures 40°, what is the measure of angle *PGH*?

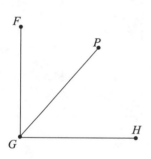

A. 40°

B. 45°

C. 50°

D. 55°

E. 90°

3. Which of the following pairs of angle measures could belong to angles that are both complementary and vertical to each other?

A. 40, 50

B. 20, 70

C. 90, 90

D. 45, 45

E. 30, 60

4. If ∠*KBF* is supplementary to ∠*DRF*, and ∠*KBF* measures 75°, what does ∠*DRF* measure?

A. 35°

B. 105°

C. 125°

D. 135°

E. 180°

5. Angles *A* and *B* are supplementary angles. If angle *A* measures 30 more than four times the measurement of angle *B*, what is the measure of angle *A*?

A. 30°

B. 90°

C. 120°

D. 150°

E. 180°

Note: Photocopying any part of this book is prohibited by law.

6. In the diagram below, lines *GH* and *JK* are parallel. Line *MN* crosses *GH* and *JK* at points *P* and *Q*, respectively. If angle *NQH* has a measure of 52°, what is the measure of angle *JPM*?

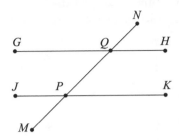

A. 26°

B. 52°

C. 104°

D. 128°

E. 180°

7. According to the diagram below, all of the following are true EXCEPT:

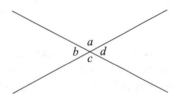

A. Angles *a* and *c* are equal to each other.

B. Angles *b* and *d* are equal to each other.

C. The total measure of angles *a, b, c,* and *d* is 360°.

D. The sum of angles *a* and *d* is equal to 90°.

E. The sum of angles *c* and *d* is equal to 180°.

ADDITIONAL PRACTICE QUESTIONS

1. Lines *AE* and *CD* intersect at point *B*. If angle *ABC* measures 40°, what is the measure of angle *DBE*?

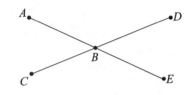

A. 20°

B. 40°

C. 50°

D. 60°

E. 140°

2. If the measure of angle *PQR* is equal to 62°, what is the measure of angle *RQS*?

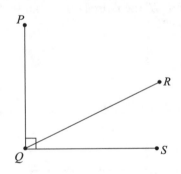

A. 18°

B. 28°

C. 62°

D. 90°

E. 152°

3. In the diagram below, point *X* lies on segment *WY*. If angle *ZXY* has measure 34°, what is the measure of angle *WXZ*?

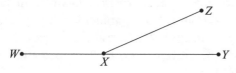

A. 34°

B. 56°

C. 124°

D. 146°

E. 180°

4. If angle *DBC* measures 72°, what is the measure of angle *ABD*?

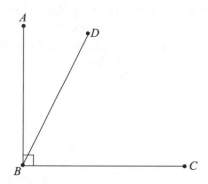

A. 9°

B. 18°

C. 36°

D. 90°

E. 108°

5. In the diagram above, point *Q* lies on segment *PR*. If angle *PQS* measures 74°, what is the measure of angle *SQR*?

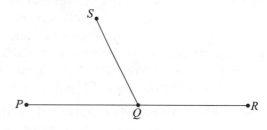

A. 58°

B. 106°

C. 116°

D. 126°

E. 126°

Note: Photocopying any part of this book is prohibited by law.

ANSWERS AND EXPLANATIONS

1. **The correct answer is (A).** Vertical angles, formed when two lines intersect each other, are always equal to each other. Angles *RVT* and *SVU* are vertical angles, so their measures will be equal. Therefore if angle *RVT* has a measure of 35°, the measure of angle *SVU* is 35° as well.

2. **The correct answer is (C).** Complementary angles share a right angle and therefore add up to 90°. Subtract 40 from 90 to find its complement:

$$90° - 40° = 50°$$

3. **The correct answer is (D).** Complementary angles add up to 90°. Vertical angles are equal to each other. The only angle pair that satisfies both of these criteria is the pair measuring 45° and 45°.

4. **The correct answer is (B).** The sum of two supplementary angles is 180°. Subtract 75 from 180 to find the measure of its supplement:

$$180° - 75° = 105°$$

5. **The correct answer is (D).** Since angle *A* is described in terms of angle *B*, let x = angle *B*. Then angle $A = 4x + 30$. Write an equation representing the fact that the sum of two supplementary angles is 180°.

$$x + 4x + 30 = 180$$
$$5x + 30 = 180$$
$$5x + 30 - 30 = 180 - 30$$
$$5x = 150$$
$$\frac{5x}{5} = \frac{150}{5}$$
$$x = 30$$

Careful! 30° is not your final answer. It is the measure of angle *B*, but the question asks for the measure of angle *A*. Plug 30 in for x in $4x + 30$:

$$4x + 30$$
$$4(30) + 30$$
$$120 + 30 = 150$$

The measure of angle *A* is 150.

6. **The correct answer is (B).** Given the fact that lines *GH* and *JK* are parallel, you know that angle *NQH* and angle *JPM* are alternate exterior angles and are therefore equal. The measure of angle *JPM* is 52°.

7. **The correct answer is (D).** In this diagram, angles *a* and *c* are vertical angles, as are angles *b* and *d*. Vertical angles, formed when two lines intersect each other, are always equal to each other.

Since the intersection of these two lines also forms the center point of a circle, the entire measure of all four angles is 360°. Angles *c* and *d* form a straight angle, and are equal to 180°. Choice (D) is the correct answer because it offers incorrect information. Angles *a* and *d* are not complementary angles, they are supplementary; they form a straight angle measuring 180°.

ADDITIONAL PRACTICE QUESTIONS

1. **The correct answer is (B).** From the diagram, you can see that angles *ABC* and angles *DBE* are vertical angles. This means that they have equal measures. Therefore, the measure of angle *DBE* is 40°.

2. **The correct answer is (B).** Angles *PQR* and *RQS* are complementary angles, which means that together they form a right angle. This means that the sum of their measures must be equal to a right angle, or 90°. Since angle *PQR* is equal to 62°, then *RQS* must equal 90° – 62° = 28°.

3. **The correct answer is (D).** Angles *WXZ* and *ZXY* are supplementary angles, which means that the sum of their measures must equal 180°. This means that the measure of angle *WXZ* is equal to 180° – 34° = 146°.

4. **The correct answer is (B).** Angles *DBC* and *ABD* are complementary, which means that the sum of their measures must equal 90°. So, the measure of angle *ABD* is equal to 90° – 72° = 18°.

5. **The correct answer is (B).** Since angles *PQS* and *SQR* are supplementary, the sum of their measures must be equal to 180°. Therefore, the measure of angle *SQR* is 180° – 74° = 106°.

TRIANGLE PROPERTIES

1. If two angles of a triangle measure 34° and 61°, what is the measure of the third angle?

    A.   34°

    B.   61°

    C.   75°

    D.   85°

    E.   180°

2. Triangle *PRT* is an isosceles triangle with sides *PT* = *PR*. If angle *R* has a measure of 50°, what is the measure of angle *T*?

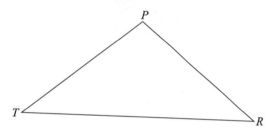

    A.   40°

    B.   50°

    C.   80°

    D.   90°

    E.   100°

3. If the perimeter of the triangle below is 15, what is the measure of angle *x*?

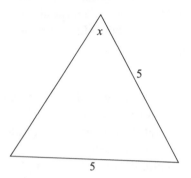

    A.   30°

    B.   45°

    C.   60°

    D.   75°

    E.   90°

4. The angles of a triangle are in a 3:5:7 ratio. What is the measure of the largest angle of the triangle?

    A.   7°

    B.   12°

    C.   15°

    D.   36°

    E.   84°

5. A triangle has a base measurement of 5 and an unknown height *h*. What is the measurement of the height *h* if the area of the triangle is 20?

6. The perimeter of an isosceles triangle is 55. The lengths of the legs are 10 less than twice the measure of the base. What does the base measure?

7. If the measures of the angles of a triangle are represented by $x, x + 10$, and $3x + 20$, the triangle must be:

A. right

B. isosceles

C. obtuse

D. equilateral

E. acute

8. In the diagram below, what is the measure of angle *A*?

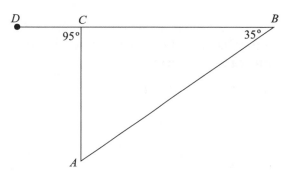

A. 15°

B. 25°

C. 30°

D. 60°

E. 95°

ADDITIONAL PRACTICE QUESTIONS

1. Triangle *ABC* has sides of the lengths indicated in the diagram above. If $x = 2$, what is the perimeter of triangle *ABC*?

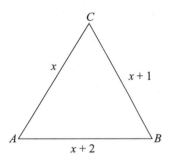

A. 2

B. 6

C. 8

D. 9

E. 12

2. In triangle *XYZ*, shown below, what is the measure of angle *Y*?

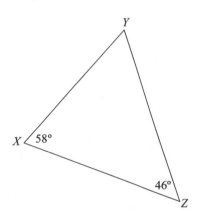

A. 76°

B. 86°

C. 114°

D. 122°

E. 134°

3. Triangle *PQR*, shown below, is an isosceles triangle with sides *PQ* = *PR*. If angle *Q* measures 50°, what is the measure of angle *R*?

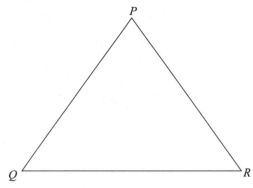

A. 40°

B. 50°

C. 80°

D. 90°

E. 130°

4. One side of an equilateral triangle has a length of 6. What is the sum of the lengths of the two other sides?

A. 6

B. 12

C. 18

D. 24

E. It cannot be determined from the information given.

5. One side of an equilateral triangle has a length of 8. What is the perimeter of the triangle?

A. 16

B. 24

C. 32

D. 64

E. It cannot be determined from the information given.

ANSWERS AND EXPLANATIONS

1. **The correct answer is (D).** This question revolves around the fact that the sum of the measures of the angles of a triangle is 180°. Since the sum of 34° and 61° is 95°, then the remaining angle must be 180° – 95°, or 85°.

2. **The correct answer is (B).** If $PT = PR$, then the measure of angle P is equal to the measure of angle T, and the angles opposite the equal legs are equal to each other. So, if angle R has a measure of 50°, angle T has a measure of 50° as well.

3. **The correct answer is (C).** If the perimeter of the triangle is 15, the remaining side must measure 5 as well, making the triangle equilateral. Since the angles of an equilateral triangle are all equal to one another, each angle measures 60° (180 ÷ 3 = 60). So, the measure of angle x is 60°.

4. **The correct answer is (E).** You know two things about the angles of the triangle: they are in a 3:5:7 ratio, and the sum of their measures must be 180°. Use these two facts to set up your equation:

$$3x + 5x + 7x = 180$$
$$15x = 180$$

$$\frac{15x}{15} = \frac{180}{15}$$
$$x = 12°.$$

If $x = 12°$, then $7x = 84°$. The largest angle of the triangle measures 84°.

5. **The correct answer is 8.** The area of a triangle can be found using the formula $A = \frac{1}{2}bh$. You can write the formula for this triangle as:

$$20 = \frac{1}{2}(5)(h)$$
$$40 = 5h$$
$$h = 8.$$

The height of the triangle is 8.

Grid in 8.

6. **The correct answer is 15.** Let x represent the measure of the base and let $2x - 10$ represent the measure of each leg. Add together the measures of the 3 sides and set the sum equal to the measure of the perimeter, 55 (be sure to account for two legs):

$$x + 2(2x - 10) = 55$$
$$x + 4x - 20 = 55$$
$$5x - 20 = 55$$
$$5x - 20 + 20 = 55 + 20$$
$$5x = 75$$
$$\frac{5x}{5} = \frac{75}{5}$$
$$x = 15.$$

So, the base measures 15.

7. **The correct answer is (C).** This question revolves around the fact that the sum of the measures of the angles of a triangle is 180°. So, add up the three measures and set them equal to 180, solve for x to find the measures of the three angles:

$$x + x + 10 + 3x + 20 = 180$$
$$5x + 30 = 180$$
$$5x + 30 - 30 = 180 - 30$$
$$5x = 150$$

$$\frac{5x}{5} = \frac{150}{5}$$
$$x = 30$$
$$x + 10 = 40$$
$$3x + 20 = 110$$

Now that you know what the three angles measure, you can determine what kind of triangle it is. Since it does not have a 90° angle, it is not a right triangle. Since none of the three angles are equal to one another, it is neither isosceles nor equilateral. In order for it to be acute, all three angles would have to measure less than 90°. The fact that the 110° measure is greater than 90° makes this triangle obtuse.

Note: Photocopying any part of this book is prohibited by law.

8. **The correct answer is (D).** Angle *DCA*, measuring 95 degrees is an exterior angle to triangle *ABC*. If you remember the rule that the exterior angle of a triangle is equal to the sum of the two remote interior angles, you can set up a basic equation to solve. The exterior angle, *DCA*, measuring 95°, is equal to the sum of the two angles inside the triangle that are furthest away from it, angle *B*, measuring 35°, and angle *A*, whose measure you are looking to find:

$$95 = 35 + A.$$

Proceed to solve by subtracting 35 from both sides of the equation:

$$95 - 35 = 35 - 35 + A$$
$$A = 60$$

So, the measure of angle *A* is 60°.

It is still possible to do this question even if you are not familiar with the rule regarding an exterior angle to a triangle.

Begin by finding the measure of the other angle of the triangle, angle *ACB*, which is supplementary to the 95° angle, *DCA*, because they share a line. Since the sum of two supplementary angles is 180°, subtract 95 from 180 to find the measure of its supplement:

$$180 - 95 = 85.$$

Now that you know that the measure of Angle *ACB* is 85, you have the measure of two angles of a triangle. You can find the measure of angle *A* by subtracting the sum of the other two angles of the triangle from 180:

$$180 - (85 + 35) = A$$
$$180 - (120) = A$$
$$A = 60$$

ADDITIONAL PRACTICE QUESTIONS

1. **The correct answer is (D).** The perimeter of a triangle is found by adding together the lengths of the three sides, which in this case is $x + (x + 1) + (x + 2) = 3x + 3$. Since $x = 2$, the perimeter of the triangle is $3(2) + 3 = 6 + 3 = 9$.

2. **The correct answer is (A).** In every triangle, the sum of the measures of the three angles is always 180°. Since the sum of the two given angles is $46° + 58° = 104°$, the measure of the missing angle must be $180° - 104° = 76°$.

3. **The correct answer is (B).** In an isosceles triangle, there are two equal sides and also two equal angles. In triangle *PQR*, since sides *PQ* and *PR* are equal, then angles *Q* and *R* are equal. We are given that angle *Q* measures 50°, which means that angle *R* must also equal 50°.

4. **The correct answer is (B).** In an equilateral triangle, all three of the sides have equal length. Since we know that one of the sides has length 6, then the other two sides must also have length 6. Therefore, the sum of the lengths of the other two sides is $6 + 6 = 12$.

5. **The correct answer is (B).** An equilateral triangle has three equal sides. Since we know the length of one side is 8, then we know that the lengths of the other two sides are also 8. The perimeter of a triangle is found by finding the sum of the lengths of the three sides, which in this case is equal to $8 + 8 + 8 = 24$.

RIGHT TRIANGLES

1. Find the area of isosceles right triangle *ABC* below.

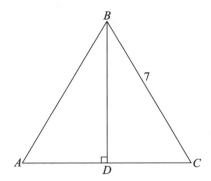

A. $2\sqrt{6}$

B. $10\sqrt{6}$

C. $20\sqrt{6}$

D. 24

E. 70

2. Find the area for a right triangle with legs measuring 5 and 12 and a hypotenuse measuring 13.

A. 16

B. 27

C. 29

D. 30

E. 31

3. A right triangle has a base measurement of 8 and an unknown height *h*. What is the measurement of the hypotenuse, *x*, if the area of the triangle is 60?

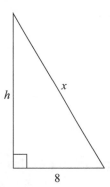

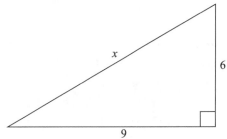

4. In the right triangle below, what is the value of *x*?

A. $\sqrt{13}$

B. $\sqrt{15}$

C. $3\sqrt{10}$

D. $\sqrt{117}$

E. 15

5. What is the value of *x*?

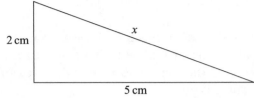

A. $\sqrt{7}$ cm

B. $\sqrt{29}$ cm

C. 7 cm

D. 10 cm

E. 29 cm

6. What is the perimeter of this right triangle?

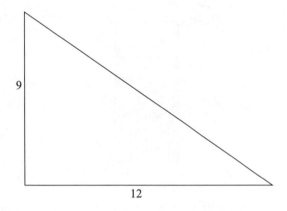

A. 15

B. 21

C. 32

D. 36

E. 54

7. What is the perimeter of the triangle below?

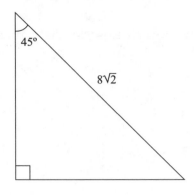

A. 8

B. $8\sqrt{2}$

C. $8 + 8\sqrt{2}$

D. $16 + 8\sqrt{2}$

E. $24 + 8\sqrt{2}$

8. What is the area of triangle *GHJ* below?

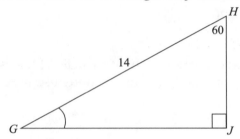

A. $14\sqrt{3}$

B. $24.5\sqrt{3}$

C. $49\sqrt{3}$

D. 73.5

E. 98

Note: Photocopying any part of this book is prohibited by law.

ADDITIONAL PRACTICE QUESTIONS

1. In the triangle below, what is the value of *C*?

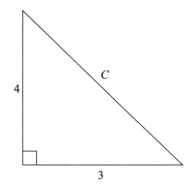

A. 5

B. 7

C. 10

D. 12

E. 25

2. What is the area of the triangle below?

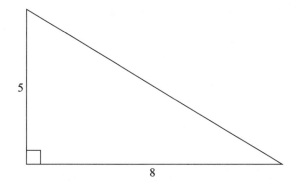

A. 13

B. 20

C. 26

D. 40

E. 89

3. In the triangle below, what is the value of *a*?

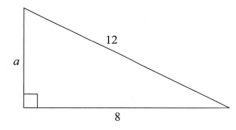

A. $\sqrt{5}$

B. 4

C. $4\sqrt{5}$

D. $5\sqrt{4}$

E. $4\sqrt{13}$

4. What is the area of the triangle shown below?

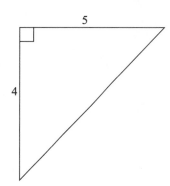

A. 9

B. 10

C. 18

D. 20

E. 41

Note: Photocopying any part of this book is prohibited by law.

5. In the triangle below, what is the value of *b*?

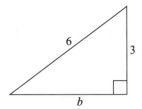

A. 3

B. $3\sqrt{3}$

C. 9

D. $3\sqrt{5}$

E. 27

ANSWERS AND EXPLANATIONS

1. **The correct answer is (B).** To find a triangle's area, you need to know the measure of the base and the height ($A = \frac{1}{2}bh$). You have the measure of the base ($AC = 10$), but how does that help you find the height? You can backtrack and work with one of the smaller triangles in the diagram first.

Segment BD, the height of the triangle, is a perpendicular bisector of line AC. AD and DC are, therefore, each equal to one half the base, or 5.

This knowledge enables you to calculate the height, BD, using the triangle BDC. The Pythagorean theorem will help you here:
$$a^2 + b^2 = c^2$$

The hypotenuse, c, will be side BC, which measures 7, while a will be side BD, which measures 5. The height, BD, will be b:
$$a^2 + b^2 = c^2$$
$$(5)^2 + b^2 = (7)^2$$
$$25 + b^2 = 49$$
$$b^2 = 24$$
$$b = \sqrt{24}$$
$$b = \sqrt{4 \times 6}$$
$$b = 2\sqrt{6}$$

Now that you know the measures of the height and the base, you can calculate the area:
$$A = \frac{1}{2}bh$$
$$= (\frac{1}{2})(10)(2\sqrt{6})$$
$$= 10\sqrt{6}.$$

2. **The correct answer is (D).** The legs, 5 and 12, constitute the base and height that is used in the area formula, $A = \frac{1}{2}bh$. The hypotenuse, 13, will not come into play in determining the area:
$$A = \frac{1}{2}bh$$
$$= \frac{1}{2}(5)(12)$$
$$= \frac{1}{2}(60)$$
$$= 30.$$

3. **The correct answer is 17.** Draw yourself a diagram:

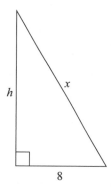

The area of a triangle can be found using the formula $A = \frac{1}{2}bh$. So, you can write the formula for this triangle as:
$$60 = \frac{1}{2}(8)h$$
$$120 = 8h$$
$$h = 15.$$

You may recognize that this will be an 8-15-17 right triangle. If not, use the Pythagorean theorem to calculate the hypotenuse:
$$a^2 + b^2 = c^2$$
$$(15)^2 + (8)^2 = c^2$$
$$225 + 64 = c^2$$
$$289 = c^2$$
$$c = 17$$

4. **The correct answer is (D).** Use the Pythagorean theorem ($a^2 + b^2 = c^2$) to answer this question.

The hypotenuse, c, is what is missing and the sides measuring 6 and 9 can represent either a or b:

$$a^2 + b^2 = c^2$$
$$(6)^2 + (9)^2 = c^2$$
$$36 + 81 = c^2$$
$$117 = c^2$$
$$c = \sqrt{117}$$

5. **The correct answer is (B).** You can eliminate choices (A), (C), (D) and (E) right away if you know that the hypotenuse must always be the longest side of the triangle, but that it will always be less than the sum of the other two sides of the triangle. If you are not aware of this fact, you can use the Pythagorean theorem ($a^2 + b^2 = c^2$) to figure out the hypotenuse.

The hypotenuse, c, is what is missing and the sides measuring 2 and 5 can represent either a or b:

$$a^2 + b^2 = c^2$$
$$(2)^2 + (5)^2 = c^2$$
$$4 + 25 = c^2$$
$$29 = c^2$$
$$c = \sqrt{29}$$

6. **The correct answer is (D).** You may recognize that this will be a 3-4-5 right triangle multiplied through by 3. If not, use the Pythagorean theorem ($a^2 + b^2 = c^2$) to determine the hypotenuse, then add together all three sides to find the perimeter.

The hypotenuse, c, is what is missing and the sides measuring 9 and 12 can be a or b alternatively.

$$a^2 + b^2 = c^2$$
$$(9)^2 + (12)^2 = c^2$$
$$81 + 144 = c^2$$
$$225 = c^2$$
$$c = 15$$

So, the sides of the triangle measure 9, 12, and 15, and the perimeter is $9 + 12 + 15 = 36$.

7. **The correct answer is (D).** You can see that the triangle contains one right angle and one 45° angle, so the missing angle is a 45° angle as well. Therefore, the triangle is a 45-45-90 isosceles right triangle, with its special characteristic of its leg:leg:hypotenuse proportions being $x : x : x\sqrt{2}$. $8\sqrt{2}$ is the hypotenuse of the right triangle. Therefore, each of the legs measures 8. So, if each of the missing legs measures 8 and the hypotenuse measures $8\sqrt{2}$, the perimeter of the triangle measures $8 + 8 + 8\sqrt{2}$, or $16 + 8\sqrt{2}$.

Even if you are not familiar with the special properties of a 45-45-90 isosceles right triangle, if you know that sides opposite equal angles are equal, you can use the Pythagorean theorem ($a^2 + b^2 = c^2$) to figure out the missing sides. Label each of the identical missing sides x and plug them in for a and b in the formula.

$$a^2 + b^2 = c^2$$
$$x^2 + x^2 = (8\sqrt{2})^2$$
$$2x^2 = (8\sqrt{2})(8\sqrt{2})$$
$$2x^2 = 128$$
$$\frac{2x^2}{2} = \frac{128}{2}$$
$$x^2 = 64$$
$$\sqrt{x^2} = \sqrt{64}$$
$$x = 8.$$

8. **The correct answer is (B).** You can eliminate choice (A) right away as the perimeter is certainly longer than one of the triangle's sides. You can see that the triangle contains one right angle and one 60° angle, so the missing angle is a 30° angle. Therefore, the triangle is a 30-60-90 triangle, with its special characteristics. If the side opposite the 30° angle measures x, then the side opposite the 60° angle measures $x\sqrt{3}$, and the side opposite the hypotenuse measures $2x$. So, in this triangle, HJ would measure 7, and GJ would measure $7\sqrt{3}$.

Note: Photocopying any part of this book is prohibited by law.

The area of a triangle can be found using the formula $A = \frac{1}{2} bh$. You can write the formula for this triangle as:

$$A = \frac{1}{2}(7)(7\sqrt{3})$$

$$= \frac{1}{2}(49\sqrt{3})$$

$$= 24.5\sqrt{3}.$$

The area of triangle GHJ is $24.5\sqrt{3}$.

ADDITIONAL PRACTICE QUESTIONS

1. **The correct answer is (A).** In this triangle, c is the hypotenuse. The length of the hypotenuse is found by using the Pythagorean theorem:

$$a^2 + b^2 = c^2$$
$$(4)^2 + (3)^2 = c^2$$
$$16 + 9 = c^2$$
$$25 = c^2$$
$$c = 5$$

2. **The correct answer is (B).** Use the formula for finding the area of a triangle:

$$A = \frac{1}{2} bh$$

$$A = \frac{1}{2} \times 8 \times 5$$

$$= \frac{1}{2} \times 40$$

$$= 20.$$

3. **The correct answer is (C).** In order to find the length of a, you need to use the Pythagorean theorem:

$$a^2 + b^2 = c^2$$
$$a^2 + (8)^2 = (12)^2$$
$$a^2 + 64 - 64 = 144 - 64$$
$$a^2 = 80$$
$$a = \sqrt{80}$$
$$a = \sqrt{16 \times 5}$$
$$a = 4\sqrt{5}$$

Note: Photocopying any part of this book is prohibited by law.

4. **The correct answer is (B).** Use the formula for finding the area of a triangle:

$$A = \frac{1}{2}bh$$

$$A = \frac{1}{2} \times 4 \times 5$$

$$= \frac{1}{2} \times 20$$

$$= 10.$$

5. **The correct answer is (B).** To find the value of b, use the Pythagorean theorem:

$$a^2 + b^2 = c^2$$
$$(3)^2 + b^2 = (6)^2$$
$$9 + b^2 = 36$$
$$9 - 9 + b^2 = 36 - 9$$
$$b^2 = 27$$
$$b = \sqrt{27}$$
$$b = \sqrt{9 \times 3}$$
$$b = 3\sqrt{3}$$

Note: Photocopying any part of this book is prohibited by law.

FACTORS AND MULTIPLES

1. The number 30 is the Least Common Multiple of which two numbers?

   A. 30 and 60

   B. 4 and 5

   C. 5 and 10

   D. 5 and 15

   E. 10 and 15

2. What are the first three multiples of 12?

   A. 12, 36, 48

   B. 1, 2, 3

   C. 3, 4, 12

   D. 12, 24, 36

   E. 48, 60, 72

3. What is the Greatest Common Factor of 12 and 30?

   A. 2

   B. 4

   C. 6

   D. 24

   E. 60

4. Which of the following sets of numbers are ALL multiples of 8?

   A. 8, 18, 28, 38

   B. 16, 20, 24, 28

   C. 12, 24, 48, 64

   D. 8, 40, 64, 88

   E. 1, 2, 4, 8

5. What is the Least Common Multiple of 16 and 40?

   A. 24

   B. 36

   C. 40

   D. 80

   E. 160

6. How many prime factors does the number 210 have?

   A. 2

   B. 3

   C. 4

   D. 6

   E. 7

7. Each of the following statements regarding the number 24 is true EXCEPT:

   A. It is a multiple of 8.

   B. It is a factor of 120.

   C. Its only prime factors are 2 and 3.

   D. It is a multiple of 6.

   E. The Greatest Common Factor of it and 72 is 12.

8. Which of the following expresses 60 as the product of prime factors?

   A. 6×10

   B. $2 \times 2 \times 3 \times 5$

   C. $2 \times 3 \times 10$

   D. 5×12

   E. $2 \times 2 \times 2 \times 2 \times 2 \times 2$

9. If a certain number is a multiple of 56, of which of the following numbers must it also be a multiple?

   A. 6

   B. 14

   C. 16

   D. 24

   E. 32

ADDITIONAL PRACTICE QUESTIONS

1. Which of the following sets of numbers are all multiples of 9?

    A. 9, 19, 29, 39

    B. 18, 27, 36, 45

    C. 1, 3, 9

    D. 3, 6, 9, 12, 15, 18

    E. 9, 90, 93, 99

2. Which of the following sets of numbers are all multiples of 4?

    A. 4, 14, 24, 34

    B. 10, 20, 40, 80

    C. 8, 16, 20, 40

    D. 4, 40, 42, 44

    E. 2, 4, 8, 10

3. What is the least common multiple of 8 and 10?

    A. 2

    B. 18

    C. 24

    D. 40

    E. 80

4. What is the greatest common factor of 12 and 36?

    A. 2

    B. 3

    C. 6

    D. 12

    E. 36

5. What is the least common multiple of 4 and 6?

    A. 2

    B. 8

    C. 12

    D. 18

    E. 24

Note: Photocopying any part of this book is prohibited by law.

ANSWERS AND EXPLANATIONS

1. **The correct answer is (E).** The Least Common Multiple (LCM) is the smallest multiple that the number pairs have in common, the smallest number they both go into evenly. Remember, the Least Common Multiple (LCM) must be at least as large as the larger of the two numbers.

You can eliminate choices (A) and (B) right off the bat. Since the Least Common Multiple (LCM) must be at least as large as the larger of the two numbers, 30 could not be a multiple of 60. 4, in choice (B), does not divide into 30 evenly.

Since choices (C), (D), and (E) only contain a total of three numbers, 5, 10 and 15, list the multiples of these three numbers and see which pair has a Least Common Multiple of 30:

    5, 10 15, 20, 25, 30
    10, 20, 30
    15, 30

You can see that 5 and 10 have 10 as their LCM, so eliminate choice (C).

You can see that 5 and 15 have 15 as their LCM, so eliminate choice (D).

That leaves choice (E). 10 and 15 do have 30 as their LCM.

2. **The correct answer is (D).** You can eliminate choices (B) and (C) right off the bat as they are listing three factors of 12, not multiples of 12. You can also eliminate choice (E), because the first multiple of 12 has to be 12. Choice (A) can be eliminated because it skips over 24, which is 2×12, right to 36, which is 3×12. The first three multiples of 12 are 12, 24, and 36.

3. **The correct answer is (C).** The Greatest Common Factor (GCF), as its name suggests is the biggest factor that will divide into two numbers evenly. Since a Greatest Common Factor (GCF) cannot be bigger than either of the numbers that it's being divided into, you can eliminate choices (D) and (E) immediately. Since all three remaining choices are factors of both 12 and 30, the greatest among them, 6, must be the Greatest Common Factor (GCF).

4. **The correct answer is (D).** The set of numbers that are all multiples of 8 must be at least as big as 8, so you can eliminate choice (E) immediately. Go through each of the remaining choices and try to identify a number in the set that is not divisible by 8. In choice (A), neither 18, 28, nor 38 are multiples of 8; they merely contain 8 as a digit. In choice (B), 20 and 28 are not multiples of 8. In choice (C), 12 is not a multiple of 8. Only choice (D) contains only numbers that are divisible by 8: 8, 40, 64, 88.

5. **The correct answer is (D).** The Least Common Multiple (LCM) is the smallest multiple that the number pair has in common, the smallest number they both go into evenly. Remember, the Least Common Multiple (LCM) must be at least as large as the larger of the two numbers.

You can eliminate choices (A) and (B) right off the bat since 24 and 36 could not be multiples of 40.

The multiples of 16 are: 16, 32, 48, 64, 80, 96…

The multiples of 40 are: 40, 80, 120, 160…

You can see that 16 and 40 have 80 as their LCM.

6. **The correct answer is (C).** The number 210 has the following four prime factors: 2, 3, 5, 7:

$$2 \times 3 \times 5 \times 7 = 210$$

7. **The correct answer is (E).** All of the statements are true except for choice (E). The Greatest Common Factor of 24 and 72 is actually the number 24 itself as it divides evenly into 72 three times.

8. **The correct answer is (B).** There are two questions that you want to consider when examining each of the choices:

Are all of the factors listed prime?

Is the product of the factors 60?

Only choice (B), $2 \times 2 \times 3 \times 5$, fits both criteria.

Note: Photocopying any part of this book is prohibited by law.

9. **The correct answer is (B).** The number that is a multiple of 56 would have to be a multiple of a number that is a factor of 56. 14 is the only number here that divides into 56 evenly: $56 \div 14 = 4$.

ADDITIONAL PRACTICE QUESTIONS

1. **The correct answer is (B).** Each number in (B) is evenly divisible by 9, so (B) is correct. Using a calculator is a good move if you aren't sure. The other choices contain numbers that aren't multiples of 9. Note that (C) contains the factors of 9, and not the multiples of 9.

2. **The correct answer is (C).** Notice that all of the numbers in choice (C) can be written in terms of 4.
$$8 = 4 \times 2$$
$$16 = 4 \times 4$$
$$20 = 4 \times 5$$
$$40 = 4 \times 10$$

    Therefore, all of the numbers in choice (C) are multiples of 4. Choice (C) is correct.

3. **The correct answer is (D).** In order to find the least common multiple of 2 numbers, it helps to list the multiples of each until you find a match:

8	10
16	20
24	30
32	40
40	50

    Since 40 is the number that shows up on both lists first, then it must be the least common multiple. Choice (D) is correct.

4. **The correct answer is (D).** In order to find the greatest common factor, you need to find the largest number that divides both 12 and 36. Since $\frac{12}{12} = 1$ and $\frac{36}{12} = 3$, choice (D) is correct.

5. **The correct answer is (C).** When looking for the least common multiple of two numbers, it is helpful to make a list of some of the multiples of each number until you find the first one that appears in both lists:

4	6
4	6
8	12
12	18
16	24

    Since 12 appears on both lists first, choice (C) is the correct answer.

Note: Photocopying any part of this book is prohibited by law.

COMBINING TERMS

1. Which of the following is equal to the expression $4a + 3a + a$?

   A. $7a$

   B. $8a$

   C. $8a^2$

   D. $7a^3$

   E. $8a^3$

2. Which of the following is equal to the expression $5x + 3y + 7x$?

   A. $5x + 10y$

   B. $5x + 10xy$

   C. $12x + 3y$

   D. $15xy$

   E. $15x$

3. Which of the following is equivalent to $7x + 3y - 3xy - x + y$?

   A. $6x - 3xy + 4y$

   B. $6x + 3y - 3$

   C. $(7x - 3y)^2$

   D. $7x + 2xy - 2y$

   E. $7xy$

4. Which of the following is equivalent to $8c^2 - 2d + 5c - 3d$?

   A. $13c - 5d$

   B. $13c^3 - 5d$

   C. $8c^2 + 5c - 5d$

   D. $8c^2 + cd$

   E. $8cd$

5. $14g - 9g^3 + g^2 - g$ can be rewritten as which of the following?

   A. $5g$

   B. $-9g^3 + g^2 + 13g$

   C. $6g^2 - g$

   D. $-9g^3 + g^2 + 15g$

   E. $9g^3 - g^2 + 13g$

ADDITIONAL PRACTICE QUESTIONS

1. Which of the following is equivalent to $3x + 4y - 2xy - x + y$?

   A. $(3x + 4y)^2$

   B. $2x - 2xy + 5y$

   C. $3y$

   D. $3x - xy + 4y$

   E. $4x - 2xy + 5y$

2. Which of the following is equivalent to $-3a - 2ab + 4b - a - b$?

   A. $(3a + 4b)^2$

   B. $4a - 2ab + 3b$

   C. $-4a - 2ab + 5b$

   D. $-4a - 2ab + 3b$

   E. $-6a + b$

3. Which of the following is equivalent to $3p - q + pq - 2q$?

   A. $3p + pq - 3q$

   B. $(3p - 2q)^2$

   C. $4p - 2q$

   D. $3p + pq + 3q$

   E. $3p + pq - q$

4. Which of the following expressions is equivalent to $4x - y + 2xy - x + xy$?

   A. $3x + xy - y$

   B. $5x + 3xy - y$

   C. $6x + 2y$

   D. $(2x - 2y)^2$

   E. $3x + 3xy - y$

5. Which of the following expressions is equivalent to $3ab + 2a - b + 3a + ab$?

   A. $(3a + b)^2$

   B. $9a + 3b$

   C. $5a + 2ab - b$

   D. $5a + 4ab - b$

   E. $5a + 4ab + b$

Note: Photocopying any part of this book is prohibited by law.

ANSWERS AND EXPLANATIONS

1. **The correct answer is (B).** The expression simplifies to $8a$.

    Remember that you can only combine terms that are exactly alike in terms of the variable(s). Each of the terms in this question is like the others.

    When combining like terms, just combine the coefficients and carry the variable along. If a variable has no coefficient, it actually has a coefficient of 1:

    $$4a + 3a + 1a = 8a.$$

2. **The correct answer is (C).** Remember that you can only combine terms that are exactly alike in terms of the variable(s). $5x$ and $7x$ are like terms. Line up the terms with the like terms side by side. When shifting the order of terms, remember that the sign in front of a term belongs to that term and moves along with it:

    $$5x + 7x + 3y.$$

    Add $5x$ and $7x$. $3y$ cannot be combined with these two x terms, since it is not a like term. When combining like terms, just combine the coefficients and carry the variable along. Make sure to include the sign of the term in front of the term (if the first term is positive, you do not need to include the sign). These signs will act as addition and subtraction signs connecting the terms in the final answer together:

    $$5x + 7x + 3y = 12x + 3y$$

    Each of the terms in the final answer should be a term unlike the others and should be connected to the next term by an addition or subtraction sign. The terms should be in alphabetical order according to what variable they contain (in this case, the x term before the y term).

    $12x + 3y$ is the final answer fitting all of these criteria.

3. **The correct answer is (A).** Remember that you can only combine terms that are exactly alike in terms of the variable(s). $7x$ and $-x$ are like terms and $3y$ and y are like terms. $-3xy$ is not like any of the other terms because it contains both an x and a y in it. Line up the terms with the like terms side by side. When shifting the order of terms, the sign in front of a term belongs to that term and moves along with it:

    $$7x - x - 3xy + 3y + y.$$

    If a variable has no coefficient, it actually has a coefficient of 1:

    $$7x - 1x - 3xy + 3y + 1y.$$

    When combining like terms, just combine the coefficients and carry the variable along. Make sure to include the sign of the term in front of the term (if the first term is positive, you do not need to include the sign). These signs will act as addition and subtraction signs connecting the terms in the final answer together:

    $$7x - 1x - 3xy + 3y + 1y = 6x - 3xy + 4y$$

    Each of the terms in the final answer should be a term unlike the others and should be connected to the next by an addition or subtraction sign. The terms should be in alphabetical order according to what variable they contain (in this case, the x-term before the y-term) and any term that contains more than one variable (in this case, the xy-term) should go between the other terms.

    $6x - 3xy + 4y$ is the final answer fitting all of these criteria.

4. **The correct answer is (C).** Remember that you can only combine terms that are exactly alike in terms of the variable(s) and powers of those variables. $8c^2$ and $5c$ are not like terms because they have different powers of the variable. $-2d$ and $-3d$ are like terms and can be combined. Line up the terms with the like terms side by side.

When shifting the order of terms, the sign in front of a term belongs to that term and moves along with it:

$$8c^2 + 5c$$

Combine $-2d$ and $-3d$ by adding the coefficients and taking their sign; carry the variable along:

$$(-2d) + (-3d) = -5d$$

List the final answer. Make sure to include the sign in front of the term (if the first term is positive, you do not need to include the sign). These signs will act as addition and subtraction signs connecting the terms in the final answer together:

$$8c^2 + 5c - 5d$$

Each of the terms in the final answer should be a term unlike the others and should be connected to the next by an addition or subtraction sign. The terms should be in alphabetical order according to what variable they contain, with the greater power of any variable coming first.

$8c^2 + 5c - 5d$ is the final answer fitting all of these criteria.

5. **The correct answer is (B).** Remember that you can only combine terms that are exactly alike in terms of the variable(s) and powers of those variables. $14g$ and $-g$ are like terms and can be combined. $-9g^3$ and g^2 are not like each other or like $14g$ and $-g$ because they have different powers of the variable.

Line up the terms with the like terms side by side.

When shifting the order of terms, the sign in front of a term belongs to that term and moves along with it:

$$-9g^3 + g^2 + 14g - g$$

Combine $14g$ and $-g$ by adding the coefficients (14 and -1); carry the variable along (remember that if a variable has no coefficient that it actually has a coefficient of 1):

$$14g + (-1g) = 13g.$$

List the final answer. Make sure to include the sign of the term in front of the term (since the first term is negative, be sure to include its sign). These signs will act as addition and subtraction signs connecting the terms in the final answer together:

$$-9g^3 + g^2 + 13g.$$

Each of the terms in the final answer should be a term unlike the others and should be connected to the next by an addition or subtraction sign. The terms should be in alphabetical order according to what variable they contain, with the greater power of any variable coming first.

$-9g^3 + g^2 + 13g$ is the final answer fitting all of these criteria.

ADDITIONAL PRACTICE QUESTIONS

1. **The correct answer is (B).** Group all of the terms with the same group of variables together, and then add them together:

$3x + 4y - 2xy - x + y =$
$(3x - x) - 2xy + (4y + y) = 2x - 2xy + 5y$

2. **The correct answer is (D).** Group all of the terms with the same group of variables together, and then add them:

$-3a - 2ab + 4b - a - b =$
$(-3a - a) - 2ab + (4b - b) = -4a - 2ab + 3b$

3. **The correct answer is (A).** Combine all of the terms that have the same variable:

$3p - q + pq - 2q =$
$3p + pq + (-q - 2q) = 3p + pq - 3q$

4. **The correct answer is (E).** Group together all of the terms with the same variables or combination of variables:

$4x - y + 2xy - x + xy =$
$(4x - x) + (2xy + xy) - y = 3x + 3xy - y$

5. **The correct answer is (D).** Combine all of the terms with the same variable, or group of variables:

$3ab + 2a - b + 3a + ab =$
$(2a + 3a) + (3ab + ab) - b = 5a + 4ab - b$

SOLVING EQUATIONS

1. If $4x + 6 = -3$, what is the value of x?

   A. $-2\frac{1}{3}$

   B. $-2\frac{1}{4}$

   C. -2

   D. $-\frac{3}{4}$

   E. $\frac{3}{4}$

2. For which of the following (x, y) pairs does $3x + 2y - 11 = 0$?

   A. $(-5, 2)$

   B. $(-2, 5)$

   C. $(2, 5)$

   D. $(5, -2)$

   E. $(5, 2)$

3. If $9x + 7 = 4x - 8$, what is the value of x?

   A. -3

   B. $-\frac{1}{5}$

   C. $-\frac{1}{13}$

   D. 3

   E. 6

4. If $p - (p + 2) = 2p + (p - 20)$, what is the value of p?

   A. -2

   B. 4

   C. 6

   D. 10

   E. 16

5. Solve for y: $-2y - 3.6 = -180$.

ADDITIONAL PRACTICE QUESTIONS

1. If $2x + 8 = -2x - 8$, what is the value of x?

   A. −16

   B. −4

   C. 0

   D. 4

   E. 16

2. If $6a + 3 = 14a - 5$, what is the value of a?

   A. −1

   B. $-\dfrac{2}{5}$

   C. $\dfrac{1}{4}$

   D. $\dfrac{2}{5}$

   E. 1

3. If $9z - 4 = 6z - 10$, what is the value of z?

   A. −6

   B. $-\dfrac{14}{3}$

   C. −2

   D. 2

   E. 6

4. If $3x - 16 = 2x + 4$, what is the value of x?

   A. −20

   B. −4

   C. $-\dfrac{12}{5}$

   D. 4

   E. 20

5. If $5b + 2 = -3b - 10$, what is the value of b?

   A. −6

   B. −4

   C. $-\dfrac{3}{2}$

   D. $-\dfrac{2}{3}$

   E. $\dfrac{3}{2}$

Note: Photocopying any part of this book is prohibited by law.

ANSWERS AND EXPLANATIONS

1. **The correct answer is (B).** Solve the equation for x by doing the same thing to both sides of the equation:

$$4x + 6 = -3$$

Subtract 6 from both sides:

$$4x + 6 - 6 = -3 - 6$$
$$4x = -9$$

Divide both sides by 4:

$$\frac{4x}{4} = \frac{-9}{4}$$
$$x = -2\frac{1}{4}.$$

2. **The correct answer is (D).** Substitute the values you are given for x and y in each answer choice until you find the pair that balances the equation.

Choice (A):

If $(x, y) = (-5, 2)$, then $x = -5$ and $y = 2$.

$3x + 2y - 11 =$
$3(-5) + 2(2) - 11 =$
$-15 + 4 - 11 =$
-22

This does not equal 0, so choice (A) is incorrect.

Choice (B):

If $(x, y) = (-2, 5)$, then $x = -2$ and $y = 5$.

$3x + 2y - 11 =$
$3(-2) + 2(5) - 11 =$
$-6 + 10 - 11 =$
-7

This does not equal 0, so choice (B) is incorrect.

Choice (C):

If $(x, y) = (2, 5)$, then $x = 2$ and $y = 5$.

$3x + 2y - 11 =$
$3(2) + 2(5) - 11 =$
$6 + 10 - 11 =$
5

This does not equal 0, so choice (C) is incorrect.

Choice (D):

If $(x, y) = (5, -2)$, then $x = 5$ and $y = -2$.

$3x + 2y - 11 =$
$3(5) + 2(-2) - 11 =$
$15 - 4 - 11 =$
0

The equation balances when $(x, y) = (5, -2)$.

3. **The correct answer is (A).** You can solve this problem by doing the algebra or by Working Backwards. Remember, you can always Work Backwards when you are asked to solve an equation and the answer choices are numbers.

To solve the equation using algebra, do the same thing to both sides of the equation until you have x on one side of the equation:

$$9x + 7 = 4x - 8.$$

First, subtract $4x$ *from both sides*:

$9x - 4x + 7 = 4x - 4x - 8$
$5x + 7 = -8$

Subtract 7 from both sides:

$5x + 7 - 7 = -8 - 7$
$5x = -15$

Divide both sides by 5:

$$\frac{5x}{5} = \frac{-15}{5}$$
$$x = -3.$$

That's choice (A).

To Work Backwards, substitute the listed answer choices for the value of x until you find the one that balances the equation. You usually always start with (C), but for this question you may want to start with one of the whole number choices that are easier to work with, like choice (D), 3:

$9(3) + 7 = 4(3) -8$
$27 + 7 = 12 - 8$
$34 = 4$

Not true. You can see that it's not even close. Rather than trying the other positive whole number, try the negative number, choice (A), –3:

$9(-3) + 7 = 4(-3) -8$
$-27 + 7 = -12 - 8$
$-20 = -20$

The equation works when $x = -3$.

4. **The correct answer is (C).** You can solve this problem by doing the algebra or by Working Backwards. Remember, you can always Work Backwards when you are asked to solve an equation and the answer choices are numbers.

To solve the equation using algebra, do the same thing to both sides of the equation until you have p on one side of the equation:

$$p - (p + 2) = 2p + (p - 20).$$

First, get rid of the parentheses:

$p - p - 2 = 2p + p - 20$
$-2 = 3p - 20$

Add 20 to both sides:

$-2 + 20 = 3p - 20 + 20$
$18 = 3p$

Divide both sides by 3:
$$\frac{18}{3} = \frac{3p}{3}$$
$$6 = p.$$

That's choice (C).

To Work Backwards, substitute the listed answer choices for the value of p until you find the one that balances the equation. Always start with (C):

$$6 - (6 + 2) = 2(6) + (6 - 20)$$
$$6 - 8 = 12 - 14$$
$$-2 = -2$$

Since the equation works when $p = 6$, choice (C) is correct.

5. **The correct answer is 88.2.** Solve this equation according to procedure the way that you would any other; don't be intimidated by the negative numbers and decimal number.

3.6 is being subtracted from $-2y$, so begin by adding 3.6 to each side of the equation:

$-2y - 3.6 = -180$
$2y - 3.6 + 3.6 = -180 + 3.6$
$-2y = -176.4$

Conclude by dividing each side by –2:

$$\frac{-2y}{-2} = \frac{-176.4}{-2}$$
$$y = 88.2.$$

ADDITIONAL PRACTICE QUESTIONS

1. **The correct answer is (B).** Solve for x by isolating all of the terms with x on one side of the equation:

$$2x + 8 = -2x - 8$$
$$2x - (-2x) + 8 = -2x - (-2x) - 8$$
$$4x + 8 = -8$$
$$4x + 8 - 8 = -8 - 8$$
$$4x = -16$$
$$x = -4$$

2. **The correct answer is (E).**

$$6a + 3 = 14a - 5$$
$$6a - 14a + 3 = 14a - 14a - 5$$
$$-8a + 3 = -5$$
$$-8a + 3 - 3 = -5 - 3$$
$$-8a = -8$$
$$a = 1$$

3. **The correct answer is (C).**

$$9z - 4 = 6z - 10$$
$$9z - 6z - 4 = 6z - 6z - 10$$
$$3z - 4 = -10$$
$$3z - 4 + 4 = -10 + 4$$
$$3z = -6$$
$$z = -2$$

4. **The correct answer is (E).**

$$3x - 16 = 2x + 4$$
$$3x - 2x - 16 = 2x - 2x + 4$$
$$x - 16 = 4$$
$$x - 16 + 16 = 4 + 16$$
$$x = 20$$

5. **The correct answer is (C).**

$$5b + 2 = -3b - 10$$
$$5b - (-3b) + 2 = -3b - 10$$
$$8b + 2 = -10$$
$$8b + 2 - 2 = -10 - 2$$
$$8b = -12$$
$$b = -\frac{12}{8}$$
$$b = -\frac{3}{2}.$$

Note: Photocopying any part of this book is prohibited by law.

FACTORING

1. $(k - 6)(k + 3) =$

   A. $k^2 - 9k - 18$

   B. $k^2 + 6k - 9$

   C. $k^2 + 18k - 3$

   D. $k^2 - 3k - 18$

   E. $k^2 - 9k - 9$

2. Which of the following is equivalent to $15x^2 - 5x + 10$?

   A. $15(x^2 - 5x + 10)$

   B. $3(5x^2 - 5x + 3)$

   C. $5(3x^2 - x + 2)$

   D. $x^2(15 - 5)$

   E. $x^2 - 5x$

3. Which of the following is equivalent to $y^4 + 3y^2$?

   A. $y^4(1 + 3)$

   B. $y^2(y^2 + 3)$

   C. $y^2(y + 3)$

   D. $y^2(y^2 + 3y)$

   E. $y(y^3 + 3)$

4. Which of the following expressions is equivalent to $3j^2k^2 + 12jk - 42k$?

   A. $3(j^2k^2 + 4jk + 14k)$

   B. $3j^2k^2(4jk - 14k)$

   C. $3k(j^2k + 4j - 14)$

   D. $j(3jk^2 + 12k - 42)$

   E. $j^2k^2(3 + 4 - 14k)$

5. Factor $3x^2 - 300$.

   A. $3(x - 100)$

   B. $3x(x - 100)$

   C. $3(x + 10)(x - 10)$

   D. $3(x + 10)(x + 10)$

   E. $3(x - 10)(x - 10)$

ADDITIONAL PRACTICE QUESTIONS

1. Which of the following expressions is equivalent to $2xy + 4yz$?

   A. $y(x + 3z)$

   B. $2y(xy + 2yz)$

   C. $2y(x + 2z)$

   D. $2(xy + yz)$

   E. $2x(y + 2z)$

2. Which of the following expressions is equivalent to $4abc - 12\,bcd$?

   A. $4bc(a - 3d)$

   B. $12bc(a - d)$

   C. $4bc(a - d)$

   D. $4bc(a - 3d)$

   E. $4ad(bc - 3bc)$

3. Which of the following expressions is equivalent to $10pqr + 15qrs + 30prs$?

   A. $5r(2pq + 3qs + 6ps)$

   B. $10r(pq + 5qs + 20ps)$

   C. $5r(2pqr + 3qrs + 6prs)$

   D. $5pqrs(2pqr + 3qrs + 6prs)$

   E. $5pqs(2r + 3r + 6r)$

4. Which of the following expressions is equivalent to $8abc + 4ac$?

   A. $4ac(2b)$

   B. $4ac(2b + 1)$

   C. $4ac(2abc + ac)$

   D. $2ac(8abc + 4ac)$

   E. $4ab(2ac + c)$

5. Which of the following expressions is equivalent to $6xz + 9xy$?

   A. $3xyz(2xz + 3xy)$

   B. $6x(z + 3y)$

   C. $3x(6xz + 9xy)$

   D. $3yz(2x + 3x)$

   E. $3x(2z + 3y)$

ANSWERS AND EXPLANATIONS

1. The correct answer is (D). There are two ways you can go here: either use FOIL or, since there are variables in the answer choices, use Plugging-in.

FOIL

Remember that FOIL stands for First, Outside, Inner, Last.

First: $k \times k = k^2$
Outside: $k \times 3 = 3k$
Inner: $-6 \times k = -6k$
Last: $-6 \times 3 = -18$

This yields $k2 + 3k - 6k - 18$. Combine like terms: $k^2 - 3k - 18$. Choice (D) is correct.

Plugging in.

Pick a value for k that is easy to work with, say, $k = 7$. Since you must subtract 6 from k, picking $k = 7$ means you can avoid dealing with negatives.

If $k = 7$, then $(k - 6)(k + 3) = (7 - 6)(7 + 3) = (1)(10) = 10$. This is your target number.

Now, plug in 7 for k in the answer choices. The correct choice will give you 10:

A. $k^2 - 9k - 18 = 7^2 - 9(7) - 18 = 49 - 63 - 18 = -32$. Discard this.

B. $k^2 + 6k - 9 = 7^2 + 6(7) - 9 = 49 + 42 - 9 = 82$. Discard this.

C. $k^2 + 18k - 3 = 7^2 + 18(7) - 3 = 49 + 126 - 3 = 172$. Discard this.

D. $k^2 - 3k - 18 = 7^2 - 3(7) - 18 = 49 - 21 - 18 = 10$. Keep this.

E. $k^2 - 9k - 9 = 7^2 - 9(7) - 9 = 49 - 63 - 9 = -23$. Discard this.

Only (D) gives 10 when $k = 7$.

2. The correct answer is (C). The first step in factoring is always to look for the Greatest Common Factor. The Greatest Common Factor is the biggest factor that divides into each of the terms evenly. For terms consisting of a number coefficient and variable, you're looking for the biggest number coefficient that divides into each of the number coefficients evenly and the greatest power of the variable that divides into the variable evenly.

The biggest number coefficient that divides into $15x^2$, $5x$, and 10 evenly is 5. $15x^2$, $5x$, and 10 have no variable in common. So, 5 is the Greatest Common Factor of $15x^2$, $5x$, and 10. The next step is to divide $15x^2 - 5x + 10$ by 5 to get the remaining factor:

$$\frac{15x^2 - 5x + 10}{5} = 3x^2 - x + 2$$

Finally, list the two factors side by side, the Greatest Common Factor multiplying the remaining factor: $5(3x^2 - x + 2)$

Choice (C) is correct.

You could have also solved this problem by Plugging-in, as you can in almost any question that has answer choices with variables.

Pick a value for x, say $x = 1$. Then:

$15x^2 - 5x + 10 =$
$15(1)^2 - 5(1) + 10 =$
$15 - 5 + 10 = 20$. This is your target number.

Now, find the answer choice that equals 20 when $x = 1$.

A. $15(x^2 - 5x + 10) = 15([1]^2 - 5[1] + 10) = 15(1 - 5 + 10) = 90$. Eliminate choice (A).

B. $3(5x^2 - 5x + 3) = 3(5[1]^2 - 5[1] + 3) = 3(5 - 5 + 3) = 9$. Eliminate choice (B).

C. $5(3x^2 - x + 2) = 5(3[1]^2 - 1 + 2) = 5(3 - 1 + 2) = 20$. Keep this.

D. $x^2(15 - 5) = (1)^2(15 - 5) = 10$. Eliminate choice (D).

E. $x^2 - 5x = (1)^2 - 5(1) = -4$. Eliminate choice (D).

Only (C) gives the same value as the target number.

3. **The correct answer is (B).** Remember the rules for multiplying exponents with the same base: you add the powers. For example, $x^2 \times x^3 = x^{(2+3)} = x^5$.

In the expression $y^4 + 3y^2$, you can factor out the Greatest Common Factor, y^2, like so:

$$y^4 + 3y^2 =$$
$$y^2(y^2) + y^2(3) =$$
$$y^2(y^2 + 3)$$

If you didn't see this, you could have solved this by Plugging-in.

Pick a value for y, say, $y = 2$. Then $y^4 + 3y^2 = (2)^4 + 3(2)^2 = 16 + 12 = 28$. This is your target number. Now, find the answer choice that equals 28 when $y = 2$.

A. $y^4(1 + 3) = (2)^4(4) = 64$. Eliminate choice (A).

B. $y^2(y^2 + 3) = 2^2(2^2 + 3) = 28$. Keep choice (B).

C. $y^2(y + 3) = 2^2(2 + 3) = 20$. Eliminate choice (C).

D. $y^2(y^2 + 3y) = 2^2(2^2 + 3(2)) = 40$. Eliminate choice (D).

E. $y(y^3 + 3) = 2(2^3 + 3) = 22$. Eliminate choice (E).

Only choice (B) yields the target number.

4. **The correct answer is (C).** You could factor out terms here:

$$3j^2k^2 + 12jk - 42k =$$
$$3kj^2k + 3k4j - 3k(14) =$$
$$3k(j^2k + 4j - 14).$$

That is choice (C).

However, it is probably easier to Plug In numbers:

Let $j = 1$ and $k = 2$.

$$3j^2k^2 + 12\,jk - 42k =$$
$$3(1)^2(2)^2 + 12(1)(2) - 42(2) =$$
$$12 + 24 - 84 = -48.$$

This is your target number; now, check to see which answer choices give the same value.

A. $3(j^2k^2 + 4jk + 14k) =$
$3([1]^2[2]^2 + 4[1][2] + 14[2]) =$
$3(4 + 8 + 28) =$
120
Discard choice (A).

B. $3j^2k^2(4jk - 14k) =$
$3(1)^2(2)^2(4[1][2] - 14[2]) =$
$12(8 - 28) =$
-240
Discard choice (B).

C. $3k(j^2k + 4j - 14) =$
$3(2)([1]^2[2] + 4[1] - 14) =$
$6(2 + 4 - 14) =$
-48
Keep choice (C).

D. $j(3jk^2 + 12k - 42) =$
$(1)(3[1][2]^2 + 12[2] - 42) =$
$(12 + 24 - 42) =$
-6
Discard choice (D).

E. $j^2k^2(3 + 4 - 14k) =$
$(1)^2(2)^2(3 + 4 - 14\,[2]) =$
$4(7 - 28) =$
-84
Discard choice (E).

Only choice (C) works.

5. **The correct answer is (C).** The first step in factoring is always to look for the Greatest Common Factor. The Greatest Common Factor is the biggest factor that divides into each of the terms evenly. For terms consisting of a number coefficient and variable, you're looking for the biggest number coefficient that divides into each of the number coefficients evenly and the greatest power of the variable that divides into the variable evenly.

The biggest number coefficient that divides into $3x^2$ and 300 evenly is 3. $3x^2$ and 300 have no variable in common. So, 3 is the Greatest Common Factor of $3x^2$ and 300. The next step is to divide $3x^2 - 300$ by 3 to get the remaining factor: $\frac{3x^2-300}{3} = x^2 - 100$. $x^2 - 100$ is the difference of two perfect squares, x^2 and 100. The factors of $x^2 - 100$ are the square root of x^2 (x) plus the square root of 100 (10) and the square root of x^2 plus the square root of 100: $(x + 10)(x - 10)$. Finally, list the three factors side by side, the Greatest Common Factor multiplying the remaining factors: $3(x + 10)(x - 10)$.

ADDITIONAL PRACTICE QUESTIONS

1. **The correct answer is (C).** Since there is a $2y$ in both terms, you can factor it out. This leaves you with $2y(x + 2z)$, which is choice (C). You can check this answer by multiplying it out to make sure that you are left with the original expression: $(2y \times x) + (2y \times 2z) = 2xy + 4yz$, which is correct. Choice (C) is correct,

2. **The correct answer is (D).** Since $4bc$ appears in both terms, you can factor it out, leaving $4bc(a - 3d)$, which is choice (D). You can check that this answer is correct by multiplying it out to make sure that you are left with the original equation: $(4bc \times a) - (4bc \times 3d) = 4abc - 12bcd$, which is correct. Choice (D) is correct.

3. **The correct answer is (A).** Since $5r$ appears in all of the terms, you can factor it out leaving $5r(2pq + 3qs + 6ps)$. You can check this answer by multiplying it out to be sure that you are left with the original expression: $(5r \times 2pq) + (5r \times 3qs) + (5r \times 6ps) = 10pqr + 15qrs + 30prs$, which is correct. Choice (A) is correct.

4. **The correct answer is (B).** Since $4ac$ appears in all of the terms, you can factor it out, leaving $4ac(2b + 1)$. You can check this answer by multiplying it out to make sure that you are left with the original expression: $(4ac \times 2b) + (4ac \times 1) = 8abc + 4ac$, which is correct. Choice (B) is correct.

5. **The correct answer is (E).** Since $3x$ appears in both terms, you can factor it out, leaving $3x(2z + 3y)$. You can check this answer by multiplying it out to make sure that you are left with the original expression: $(3x \times 2z) + (3x \times 3y) = 6xz + 9xy$, which is correct. Choice (E) is correct.

INEQUALITIES

1. Which of the following identifies exactly those values of x that satisfy $9 - 2x \leq -3$?

   A. $x \leq -6$

   B. $x > -3$

   C. $x \leq -6$

   D. $x \geq 3$

   E. $x \geq 6$

2. Which of the following values of y satisfies the inequality $9y + 6 > 7y - 8$?

   A. $y < -7$

   B. $y > -\frac{1}{8}$

   C. $y > -7$

   D. $y < 1$

   E. $y > -1$

3. Which of the following inequalities results from the inequality $10 > 15x - 5y$ being solved for y?

   A. $y > 6x$

   B. $y > 15x - 2$

   C. $y < 3x - 2$

   D. $y > 3x - 2$

   E. $y > 3x - 10$

4. Which of the following is a member of the solution set of $5 < x \leq 9$?

   A. 3

   B. $4\frac{1}{2}$

   C. 5

   D. $7\frac{1}{2}$

   E. 10

5. If $\frac{x}{4} - \frac{x}{3} > 2$, which of the following represents the range of x on the number line?

   A. ────○──────────→
         24

   B. ────○──────────→
         12

   C. ────○──────────→
        −24

   D. ←──────○──────
              −12

   E. ←──────○──────
              −24

6. If $-2 - 7x =$ an integer, and $6 > -2 - 7x > 4$, then which of the following must be true?

   A. $x = -1$

   B. $x > 5$

   C. $6 > x > 5$

   D. $x = 1$

   E. $x < -2$

7. If $5x + 3 \geq x + 4$, what is the value of x?

   A. $x = 0$

   B. $x < \frac{1}{2}$

   C. $x < 2$

   D. $x \leq -\frac{1}{2}$

   E. $x \geq \frac{1}{4}$

8. If a and b are positive integers and $a + b < 11$, what is the greatest possible value of $a - b$?

ADDITIONAL PRACTICE QUESTIONS

1. Which of the following indicates exactly the values of x if $2 + x \leq 8$

   A. $x \leq 4$

   B. $x < 6$

   C. $x \geq -6$

   D. $x \leq 6$

   E. $x \leq 10$

2. Which of the following identifies exactly those values of x that satisfy $2x + 4 \geq 14$?

   A. $x \geq 5$

   B. $x \geq -5$

   C. $x < 5$

   D. $x \geq 9$

   E. $x \geq 10$

3. Which of the following is the graph of the solution set for $x \leq -2$ and $x > 1$?

   A.

   B.

   C.

   D.

   E.

4. Which of the following identifies exactly those values of x that satisfy $4 - 3x \leq 22$?

   A. $x \leq -6$

   B. $x \geq 6$

   C. $x \geq -\frac{26}{3}$

   D. $x \leq 15$

   E. $x \geq -6$

5. Which of the following identifies exactly the values of x that satisfy $5x - 3 \leq 8x + 6$?

   A. $x \leq -3$

   B. $x \leq \frac{3}{14}$

   C. $x \geq 3$

   D. $x \geq -3$

   E. $x \leq 9$

Note: Photocopying any part of this book is prohibited by law.

ANSWERS AND EXPLANATIONS

1. **The correct answer is (E).** You need to get x to stand on its own on one side of the inequality sign.

$$9 - 2x \leq -3$$

Remember that you work with inequalities the same way you work with equations: what you do to one side of the inequality, you must also do to the other side.

Begin by subtracting 9 from both sides:

$$9 - 9 - 2x \leq -3 - 9$$
$$-2x \leq -12$$

The next step is to isolate x by dividing both sides by -2. Remember, there is another special rule when working with inequalities: when you divide or multiply by a negative number, you must flip the inequality sign. Because you need to divide by a negative number to solve this inequality, you need to flip the inequality sign. $\leq$ becomes $\geq$:

$$\frac{-2x}{-2} \leq \frac{-12}{-2}$$
$$x \geq 6$$

You can check your work by plugging any value that is greater than or equal to 6 into the inequality. Let's try 8:

$9 - 2x \leq -3$
$9 - 2(8) \leq -3$
$9 - 16 \leq -3$
$-7 \leq -3$

This is a true inequality.

2. **The correct answer is (C).** You need to get y to stand on its own on one side of the inequality sign.

Remember that you work with inequalities the same way you work with equations: what you do to one side of the inequality, you must also do to the other side.

First, subtract $7y$ from both sides:

$$9y - 7y + 6 > 7y - 7y - 8$$
$$2y + 6 > -8$$

Now, subtract 6 from both sides:

$$2y + 6 - 6 > -8 - 6$$
$$2y > -14$$

Finally, to isolate y, divide both sides by 2:

$$\frac{2y}{2} > \frac{-14}{2}$$
$$y > -7$$

3. **The correct answer is (D).** Since all of the answer choices are expressed in terms of values for y, you need to get y to stand on its own on one side of the inequality sign.

Remember that you work with inequalities the same way you work with equations: what you do to one side of the inequality, you must also do to the other side.

$$10 > 15x - 5y$$

Add $5y$ to both sides:

$$10 + 5y > 15x - 5y + 5y$$
$$10 + 5y > 15x$$

Now, subtract 10 from both sides:

$$10 + 5y - 10 > 15x - 10$$
$$5y > 15x - 10$$

Now, to isolate y, divide both sides by 5:

$$\frac{5y}{5} > \frac{15x - 10}{5}$$
$$y > 3x - 2$$

4. **The correct answer is (D).** The inequality, $5 < x \leq 9$, contains all numbers between 5 and 9, including 9, but not including 5. $7\frac{1}{2}$ is the only number that fits the criteria.

5.   **The correct answer is (E).** Begin by multiplying both sides of the inequality by 12 to clear the fractions:

$$(12) \frac{x}{4} - \frac{x}{3} > 2 (12)$$
$$3x - 4x > 24$$

Now, perform the subtraction on the left-hand side of the equation and you'll get:
$$-x > 24$$

You're almost there. Now, divide both sides of the equation by –1, but remember that when you divide by a negative number in an inequality, you must flip the inequality sign.

$$\frac{-x}{-1} > \frac{24}{-1}$$
$$x < -24$$

Which choice is the right visual representation of this inequality? Choice (E):

$$-24$$

On the number line, the fact that the arrow is pointing to the left means, "less than." The fact that there is an open circle at –24 means that –24 is not included in the solution set, which is what you want since you found that $x < -24$.

If the answer had been $x \leq -24$, then the circle would have had to have been filled in because, in that case, –24 *would* be included in the solution set.

Choice (E) is correct.

6.   **The correct answer is (A).** Don't be daunted by the terminology and the two inequality signs! Just think it through logically. All the problem is saying is, "if $-2 - 7x$ is an integer, and that integer is between 4 and 6, then that integer has to be 5. Thus, $-2 - 7x$ has to equal 5."

All you have to do is some basic algebra:
$$-2 - 7x = 5$$

Add 2 to both sides:
$$-7x = 7$$

Divide both sides by –7:
$$x = -1$$

7.   **The correct answer is (E).** You want to eventually get x standing alone to one side so that you can check its value against the answer choices.
$$5x + 3 \geq x + 4$$

Start by subtracting 3 from both sides of the inequality:
$$5x + 3 - 3 \geq x + 4 - 3$$
$$5x \geq x + 1$$

Subtract x from both sides:
$$5x - x \geq x + 1 - x$$
$$4x \geq 1$$

Divide both sides of the inequality by 4:

$$\frac{4x}{4} \geq \frac{1}{4}$$

$$x \geq \frac{1}{4}$$

8.   **The correct answer is 8.** The greatest value of $a - b$ will occur when a is as large as possible and b is as small as possible.

It's easier to start with the value of b. Since b is a positive integer, then the least possible value of b is 1. When $b = 1$, then the largest possible value of a is 9, since $a + b < 11$, that is, the most they can add up to is 10.

So, the greatest possible value of $a - b = 9 - 1 = 8$.

Grid in 8 as your answer.

Note: Photocopying any part of this book is prohibited by law.

ADDITIONAL PRACTICE QUESTIONS

1. **The correct answer is (D).** Solve the inequality the same way you would if it was a linear equation:

$$2 + x \leq 8$$
$$2 - 2 + x \leq 8 - 2$$
$$x \leq 6$$

2. **The correct answer is (A).** Solve the inequality as if it were a linear equation:

$$2x + 4 \geq 14$$
$$2x + 4 - 4 \geq 14 - 4$$
$$2x \geq 10$$
$$\frac{2x}{2} \geq \frac{10}{2}$$
$$x \geq 5$$

3. **The correct answer is (B).** Since we are looking for the graph of the solution set $x \leq 2$ and $x > 1$, we need to find the graph that has a closed point at –2 with a line extending to the left and an open point at 1 with a line extending to the right. The only answer that fits this description is choice (B).

4. **The correct answer is (E).** Solve the inequality as if it were a linear equation. Remember, when dividing by negative numbers you have to switch the direction of the inequality sign:

$$4 - 3x \leq 22$$
$$4 - 4 - 3x \leq 22 - 4$$
$$-3x \leq 18$$
$$\frac{-3x}{-3} \leq \frac{18}{-3}$$
$$x \geq -6$$

Choice (E) is correct.

5. **The correct answer is (D).** Solve the inequality as if it were a linear equation. Remember that when you divide by a negative number, you have to switch the direction of the inequality sign:

$$5x - 3 \leq 8x + 6$$
$$5x - 8x - 3 \leq 8x - 8x + 6$$
$$-3x - 3 \leq 6$$
$$-3x - 3 + 3 \leq 6 + 3$$
$$-3x \leq 9$$
$$\frac{-3x}{-3} \leq \frac{9}{-3}$$
$$x \geq -3$$

QUADRILATERALS

1. Find the length of a rectangle whose area is 72 square meters and whose width is 6 meters.

    A. 8 meters

    B. 9 meters

    C. 11 meters

    D. 12 meters

    E. 15 meters

2. Martin has a backyard whose length and width are identical. He lines each length of the yard with hedges. Martin then lines hedges across the entire back width of the yard, which is 50 feet. At the end of his gardening project, how many feet of hedges has Martin laid?

3. Each of the following statements about rectangles and squares is true EXCEPT:

    A. Both shapes are parallelograms.

    B. Both shapes have equal lengths.

    C. Both shapes have equal widths.

    D. Both shapes have 4 equal angles.

    E. Both shapes can be divided into isosceles right triangles.

4. A rectangular playing field with an area of 100 could have all of the following length/width dimensions EXCEPT:

    A. 50 and 2

    B. 25 and 4

    C. 75 and 3

    D. 100 and 1

    E. 20 and 5

5. What is the perimeter of a square whose area is 64?

    A. 5

    B. 16

    C. 25

    D. 32

    E. 64

6. The length of the diagonal of a square is $4\sqrt{2}$. What is area of the square?

    A. 4

    B. 12

    C. $12\sqrt{2}$

    D. 16

    E. $16\sqrt{2}$

7. The perimeter of a square is $4x + 20$. Which of the following expressions represents the area of the square?

    A. $x + 5$

    B. $2x + 10$

    C. $x^2 + 25$

    D. $x^2 + 10x + 25$

    E. $x^2 - 25$

Note: Photocopying any part of this book is prohibited by law.

8. What is the measure of *Z* in the figure below?

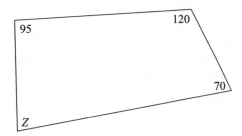

A. 55

B. 75

C. 105

D. 145

E. 285

ADDITIONAL PRACTICE QUESTIONS

1. What is the area of the rectangle shown below?

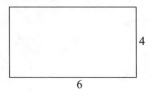

A. 10

B. 12

C. 20

D. 24

E. 48

2. A farmer wants to fertilize his 40 foot by 50 foot garden. If one bag of fertilizer covers 20 square feet, how many bags of fertilizer are needed to cover the entire garden?

A. 100

B. 180

C. 200

D. 1,000

E. 2,000

3. What is the perimeter of the square below?

A. 10

B. 20

C. 25

D. 40

E. 50

Note: Photocopying any part of this book is prohibited by law.

4. The Murray's want to build a fence around their yard that measures 35 feet by 65 feet. How many feet of the fencing material do they need?

A. 70

B. 100

C. 130

D. 200

E. 2,275

5. A television has a length of 30 inches and a height of 40 inches. What is the length of the diagonal?

A. 35

B. 50

C. 55

D. 70

E. 100

ANSWERS AND EXPLANATIONS

1. **The correct answer is (D).** Draw yourself a diagram:

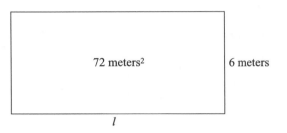

Use the formula for finding the area of a rect-angle:

$$A = l \times w$$
$$72 = 6 \times l$$
$$l = 12$$

The length is 12.

2. **The correct answer is 150.** You know that Martin's yard is a square if it has identical lengths and widths. If he lines the width with 50 feet of hedges, then the sides must also equal 50. The measures of the sides plus the measure of the back would be $50 + 50 + 50 = 150$. At the end of his gardening project, Martin has laid 150 feet of hedges.

3. **The correct answer is (E).** This question de-pends on your knowledge of the properties shared by squares and rectangles. Only squares can be divided into two isosceles right triangles.

4. **The correct answer is (C).** The area of a rect-angle is found by multiplying the length times the width. The only answer choice that doesn't yield a product of 100, the given area of the playing field, is answer choice (C).

5. **The correct answer is (D).** If the area of the square is 64, you know that each side is equal to 8, since the area of a square is equal to a side squared. The perimeter is measured by adding all four sides or by multiplying a side by 4: $8 \times 4 = 32$.

6. **The correct answer is (D).** Remember that the diagonal of a square divides the square into two 45-45-90 isosceles right triangles whose

leg:leg:hypotenuse proportions are $x:x:x\sqrt{2}$. $4\sqrt{2}$ is the hypotenuse of each of the right triangles formed. Therefore, each of the legs (in this case, each of the four sides of the square) measures 4. Squaring one of these legs gives you the area of the square: $4^2 = 16$.

Even if you were not familiar with the special properties 45-45-90 isosceles right triangle, if you know that sides opposite equal angles are equal, you can use the Pythagorean theorem $(a^2 + b^2 = c^2)$ to figure out the missing sides. Label each of the identical missing sides x and plug them in for a and b in the formula:

$$a^2 + b^2 = c^2$$
$$x^2 + x^2 = (4\sqrt{2})^2$$
$$2x^2 = (4\sqrt{2})(4\sqrt{2})$$
$$2x^2 = 32$$
$$\frac{2x^2}{2} = \frac{32}{2}$$
$$x^2 = 16$$
$$x = 4$$

Again, if each of the missing legs measures 4, the area of the square will be the square of the measure of one of the sides, 4, which is 16.

7. **The correct answer is (D).** This question must be done in two steps: First, determine the mea-sure of a side of the square.

If the perimeter of the square is $4x + 20$, you need to divide $4x + 20$ by 4 to find the measure of a side of the square:

$$\frac{4x + 20}{4} = x + 5$$

You know that a square has four equal sides, so the area of the square will be the square of the measure of one of the sides, which is $x + 5$:

$$(x + 5)^2 = (x + 5)(x + 5)$$
$$= x^2 + 5x + 5x + 25$$
$$= x^2 + 10x + 25$$

8. **The correct answer is (B).** Even though this quadrilateral is irregularly shaped, it has the one characteristic that all quadrilaterals share: the sum of the measures of its angles is 360 degrees. Use this basic fact about quadrilaterals to answer this question. First, add the measures of the other three angles that you are given:
$$70 + 120 + 95 = 285.$$

Then, subtract the total from 360 to get the measure of the remaining angle:
$$360 - 285 = 75.$$

The remaining angle z measures 75.

ADDITIONAL PRACTICE QUESTIONS

1. **The correct answer is (D).**
   The area of a rectangle is found by calculating the length times the width:
   $$A = l \times w$$
   $$= 6 \times 4$$
   $$= 24$$

2. **The correct answer is (A).** First calculate the area of the garden:
   $$A = l \times w$$
   $$= 40 \times 50$$
   $$= 2,000$$

   Now determine how many bags of fertilizer are needed:
   $$2,000 \text{ sq. ft} \times \frac{1 \text{ bag}}{20 \text{ sq. ft}} = 100 \text{ bags.}$$

3. **The correct answer is (B).** The perimeter of a square is found by adding together the lengths of the four sides. In this case, the length of each side is 5, so the perimeter is equal to $5 + 5 + 5 + 5 = 20$. Choice (B) is correct.

4. **The correct answer is (D).**
   First find the perimeter of the yard by adding together the lengths of the four sides:
   $$P = 2l + 2w$$
   $$= 2(35) + 2(65)$$
   $$= 70 + 130$$
   $$= 200$$

   The Murray's will need 200 feet of fencing to go around the yard. Choice (D) is correct.

5. **The correct answer is (B).** Think of the length and height as two lengths of a triangle and the diagonal as the hypotenuse. Use the Pythagorean theorem to find the length of the diagonal:
   $$a^2 + b^2 = c^2$$
   $$(30)^2 + (40)^2 = c^2$$
   $$900 + 1,600 = c^2$$
   $$c^2 = 2,500$$
   $$c = 50$$

   The length of the diagonal is 50 inches. Choice (B) is correct.

CIRCLES

1. What is the circumference of a circle with area 25π?

    A. 2π

    B. 5π

    C. 10π

    D. 15π

    E. 25π

2. All of the following statements regarding the circle with center point P are true EXCEPT:

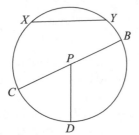

    A.   Segment XY is a chord.

    B.   Line BC is the circle's diameter.

    C.   Segment PD is a radius.

    D.   Segment PB is a radius.

    E. $XY = PD$.

3. What is the degree measurement of arc DAM?

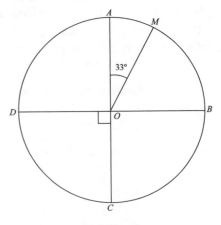

4. What is the area, in square feet, of a circle whose diameter measures 18 feet?

    A. 9π

    B. 18π

    C. 36π

    D. 81π

    E. 123π

5. Four circular fields of equal area are placed adjacent to one another according to the diagram below. Line segment *MO* extends from the center points of the middle two circles. If segment *MO* measures 20 feet across, and the length of the portion of segment *MO* that lies outside the circles is 4 feet, then what is the total area of all four circular playing fields?

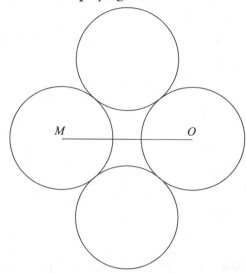

A. 128π

B. 150π

C. 256π

D. 300π

E. 428π

6. If a circle with radius 6 meters has a central angle of 60°, what is the length of the arc intercepted by this central angle?

Note: The length of an arc is found using the formula:

$$\text{Arc} = \left(\frac{\text{central angle}}{360}\right) \times (\text{Circumference}).$$

A. π meters

B. 2π meters

C. 4 meters

D. 4π meters

E. 6 meters

7. The area of a large circular rug whose radius is 12 feet is how much greater, in square feet, than the area of a circular rug whose radius is 8 feet?

A. 4π

B. 8π

C. 80π

D. 144π

E. 320π

8. What is the measure of angle *q* in the diagram of the circle with center *z* below?

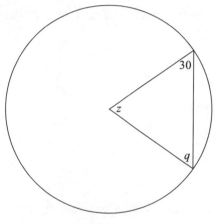

ADDITIONAL PRACTICE QUESTIONS

1. The radius of a circle is 24 centimeters. What is the diameter of the circle?

    A. 12 centimeters

    B. 24 centimeters

    C. 36 centimeters

    D. 48 centimeters

    E. 48π centimeters

2. What is the circumference of a circle with radius 6?

    A. 6

    B. 6π

    C. 12π

    D. $12\pi^2$

    E. 24π

3. What is the area of a circle with a diameter of 20?

    A. 10π

    B. 20π

    C. 100π

    D. 200π

    E. 400π

4. In the diagram below, point O is the center of the circle, and segment AO has length 3. What is the length of arc AB?

    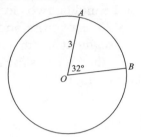

    A. $\dfrac{3}{16}\pi$

    B. $\dfrac{8}{15}\pi$

    C. $\dfrac{4}{15}\pi$

    D. $\dfrac{16}{15}\pi$

    E. 96π

5. In the circle below, point O is the center and segment AO has length 6. What is the area of the sector formed by AOB?

    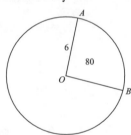

    A. $\dfrac{1}{8}\pi$

    B. $\dfrac{2}{3}\pi$

    C. $\dfrac{4}{3}\pi$

    D. $\dfrac{8}{3}\pi$

    E. 8π

Note: Photocopying any part of this book is prohibited by law.

ANSWERS AND EXPLANATIONS

1. **The correct answer is (C).** Work backwards from the given area to the find the radius; use the radius to find the circumference. Often, the key to circle problems is knowing the radius.

$$A = \pi \times r^2$$
$$25\pi = \pi \times r^2$$
$$25 = r^2$$
$$r = 5$$

The circumference of the circle is:

$$C = 2\pi \times r$$
$$= 2\pi(5)$$
$$= 10\pi$$

2. **The correct answer is (E).** A chord can never equal a radius.

3. **The correct answer is 123.** An intercepted arc is always equal to its central angle. If $AC \perp DB$, then angle AOD is 90°, and its intercepted arc, AD, is 90° as well. If angle AOM is equal to 33°, then arc AM is also equal to 33°. $90 + 33 = 123$. The measure of arc DAM is 123.

4. **The correct answer is (D).** The area of a circle is determined using the formula, $A = \pi r^2$. The radius of a circle is equal to one half the diameter. In this case, if the diameter measures 18 feet, the radius must equal 9 feet.

$$A = \pi(9)^2$$
$$A = 81\pi$$

The area of the circle is 81π.

5. **The correct answer is (C).** Segment MO is 20 feet across. Four feet lie outside the circles leaving 16 feet inside. The portions of MO lying inside the circle are both radii, each measuring 8 feet: $r = 8$. Find the area of one circle using $A = \pi r^2$ and multiply it by four to get the total area of all four circles.

$$A = \pi \times r^2$$
$$A = \pi(8)^2$$
$$A = 64\pi \text{ for one circle}$$
$$A = 64\pi(4)$$
$$A = 256\pi \text{ for all four circles}$$

6. **The correct answer is (B).** Remember that the formula for determining the circumference is $C = 2\pi r$.

$$\text{Arc} = \left(\frac{\text{central angle}}{360} \right) \times (\text{Circumference})$$
$$= \frac{60}{360}(2\pi)(6)$$
$$= \frac{1}{6}(12\pi)$$
$$= 2\pi \text{ meters.}$$

7. **The correct answer is (C).** Compute the area of each circle and subtract:

$$\text{Area large rug} = \pi \times r^2$$
$$= \pi(12)^2$$
$$= 144\pi$$

$$\text{Area small rug} = \pi \times r^2$$
$$= \pi(8)^2$$
$$= 64\pi$$

$$\text{Difference} = 144\pi - 64\pi$$
$$= 80\pi$$

8. **The correct answer is 30.** Since z is the center point of the circle, you know that the two legs of the triangle extending from it are radii and are therefore equal to each other. Since the angles opposite the legs are equal as well, angle q must equal 30°.

Note: Photocopying any part of this book is prohibited by law.

ADDITIONAL PRACTICE QUESTIONS

1. **The correct answer is (D).** The diameter of a circle is equal to two times the radius:

$$d = 2r$$
$$= 2(24)$$
$$= 48 \text{ centimeters}$$

2. **The correct answer is (C).** The circumference of a circle is equal to the diameter times π:

$$C = 2 \times \pi \times r$$
$$= 2\pi(6)$$
$$= 12\pi$$

3. **The correct answer is (C).** First, calculate the radius of the circle:

$$d = 2r$$
$$20 = 2r$$
$$\frac{20}{2} = \frac{2r}{2}$$
$$r = 10.$$

Now use the formula for finding the area of a circle:

$$A = \pi r^2$$
$$= \pi(10)^2$$
$$= 100\pi$$

4. **The correct answer is (B).** First find the circumference of the circle, given that the radius is 3:

$$C = 2 \times \pi \times r$$
$$= 2\pi(3)$$
$$= 6\pi$$

Let x represent the length of the arc AB. The proportion of x to the circumference must be the same as the proportion of the angle $32°$ to $360°$:

$$\frac{x}{6\pi} = \frac{32°}{360°}$$
$$360x = 192\pi$$
$$x = \frac{8}{15}\pi.$$

5. **The correct answer is (E).** First find the area of the circle given that the radius is 6:

$$A = \pi \times r^2$$
$$= \pi(6)^2$$
$$= 36\pi$$

Let x represent the area of the shaded area. The proportion of x to the total area of the circle must be the same as the proportion of $80°$ to the entire circle, $360°$:

$$\frac{x}{36\pi} = \frac{80°}{360°}$$
$$360x = 2,880\pi$$
$$x = \frac{2,880\pi}{360}$$
$$x = 8\pi.$$

GEOMETRY STRATEGY

1. A wire extends from the top of a 30-foot telephone pole to a point on the ground that is 16 feet from the base of the pole. What is the length of the wire?

   A.   14 feet

   B.   17 feet

   C.   28.5 feet

   D.   34 feet

   E.   46 feet

2. What is the area of a circle with circumference 20π?

   A. 10π

   B. 20π

   C. 40π

   D. 50π

   E. 100π

3. What is the value of angle b?

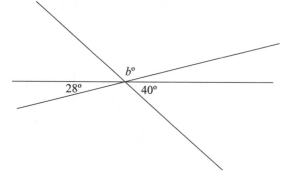

   A.   68

   B.   82

   C.   108

   D.   112

   E.   145

4. One side of a square is decreased by 20% while its adjacent side is increased by 10% forming a new rectangle. The area of the new rectangle formed is what percentage of the area of the original square?

   A.   80%

   B.   85%

   C.   88%

   D.   99%

   E.   110%

5. What is the value of $a + b$?

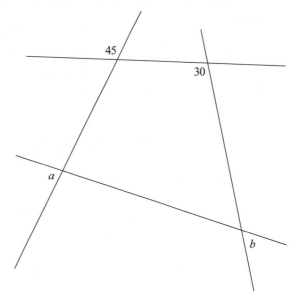

Note: Photocopying any part of this book is prohibited by law.

6. Alana drives from point X and heads due west to point Y covering a distance of 20 miles. She makes a turn of exactly 90 degrees from her previous course and drives due south to point Z. The distance from point Y to point Z is 15 miles. What is the distance from point X to point Z in miles?

 A. 5

 B. 10

 C. 25

 D. 35

 E. 50

7. In the figure below, the area of triangle QRT is $\frac{2}{3}$ of the area of square $PQRS$. What is the length of segment QT?

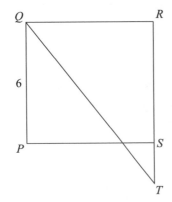

 A. 4

 B. 8

 C. 10

 D. 12

 E. 24

8. What is the ratio of the area of a square with a diagonal of length $2\sqrt{2}$ to the area of a square with a diagonal of length $5\sqrt{2}$?

 A. $2 : 5\sqrt{2}$

 B. $2 : 5$

 C. $2 : 25$

 D. $4 : 10$

 E. $4 : 25$

9. A square with a side of 7 has exactly one point in common with another square with the same dimensions. If S is a point on one square and W is a point on the other square, what is the maximum possible length of segment SW?

 A. 7

 B. $7\sqrt{2}$

 C. 14

 D. $14\sqrt{2}$

 E. 28

Note: Photocopying any part of this book is prohibited by law.

ADDITIONAL PRACTICE QUESTIONS

1. A 12-foot ladder reaches to the top of an 8-foot wall. How far away from the bottom of the wall is the ladder?

    A.   4 feet

    B. $4\sqrt{5}$ feet

    C.   10 feet

    D. $4\sqrt{13}$ feet

    E.   20 feet

2. What is the area of a circle with a circumference of 8π?

    A. 4π

    B. 8π

    C. 16π

    D. 32π

    E. 64π

3. The width of rectangle A is 20% longer than a side of square J. The length of rectangle A is 20% shorter than a side of square J. The area of rectangle A is what percentage of the area of square J?

    A.   40%

    B.   96%

    C.   100%

    D.   200%

    E.   400%

4. In the figure below, the area of rectangle $PQRS$ is equal to the area of triangle PRT. If the length of RS is equal to 5, what is the length of segment PT?

    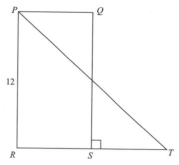

    A.   10

    B. $2\sqrt{61}$

    C.   17

    D.   22

    E.   60

5. In the figure below, the circle with center O is inscribed in square $ABCD$. If the length of AB is 6, what is the approximate area of the shaded region? (Assume that $\pi = 3.14$).

    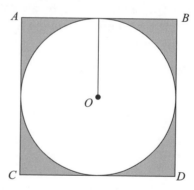

    A.   3.14

    B.   7.74

    C.   9.42

    D.   15.48

    E.   18.84

Note: Photocopying any part of this book is prohibited by law.

ANSWERS AND EXPLANATIONS

1. **The correct answer is (D).** Draw yourself a diagram:

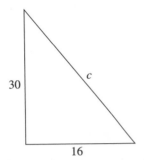

You can always use the Pythagorean theorem (and your calculator) to solve for the length of the wire which is the hypotenuse of the triangle:

$$a^2 + b^2 = c^2$$
$$16^2 + 30^2 = c^2$$
$$256 + 900 = c^2$$
$$1,156 = c^2$$
$$\sqrt{1,156} = \sqrt{c^2}$$
$$34 = c$$

2. **The correct answer is (E).** Work Backwards from the given circumference to the find the radius; use the radius to find the area. Often, the key to circle problems is knowing the measurement of the radius.

Circumference of a circle:

$$C = 2\pi r$$

$$20\pi = 2\pi r$$

$$\frac{20\pi}{2\pi} = \frac{2\pi r}{2\pi}$$

$$10 = \pi$$

Area of a circle:

$$A = \pi r^2$$
$$A = \pi (10)^2$$
$$A = 100\pi$$

3. **The correct answer is (D).** Your knowledge about vertical angles tells you that that the angle directly opposite angle b is equal to b. This angle, along with the 28° angle and the 40° angle, form

a straight line and are therefore supplementary angles and add up 180°. So, you can write the following equation:

$$28 + b + 40 = 180$$

And then, solve for b.

$$b + 68 = 180$$
$$b = 112$$

4. **The correct answer is (C).**

Step 1: Pick a Simple Number to Replace the Variables.

Plug-in for the sides of the square.

Make the square have sides of length 10. The side of a square that is decreased by 20% will become the width of the new rectangle. The adjacent side of the square that is increased by 10% will form the length of the new rectangle.

Since the width of the new rectangle is 20% shorter than a side of the original square, then the width = $0.8 \times 10 = 8$.

Since the length of the new rectangle is 10% more than a side of the original square, then length = $1.1 \times 10 = 11$.

Step 2: Plug that number into the equation in the question. Now you can solve the areas of both the new rectangle and the original square.

Original square's area = (side)^2 = 10^2 = 100

New rectangle area = (length)(width) = (11)(8) = 88.

The area of new rectangle is what percentage of the area of the original square?

Percent = $\frac{\text{Part}}{\text{Whole}}$ = $\frac{88}{100}$ = .88 = 88%.

5. **The correct answer is 285.** Do not assume that it is necessary to find the measures of angles a and b individually to answer the question. See if there is a way to find this sum directly.

Since you know that each of the labeled angles has at least a vertical angle (and therefore an equal angle) you know the internal angles of the quadrilateral formed. Your knowledge of

Note: Photocopying any part of this book is prohibited by law.

geometry also tells you that all quadrilaterals have an interior angle total of 360°. You can therefore write a formula:

$$360 = 45 + 30 + a + b$$
$$360 = 75 + a + b$$
$$a + b = 285$$

6. **The correct answer is (C).** The best strategic approach here is to draw a diagram:

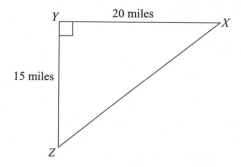

The triangular map shown is a right triangle where segment XZ is the hypotenuse. You can therefore apply the Pythagorean theorem to figure out the length of XZ:

$a^2 + b^2 = c^2$ where c is the measure of the hypotenuse.

$$(15)^2 + (20)^2 = c^2$$
$$225 + 400 = c^2$$
$$625 = c^2$$
$$\sqrt{625} = \sqrt{c^2}$$
$$25 = c$$

So, $XZ = 25$ miles.

7. **The correct answer is (C).** This question contains overlapping figures with sides in common. You need to use your knowledge of two geometric formulas to answer it. It is not possible to find the length of segment QT directly in one step—you will first have to find the length of a side that you are not being asked to find: segment RT.

Also, since you are told that the figure is not drawn to scale, you cannot rely on it to estimate measurements.

You can see from the diagram that area of square $PQRS$ is 36, as you are given the measure of its side PQ, (6), and $6^2 = 36$.

So, you know that the area of triangle QRT must be $\frac{2}{3}$ of 36, or 24. You need to use the formula for the area of a triangle to determine the height, segment RT:

$$\text{Area} = \frac{\text{base} \times \text{height}}{2}$$

You can see that the base of the triangle is the side of the square, segment QR, which measures 6, since all sides of the square will have the same measure. Since the area is 24 and the base is 6, the height, segment RT, measures 8:

$$\text{Area} = \frac{\text{base} \times \text{height}}{2}$$
$$24 = \frac{6h}{2}$$
$$(2)24 = \frac{6h}{2}(2)$$
$$\frac{48}{6} = \frac{6h}{6}$$
$$8 = h$$

Since you know that a square, by definition, has four right angles, you know that angle R is a right angle and that triangle QRT is a right triangle. Segment QT, whose measure the question asks you to find, is the hypotenuse of this right triangle. You can therefore find the measure of segment QT by using the Pythagorean theorem:

$$a^2 + b^2 = c^2$$
$$8^2 + 6^2 = c^2$$
$$64 + 36 = c^2$$
$$100 = c^2$$
$$\sqrt{100} = \sqrt{c^2}$$
$$\sqrt{100} = c$$
$$10 = c$$

Segment QT measures 10.

8. **The correct answer is (E).** If the first square has a diagonal measuring $2\sqrt{2}$, its sides will measure 2, like so:

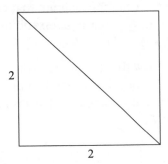

The length of the side of the square can be derived from the Pythagorean theorem: $a^2 + b^2 = c^2$. In this case, you have:

$$x^2 + x^2 = (2\sqrt{2})^2$$
$$2x^2 = (2\sqrt{2})(2\sqrt{2})$$
$$2x^2 = 8$$
$$\frac{2x^2}{2} = \frac{8}{2}$$
$$x^2 = 4$$
$$\sqrt{x^2} = \sqrt{4}$$
$$x = 2$$

The second square has a measuring $5\sqrt{2}$, its sides will measure 5, like so:

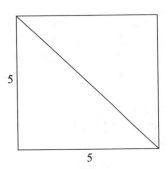

The length of this line can be derived from the Pythagorean theorem: $a^2 + b^2 = c^2$. In this case, you have:

$$x^2 + x^2 = (5\sqrt{2})^2$$
$$2x^2 = (5\sqrt{2})(5\sqrt{2})$$
$$2x^2 = 50$$
$$\frac{2x^2}{2} = \frac{50}{2}$$
$$x^2 = 25$$
$$\sqrt{x^2} = \sqrt{25}$$
$$x = 5$$

<u>Step 2: Plug that Number into the Equations in the Question.</u>

The first square has sides measuring 2, so its area will be 2^2, or 4. The second square has sides measuring 5, so its area will be 5^2, or 25. That's a ratio of 4 : 25.

9. **The correct answer is (D).** The diagonal marks the longest measurement across each of the squares. If the squares touched at the point at which their diagonals lined up as shown, then the maximum possible length of segment SW would be the sum of the diagonals SU and UW.

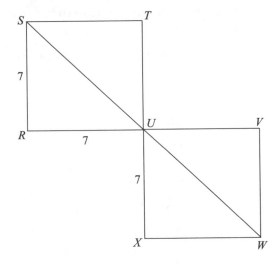

Since you know the dimensions of each of the squares, you can determine the measures of their diagonals using the Pythagorean theorem. Then, add up measures of the diagonals to find the maximum possible length of segment SW.

If you're familiar with the fact that a diagonal divides a square into two 45-45-90 isosceles right triangle, you know that the leg : leg : hypotenuse ratio of the triangles formed is $x : x : x\sqrt{2}$.

Note: Photocopying any part of this book is prohibited by law.

Since each of the legs measures 7, the hypotenuse (diagonal) will measure $7\sqrt{2}$.

Even if you are not familiar with the special properties 45-45-90 isosceles right triangle, you can use the Pythagorean theorem ($a^2 + b^2 = c^2$) to figure out the measure of the missing hypotenuse (diagonal).

$$a2 + b2 = c2$$
$$7^2 + 7^2 = c2$$
$$49 + 49 = c2$$
$$98 = c2$$
$$\sqrt{98} = c$$
$$7\sqrt{2} = c$$

So, the diagonals SU and UW each measure $7\sqrt{2}$.

$$7\sqrt{2} + 7\sqrt{2} = 14\sqrt{2}.$$

The maximum possible length of segment SW is $14\sqrt{2}$.

Choice (D) is correct.

ADDITIONAL PRACTICE QUESTIONS

1. **The correct answer is (B).** It may be helpful to start off by drawing a diagram:

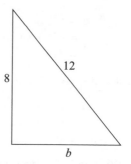

As you can see, this situation represents a right triangle with a height of 8 and a hypotenuse of 12. Since you are looking for the base of the triangle, b, you can use the Pythagorean theorem:

$$a^2 + b^2 = c^2$$
$$(8)^2 + b^2 = (12)2$$
$$64 + b^2 = 144$$
$$64 - 64 + b^2 = 144 - 64$$
$$b^2 = 80$$
$$b = \sqrt{80}$$
$$= \sqrt{5} \times \sqrt{16}$$
$$= 4\sqrt{5}.$$

2. **The correct answer is (C).** Work backwards using the circumference to find the radius:

$$C = 2\pi \times r$$
$$8\pi = 2\pi \times r$$
$$r = \frac{8\pi}{2\pi}$$
$$= 4$$

Now that you know that the radius is equal to 4, you can calculate the area:

$$A = \pi \times r^2$$
$$= \pi(4)^2$$
$$= 16\pi$$

Note: Photocopying any part of this book is prohibited by law.

3. **The correct answer is (B).** Suppose square J has sides of length 10. If the width of A is 20% longer, then the width of A is equal to $1.2 \times 10 = 12$. If the length of A is 20% shorter, then the length is $0.80 \times 10 = 8$. Now calculate the area of J:

$$A = l \times w$$
$$= (10) \times (10)$$
$$= 100$$

Now calculate the area of A:

$$A = l \times w$$
$$= (8) \times (12)$$
$$= 96$$

Since 96 is 96% of 100, choice (B) is correct.

4. **The correct answer is (B).**

From the diagram, you can calculate the area of rectangle $PQRS$:

$$A = l \times w$$
$$= (5) \times (12)$$
$$= 60$$

You now know that the area of PRT must also be equal to 60. Using this information and the length of segment PR, you can calculate the length of RT:

$$A = \frac{1}{2} \times b \times b$$
$$60 = \frac{1}{2} \times b \times (12)$$
$$60 = 6b$$
$$b = 10.$$

Now that you know the lengths of segments PR and RT you can use the Pythagorean theorem to find the length of PT:

$$a^2 + b^2 = c^2$$
$$(12)^2 + (10)^2 = c^2$$
$$144 + 100 = c^2$$
$$c^2 = 244$$
$$c = \sqrt{4 \times 61}$$
$$= 2\sqrt{61}$$

5. **The correct answer is (B).** In order to find the area of the shaded region, you must first find the area of the circle and subtract it from the area of the square. Since we know the length of AB is 6, we can calculate the area of $ABCD$:

$$A = l \times w$$
$$= (6) \times (6)$$
$$= 36$$

Since the diameter of the circle is 6, the radius must be $6 \times \frac{1}{2} = 3$. Now find the area of the circle:

$$A = \pi \times r^2$$
$$= \pi \times (3)^2$$
$$= 9\pi$$
$$\approx 9 \times 3.14$$
$$\approx 28.26$$

Now subtract the area of the circle from the area of the square to find the area of the shaded region:

$$A = 36 - 28.26$$
$$= 7.74$$

Note: Photocopying any part of this book is prohibited by law.

ARITHMETIC STRATEGY

1. Norah has gotten hits 4 times of her last 10 times at bat. If she gets hits her next b times at bat, she will have gotten hits 50% of her times at bat. What is the value of b?

A. 1

B. 2

C. 3

D. 4

E. 5

2. A store charges $4.00 for a burger on the lunch menu and $5.00 for a burger on the dinner menu. If 220 burgers were sold on a given day for a total of $985.00, how many were sold at lunch?

A. 98

B. 104

C. 111

D. 115

E. 119

3. 80 percent of the stores at a certain mall are clothing stores. 25 percent of the clothing stores specialize in children's clothing. What percent of the stores at this mall specialize in children's clothing?

A. 10%

B. 15%

C. 20%

D. 25%

E. 30%

4. For any positive integer, b, let the symbol $\S b$ represent the sum of the digits of b. For example, $\S 32 = 3 + 2 = 5$. What is the value of $\S 27 \times \S 63$?

A. 9

B. 45

C. 81

D. 90

E. 1,701

5. 30 percent of the members of a swim club are adults, and 70 percent are children. If a number of children equal to the number of original club members join the club, what percent of the new club membership is comprised of adults?

A. 10%

B. 15%

C. 20%

D. 25%

E. 30%

6. During a trip to an amusement park, Ellen, Kathy, and Maryjane each bought ride tickets at a cost of $1 per ticket. If Ellen bought 20 more tickets than Kathy, and Kathy bought twice as many tickets as Maryjane, how many tickets did Maryjane purchase if the three of them spent $145 on tickets altogether?

A. 10

B. 15

C. 20

D. 25

E. 30

Note: Photocopying any part of this book is prohibited by law.

7. What is the average (arithmetic mean) of $3a + 5, 5a - 3$ and $4a + 1$ in terms of a?

    A. $2a + 1$

    B. $3a - 2$

    C. $3a + 1$

    D. $4a + 1$

    E. $12a + 3$

8. Which of the following values of x and y will make the ratio of $x : (x + y)$ be $3 : 7$?

    A. $x = 3, y = 7$

    B. $x = 3, y = 10$

    C. $x = 4, y = 3$

    D. $x = 6, y = 8$

    E. $x = 9, y = 18$

9. How many positive integers less than 999 are divisible by either 3 or 10 or both?

    A. 333

    B. 343

    C. 431

    D. 432

    E. 433

ADDITIONAL PRACTICE QUESTIONS

1. Justin's baseball team has won 12 out of their last 20 games. If his team wins w more games, they will have won 68% of their games. What is the value of w?

    A. 5

    B. 8

    C. 9

    D. 12

    E. 14

2. A train station charges $7.50 for tickets purchased before 5:00 pm and $9.25 for tickets purchased after 5:00 pm. If 80 tickets were sold on a certain day for a total of $699.75, how many were sold after 5:00 pm?

    A. 13

    B. 23

    C. 40

    D. 57

    E. 75

3. Sixty percent of the students at a certain high school play a sport. Twenty percent of the students who play a sport are also involved in the drama club. What percent of the students at the high school play a sport and are involved in the drama club?

    A. 3%

    B. 12%

    C. 30%

    D. 40%

    E. 48%

Note: Photocopying any part of this book is prohibited by law.

4. Nicole, Chad, and Bill each purchased raffle tickets for $5.00 each. Nicole purchased 13 more tickets than Chad, and Chad bought four times as many tickets as Bill. How many tickets did Bill purchase if together they spent a total of $245?

A. 4

B. 7

C. 16

D. 17

E. 20

5. What is the average of $x + 4$, $2x + 6$, and $3x + 2$ in terms of x?

A. $2x + 4$

B. $2x + 12$

C. $3x + 6$

D. $4x + 2$

E. $6x + 4$

ANSWERS AND EXPLANATIONS

1. **The correct answer is (B).** Work Backwards here plugging in each of the choices for b, starting with (C), 3. The key is to add the value replacing b to both the hits made and at-bat attempts.

$$\frac{\text{hits made}}{\text{at bats}} = \frac{4+3}{10+3} = \frac{7}{13}$$

$$13\overline{)7.00}^{.53} \cong 53\%$$

No need to work out the division any further. You can see that this answer is bigger than 50%. It is not much bigger, however. Chances are that the next smallest choice, (B), 2, will be the answer.

$$\frac{\text{hits made}}{\text{at bats}} = \frac{4+2}{10+2} = \frac{6}{12} = \frac{1}{2}$$

$$2\overline{)1.00}^{.50} = 50\%$$

Choice (B) works, so you don't have to try any more choices.

2. **The correct answer is (D).** Start by Working Backwards with choice (C).

Lunch menu: $111 \times \$4.00 = \$444.00$

Dinner menu: $(220 - 111) \times \$5.00 = 109 \times \$5.00 = \$545.00$

$\$444.00 + \$545.00 = \$989.00$

The total, \$989.00, is too big, so you want to increase the number of less costly lunch burgers. Try choice (D).

Lunch menu: $115 \times \$4.00 = \$460.00$

Dinner menu: $(220 - 115) \times \$5.00 = 105 \times \$5.00 = \$525.00$

$\$460.00 + \$525.00 = \$985.00$

3. **The correct answer is (C).** Since this question deals with percents, select 100 as the total number of stores at the mall.

So, there are 80 clothing stores. 25% of these 80 clothing stores will specialize in children's clothing:

$$\frac{x}{80} = \frac{25}{100}$$

$$\frac{x}{80} = \frac{1}{4}$$

$$\frac{4x}{4} = \frac{80}{4}$$

$$x = 20$$

$$\frac{\substack{\text{clothing stores specializing} \\ \text{in children's clothing}}}{\text{total stores}} = \frac{20}{100} = 20\%$$

So, 20% of the stores at the mall specialize in children's clothing.

4. **The correct answer is (C).** Divide the question into two parts. First determine the individual values of §27 and §63.

$$\S27 = 2 + 7 = 9$$
$$\S63 = 6 + 3 = 9$$

Then multiply the results.
$$9 \times 9 = 81$$

5. **The correct answer is (B).** Since the question deals with percents, select 100 as the number of original club members.

So, there will be 30 adults and 70 children with 100 additional children joining the club, resulting in a total of 200 club members.

$$\frac{\text{adults}}{\text{total club members}} = \frac{30}{200} = \frac{3}{20}$$

$$20\overline{)3.0}^{.15}$$

So, 15% of the new club membership is comprised of adults.

6. **The correct answer is (D).** The number of dollars spent on tickets is equal to the number of tickets purchased, since the cost of each ticket is $1. The best approach to this question is to Work Backwards, starting with (C):

Maryjane:	20
Kathy:	$2 \times 20 = 40$
Ellen:	$40 + 20 = 60$
	$20 + 40 + 60 = 120$

This sum is too small, so (A) and (B) are incorrect as well. Try (D):

Maryjane:	25
Kathy:	$2 \times 25 = 50$
Ellen:	$50 + 20 = 70$
	$25 + 50 + 70 = 145$

7. **The correct answer is (D).** Plug in a value for *a* that's easy to work with and work out the average quickly.

Avoid selecting 1, 3, 4 or 5 since they are already contained in the given algebraic expressions.

Let *a* be 2:
$$3(2) + 5 = 6 + 5 = 11$$
$$5(2) - 3 = 10 - 3 = 7$$
$$4(2) + 1 = 8 + 1 = 9$$

Write out the equation for determining an average:

$$\text{Average} = \frac{\text{The sum of the values}}{\text{The number of values}}$$

First, add up the values to determine the total to put in the numerator of the fraction:
$$11 + 7 + 9 = 27$$

Then, count the total number of values to put in the denominator of the fraction.

There are 3 values in this set, so the fraction is $\frac{27}{3}$.

Finally, reduce the fraction:
$$\frac{27}{3} = 9$$

The average is 9. Plug 2 into the answer choices and see which one comes out to be 9:

A. $2(2) + 1 = 5$

B. $3(2) - 2 = 4$

C. $3(2) + 1 = 7$

D. $4(2) + 1 = 9$

E. $12(2) + 3 = 27$

Only choice (D) comes out to be 9.

If you know how to do this question algebraically, it is a fairly basic solution. You need to quickly assess each question and determine which method will be most efficient for you. Here's how this solution works algebraically:

$$\begin{array}{r} 3a + 5 \\ 5a - 3 \\ + \underline{4a + 1} \\ 12a + 3 \end{array}$$

$$\frac{12a + 3}{3} = 4a + 1$$

Either way you get (D).

8. **The correct answer is (D).** Plug in the values given in each choice for *x* and *y* in the ratio of $x : (x + y)$ and see which one comes out to be 3:7

A. $x = 3, y = 7$ 3 : (3 + 7) 3:10

B. $x = 3, y = 10$ 3 : (3 + 10) 3:13

C. $x = 4, y = 3$ 4 : (4 + 3) 4:7

D. $x = 6, y = 8$ 6 : (6 + 8) 6:14 = 3:7

E. $x = 9, y = 18$ 9 : (9 + 18) 9:27 = 1:3

Note: Photocopying any part of this book is prohibited by law.

9. **The correct answer is (C).** First determine the greatest number less than 999 that is a multiple of 3:

996 is the greatest number less than 999 that is a multiple of 3.

Then divide 996 by 3:
$$996 \div 3 = 332$$

So, there are 332 numbers that are divisible by 3.

Next, determine the greatest number less than 999 that is a multiple of 10:

990 is the greatest number less than 999 that is a multiple of 10.

Then divide 990 by 10:
$$990 \div 10 = 99$$

Finally, add up the quotients:
$$332 + 99 = 431$$

Since the question stipulates that the numbers can be either 3 or 10 <u>or both</u>, you do not need to worry about subtracting any overlap.

The correct answer is 431.

ADDITIONAL PRACTICE QUESTIONS

1. **The correct answer is (A).**

Plug in each of the answer choices to find the correct one. Start with choice (C):

$$\frac{\text{games won}}{\text{games played}} = \frac{12+9}{20+9}$$
$$= \frac{21}{29}$$
$$\approx 72\%.$$

Choice (C) is not correct, and can therefore be eliminated. Since 72% is higher than 68%, you can also eliminate choices (D) and (E). Now try choice (A):

$$\frac{\text{games won}}{\text{games played}} = \frac{12+5}{20+5}$$
$$= \frac{17}{25}$$
$$= 68\%.$$

2. **The correct answer is (D).** Try each answer choice until you find the one that is correct. Start with choice (C):

After 5 pm: $40 \times \$9.25 = \$370$

Before 5 pm: $80 - 40 = 40$
$40 \times \$7.50 = \$300$

Total: $\$370 + \$300 = \$670$

Choice (D) is incorrect, and can therefore be eliminated. Since $670 is less than $699.75, choices (A) and (B) can also be eliminated. Now try choice (D):

After 5 pm: $57 \times \$9.25 = \$527.25$

Before 5 pm: $80 - 57 = 23$
$23 \times \$7.50 = \$172.50$

Total: $\$527.25 + \$172.50 = \$699.75$

3. **The correct answer is (B).** Suppose there are 100 total students at the high school. If 60% of them play a sport, then 60 students play a sport. Twenty percent of the 60 students are also involved in the drama club:

$$\frac{x}{60} = \frac{20}{100}$$

$$\frac{x}{60} = \frac{1}{5}$$

$$5x = 60$$

$$\frac{5x}{5} = \frac{60}{5}$$

$$x = 12\%.$$

4. **The correct answer is (A).** Work backwards with each answer choice until you find the correct one. Start with choice (C):

Bill:	16 tickets
	$16 \times \$5 = \$80$
Chad:	$4 \times 16 = 64$ tickets
	$64 \times \$5 = \$320$
Nicole:	$64 + 13 = 77$ tickets
	$77 \times \$5 = \$385$
Total:	$\$80 + \$320 + \$385 = \$785$

Choice (C) is too high, so choices (C), (D), and (E) can be eliminated. Now try choice (A):

Bill:	4 tickets
	$4 \times \$5 = \$20$
Chad:	$4 \times 4 = 16$ tickets
	$16 \times \$5 = \$80$
Nicole:	$16 + 13 = 29$ tickets
	$29 \times \$5 = \$145$
Total:	$\$20 + \$80 + \$145 = \$245$

5. **The correct answer is (A).** Choose a value for x, for example 5. The three terms are now

$5 + 4 = 9$, $10 + 6 = 16$, and $15 + 2 = 17$. Now calculate the average:

$$\text{Average} = \frac{\text{sum of values}}{\text{number of values}}$$

$$= \frac{9 + 16 + 17}{3}$$

$$= \frac{42}{3}$$

$$= 14.$$

Plug 5 into each of the answer choices to find the one that gives you 14:

A.	$2(5) + 4 = 14.$	Keep this.
B.	$2(5) + 12 = 22.$	Eliminate.
C.	$3(5) + 6 = 21.$	Eliminate.
D.	$4(5) + 2 = 22.$	Eliminate.
E.	$6(5) + 4 = 34.$	Eliminate.

ALGEBRA STRATEGY

1. How old will Jacob be *a* years from now if he was *b* years old *c* years ago?

   A. $b - c + a$

   B. $c - b + a$

   C. $b + c - a$

   D. $b + c + a$

   E. $b - c - a$

2. If *x* is an even integer, which of the following is an odd integer?

   A. $x + 4$

   B. $x - 2$

   C. $2x - 3$

   D. $3x + 2$

   E. $5x - 8$

3. At a particular resort, renting a beach umbrella costs $5 for the first hour and $2 per hour for each hour after that. If a family rents three beach umbrellas for the same amount of time for a total cost of $39 dollars, for how many hours did they rent the three beach umbrellas?

   A. 3

   B. 4

   C. 5

   D. 6

   E. 7

4. For any positive integer, *k*, where $k \neq 5$ let **k** be equal to $\frac{k+4}{k-5}$. What is the value of **7**?

   A. -2

   B. $-\frac{4}{5}$

   C. $\frac{3}{2}$

   D. 4

   E. $\frac{11}{2}$

5. Lyle has put a $1,500 down payment on a car which represents 8% of the total cost of the car. What was the total cost of the car?

   A. $18,750

   B. $15,000

   C. $13,800

   D. $12,000

   E. $7,500

6. An usher has to seat *p* patrons into aisles of seats that can each accommodate *q* patrons. If there are *r* patrons remaining after the usher has filled all of the seats, how many aisles are there in terms of *p*, *q*, and *r*?

   A. $\frac{q-r}{p}$

   B. $\frac{q+r}{p}$

   C. $\frac{p-r}{q}$

   D. $\frac{q-p}{r}$

   E. $\frac{p+q}{r}$

7. If $a - 3 = b$, then which of the following is equivalent to $3a - 2b$?

   A. $b - 5$

   B. $b + 6$

   C. $b + 9$

   D. $2b - 3$

   E. $5b + 2$

Note: Photocopying any part of this book is prohibited by law.

8. For all whole numbers y, let the "petal" of y be defined as the difference between y and the greatest prime number that is a factor of y. What is the "petal" of 21?

A. 1

B. 3

C. 7

D. 14

E. 21

9. If $x^y = 64$ and x and y are integers, which of the following could NOT be a value of x?

A. 64

B. 32

C. 8

D. 4

E. −2

ADDITIONAL PRACTICE QUESTIONS

1. If p is an even integer, which of the following must also be even?

A. $p + 3$

B. $4 + 2p$

C. $6p - 5$

D. $9 - p$

E. $15 - 3p$

2. A candy store sells chocolate fudge for $4.00 for the first pound and $2.50 for each additional pound. How many pounds of fudge could be purchased with $29?

A. 4.5

B. 7.25

C. 10

D. 11

E. 19

3. In the month of May, Richard earned $4.36 in interest on his savings account. If his interest rate is 0.2%, how much money was in his account during the month?

A. $218

B. $436

C. $872

D. $1,090

E. $2,180

4. A worker at a canning factory is packing cans into boxes. He has a cans that have to be packed into boxes that hold b cans each. If there are c cans left over after filling all of the boxes, how many boxes are there?

A. $\dfrac{a-c}{b}$

B. $\dfrac{a+b}{c}$

C. $\dfrac{a-b}{c}$

D. $\dfrac{a+c}{b}$

E. $\dfrac{b-a}{c}$

5. If $5j - 2 = r$, which of the following is equivalent to $4r + 3j$?

A. $20j - 8$

B. $23j - 2$

C. $23j - 8$

D. $17r + 8$

E. $18r - 6$

ANSWERS AND EXPLANATIONS

1. **The correct answer is (D).** Select easy numbers to plug in for a, b, and c. Let $a = 5$, $b = 15$ and $c = 10$. So, if Jacob was 15 years old 10 years ago, he is 25 now. 5 years from now, he'll be 30. See which of the choices comes out to be 30 when you plug in $a = 5$, $b = 15$ and $c = 10$:

    A. $15 - 10 + 5 = 10$

    B. $10 - 15 + 5 = 0$

    C. $15 + 10 - 5 = 20$

    D. $15 + 10 + 5 = 30$

    E. $15 - 10 - 5 = 0$

2. **The correct answer is (C).** There are variables as answer choices—a good sign that this is a candidate for Plugging-in.

    Pick a value for x. It has to be an even integer so, say, $x = 4$.

    Now, plug this value in for x in the answer choices—the one that gives an odd answer will be correct:

    A. $x + 4 = 4 + 4 = 8$. This is even. Eliminate this answer.

    B. $x - 2 = 4 - 2 = 2$. This is even. Eliminate this answer.

    C. $2x - 3 = 2(4) - 3 = 5$. This is odd and is the correct answer.

    D. $3x + 2 = 3(4) + 2 = 14$. This is even. Eliminate this answer.

    E. $5x - 8 = 5(4) - 8 = 12$. This is even. Eliminate this answer.

3. **The correct answer is (B).** An equation is contained in this word problem. Note that all of the answer choices are numbers. You have a perfect Working Backwards question!

    The right answer will be the one that gives a value of $39 when you run it through the question.

    <u>Step 1: Start with Answer Choice (C).</u>

    Run choice (C) through the question and see if it gives a cost of $39.

    Find the cost of renting one beach umbrella for 5 hours and then multiply that answer by 3:

    1st hour = $5
    4 subsequent hours = $4 \times \$2 = \$8$
    $\$5 + \$8 = \$13$
    $\$13 \times 3$ beach umbrellas = $39.

    Sometimes, you get lucky on the first try.

4. **The correct answer is (E).** The value of **7** is: $\frac{7+4}{7-5} = \frac{11}{2}$.

5. **The correct answer is (A).**

    <u>Step 1: Read Through the Question.</u> You know that $1,500 equals 8% of total cost of the car. Knowing what the numerical value of the percentage is makes it possible to answer, "What was total cost of the car?"

    <u>Step 2: Reread the Question and Translate the English into Math.</u> Lyle paid $1,500 towards the cost of a car and this payment represents 8% of the total cost of the car. Essentially, you're asking yourself this question: "Eight percent of what number is equal to 1,500?"

    Percent questions call for a three-part equation: Percent $= \frac{\text{Part}}{\text{Whole}}$.

    In this case, you are given the Percent, (8%, or 0.08), and Part, ($1,500), and are looking for the Whole, (the total cost of the car).

    $$\text{So, } 0.08 = \frac{1,500}{\text{Total Cost of Car}}$$

    <u>Step 3: Solve the Math.</u>

    $$0.08 = \frac{1,500}{\text{Total Cost of Car}}$$

    $$0.08 \times \text{Total Cost of Car} = 1,500$$

    $$\text{Total Cost of Car} = \frac{1,500}{0.08}$$

    Total cost of the car = $18,750.

Note: Photocopying any part of this book is prohibited by law.

6. The correct answer is (C). Select values for p, q, and r, making sure that the number that you select for q doesn't divide into the number that you select for p evenly, since there needs to be a remainder. Be sure that the value that you select for r is the remainder that you get when you divide p by q.

Say, for instance that you set up the values as follows: $p = 504$, $q = 20$, and $r = 4$, indicating that there are 504 patrons, each aisle contains 20 seats, and there are 4 patrons remaining after all of the seats are filled.

If each aisle contains 20 seats, 504 patrons will go into 25 aisles, with 4 patrons left over. Plug the same values into the choices, and see which one comes out to be 25:

A. $\dfrac{20-4}{504} = \dfrac{16}{504} = \dfrac{2}{63}$

B. $\dfrac{20+4}{504} = \dfrac{24}{504} = \dfrac{3}{63}$

C. $\dfrac{504-4}{20} = \dfrac{500}{20} = 25$

D. $\dfrac{20-504}{4} = -\dfrac{484}{4} = 121$

E. $\dfrac{504+20}{4} = \dfrac{524}{4} = 131$

7. The correct answer is (C). Whenever you see unknowns in the answer choices, don't do the algebra unless you have to. Remember that those variables are there to take the place of actual numbers. So…Plug In a number in place of the variable and work with the question that way. Follow these three steps for Plugging In:

<u>Step 1: Pick Simple Numbers to Replace the Variables.</u>

In this question, you have two variables, a and b. If you pick a number for a, you derive a value for b. Choose something easy to work with. Since you are subtracting 3 from a, make a bigger than 3, say $a = 5$.

Then, since $a - 3 = b$, then $(5) - 3 = b$, or $2 = b$

<u>Step 2: Plug those numbers into the equations in the question</u>

You have $a = 5$ and $b = 2$.

Plug these values into the expression in the question:

$3a - 2b = 3(5) - 2(2) = 15 - 4 = 11$

11 is your target number. All you have to do now is find an answer choice that also yields 11 when you Plug In $b = 2$.

<u>Step 3: Plug the Numbers into the Answers Choices. Eliminate Those that Give a Different Result than the Target Number.</u>

(A): $b - 5 = 2 - 5 = -3$. Eliminate.

(B): $b + 6 = 2 + 6 = 8$. Eliminate.

(C): $b + 9 = 2 + 9 = 11$. Keep this.

(D): $2b - 3 = 2(2) - 3 = 4 - 3 = 1$. Eliminate.

(E): $5b + 2 = 5(2) + 2 = 10 + 2 = 12$. Eliminate.

Only (C) gives the right answer.

8. The correct answer is (D). When working on symbolism questions, you need to follow the instructions exactly.

In this case, the definition of "petal" is that it is the difference between y and the greatest prime number that is a factor of y. That is, to find the "petal" of a number, find the prime number that is a factor of that number, but closest to that number in value and subtract it from that number.

In this case, the "petal" of 21 is 14, since the greatest prime number that is a factor of 21 is 7, and $21 - 7 = 14$.

9. The correct answer is (B). The easiest way to tackle this question is by considering each of the answer choices:

A. 64 $x^y = 64$. If $x = 64$ and $y = 1$, then $64^1 = 64$.

B. 32 $x^y = 64$. If $x = 32$, there is no integer value for y that will make $32y = 64$.

C. 8 $x^y = 64$. If $x = 8$ and $y = 2$, then $8^2 = 64$.

D. 4 $x^y = 64$. If $x = 4$ and $y = 3$, then $4^3 = 64$

E. 2 $x^y = 64$. If $x = -2$ and $y = 6$, then $(-2)^6 = 64$. Remember that a negative number raised to an even power is positive.

ADDITIONAL PRACTICE QUESTIONS

1. **The correct answer is (B).** Choose an even integer for p, such as 2. Plug 2 into each of the answer choices and eliminate the ones that are not even:

A: $2 + 3 = 5$. This is odd. Eliminate.

B: $4 + 4 = 8$. This is even. Keep this.

C: $12 - 5 = 7$. This is odd. Eliminate.

D: $9 - 2 = 7$. This is odd. Eliminate.

E: $15 - 6 = 9$. This is odd. Eliminate.

2. **The correct answer is (D).** Work backwards with each answer choice to find the correct answer.

Start with choice (C):

First pound: $4

Remaining 9 pounds: $2.50 \times 9 = 22.50

Total: $4 + $22.50 = 26.50

Choice (C) is too low, which means that choices (C), (A), and (B) can be eliminated. Now try choice (D):

First pound: $4

Remaining 10 pounds: $2.50 \times 10 = 25

Total: $4 + $25 = 29

3. **The correct answer is (E).** We know that $4.36 is 0.2% of the total amount of money in Richard's bank account. Plug these values into the percent formula, and solve for the missing value:

$$\frac{\%}{100} = \frac{\text{part}}{\text{whole}}$$

$$\frac{0.2}{100} = \frac{\$4.36}{w}$$

$$0.002 = \frac{\$4.36}{w}$$

$$0.002w = \$4.36$$

$$w = \$2,180$$

4. **The correct answer is (A).** Choose values to represent a, b, and c. Suppose there are 24 cans that need to be packed, each box holds 5 cans, and you have 4 cans left over. This means that there are $24 - 4 = 20$ cans that were packed. Since each box holds 5 cans, there are 20 cans $\times \frac{1 \text{ box}}{5 \text{ cans}} = 4$ boxes. Now plug these values into each of the answer choices to see which one gives you 4 as the answer:

A. $\frac{a-c}{b} = \frac{24-4}{5} = \frac{20}{5} = 4$. Keep this.

B. $\frac{a+b}{c} = \frac{24+5}{4} = \frac{29}{4}$. Eliminate.

C. $\frac{a-b}{c} = \frac{24-5}{4} = \frac{19}{4}$. Eliminate.

D. $\frac{a+c}{b} = \frac{24+4}{5} = \frac{28}{5}$. Eliminate.

E. $\frac{b-a}{c} = \frac{5-24}{4} = -\frac{19}{4}$. Eliminate.

Note: Photocopying any part of this book is prohibited by law.

5. **The correct answer is (C).** Choose a value for j, for example 2. Then:

$$r = 5j - 2$$
$$= 5(2) - 2$$
$$= 10 - 2$$
$$= 8$$

If $j = 2$ and $r = 8$, then:

$$4r + 3j = 4(8) + 3(2)$$
$$= 32 + 6$$
$$= 38$$

Now plug these values for j and r into each answer choice and eliminate the ones that do not give you 34:

A: $20j - 8 = 20(2) - 8$
$$= 40 - 8$$
$$= 32. \text{ Eliminate.}$$

B: $23j - 2 = 23(2) - 2$
$$= 46 - 2$$
$$= 44. \text{ Eliminate.}$$

C: $23j - 8 = 23(2) - 8$
$$= 46 - 8$$
$$= 38. \text{ Keep this.}$$

D: $17r + 8 = 17(8) + 8$
$$= 136 + 8$$
$$= 144. \text{ Eliminate.}$$

E: $18r - 6 = 18(8) - 6$
$$= 144 - 6$$
$$= 138. \text{ Eliminate.}$$

POINTS AND DISTANCE

1. In the figure shown below, what is the length of line segment *AB*?

A. −4

B. 3

C. 4

D. 7

E. 8

2. Quadrant II contains which of the following points?

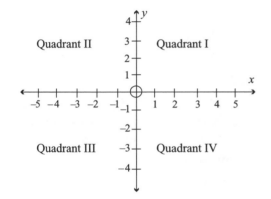

A. (1,5)

B. (−2,−3)

C. (−2,4)

D. (0,−6)

E. (5,2)

3. What is the length of segment $\overline{CD}$?

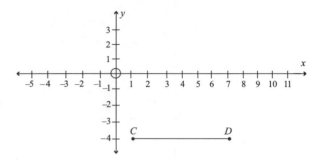

4. In the *xy*-plane below, $\overline{AC} = 10$. What is the value of *W*?

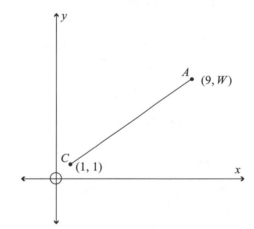

A. 5

B. 6

C. 7

D. 8

E. 9

5. In the figure below, if line segment $\overline{GH}$ is parallel to the x-axis and has length 7, what is the value of r?

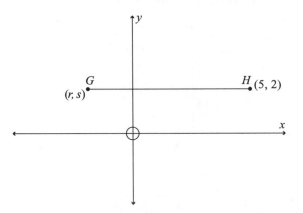

A. –4

B. –3

C. –2

D. 2

E. 3

6. Square WXYZ is graphed in the xy-plane as shown below. What is the area of right triangle XYZ, in square units?

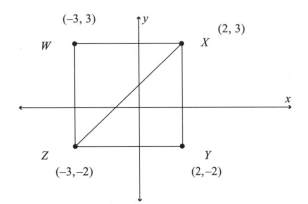

A. 5

B. $6\frac{1}{4}$

C. 10

D. $12\frac{1}{2}$

E. 25

7. What are the coordinates of the midpoint of $\overline{ST}$?

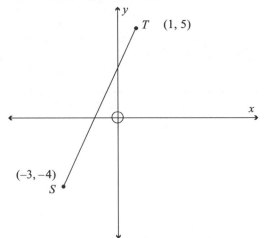

Note: Figure not drawn to scale.

A. (–1, –1)

B. $(-1, \frac{1}{2})$

C. $(0, 1\frac{1}{2})$

D. (1, 1)

E. $(2, 4\frac{1}{2})$

8. The midpoint of $\overline{HJ}$ is K. If the coordinates of point H are (–1, 4) and the coordinates of point K are (2, –1), what are the coordinates of point J?

A. (0, 2)

B. $(\frac{1}{2}, 1\frac{1}{2})$

C. (1, 0)

D. $(1\frac{1}{2}, 2\frac{1}{2})$

E. (5, –6)

ADDITIONAL PRACTICE QUESTIONS

1. In which quadrant does the point (2, –3) lie?

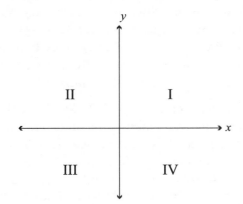

   A.   Quadrant I

   B.   Quadrant II

   C.   Quadrant III

   D.   Quadrant IV

   E.   Quadrants I and IV

2. What is the midpoint of the segment beginning at the point (3, 4) and ending at the point (–1, 2)?

   A.   (1, 2)

   B.   (1, 3)

   C.   (2, 6)

   D.   (3, 1)

   E.   (4, 2)

3. What is the distance between the points (–2, 3) and (4, –1)?

   A. $2\sqrt{6}$

   B. $2\sqrt{13}$

   C. $2\sqrt{26}$

   D. $5\sqrt{2}$

   E.   52

4. Calculate the slope of the line passing through the points (8, –2) and (–4, 6).

   A. $-\dfrac{2}{3}$

   B.   –1

   C. $-\dfrac{3}{2}$

   D. $\dfrac{2}{3}$

   E. $\dfrac{3}{2}$

5. What is the slope of the line passing through the points (5, –3) and (–1, 7)?

   A. $-\dfrac{5}{3}$

   B. $-\dfrac{2}{5}$

   C.   1

   D. $\dfrac{2}{5}$

   E. $\dfrac{5}{2}$

ANSWERS AND EXPLANATIONS

1. **The correct answer is (E).** The length of a segment is the same as the distance between its endpoints.

    The length of line segment $\overline{AB}$ is the distance between its endpoints A and B. Since these points are 8 units apart, the length of $\overline{AB}$ is 8.

    Part of line segment $\overline{AB}$ is to the left of the origin where x-coordinates are negative. This part still has a positive length value because distance is always a positive quantity. A distance of five units to the left is still a distance of 5 units. The piece of $\overline{AB}$ to the left of the origin starts at 0 (the origin) and extends 5 units (to point A with x-coordinate -5). The piece of $\overline{AB}$ to the right of the origin starts at 0 (the origin) and extends 3 units to point B (with x-coordinate 3). So, the total length of the segment is $5 + 3 = 8$ units.

2. **The correct answer is (C).** This question requires you to be familiar with the location of the quadrants on the coordinate grid. Quadrant I is located in the upper right and the rest run consecutively in a counter-clockwise fashion.

    As you can see from the diagram of the coordinate grid below, all points in Quadrant II have a negative x-coordinate and a positive y-coordinate. The only point among the choices that resides in Quadrant II is $(-2, 4)$.

    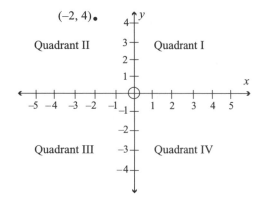

3. **The correct answer is 6.** When the endpoints have the same y-coordinate, the length of the segment is the difference between its x-coordinates. The coordinates of C are $(1, -4)$ and the coordinates of D are $(7, -4)$. Since both points have a y-coordinate of -4, the length of $\overline{CD}$ is the difference of its x-coordinates: $7 - 1 = 6$.

4. **The correct answer is (C).** Determine the endpoints of the segment. One of the endpoints of the segment has coordinates $(1, 1)$. The other endpoint has coordinates $(9, w)$. You're not asked to solve for the length of the segment—you're told that it's 10. You're asked to solve for w, the y-coordinate of one endpoint. So, instead of plugging in two sets of known endpoints to solve for an unknown length, you'll plug in the length and the information you do have about the endpoints to solve for the unknown coordinate.

    The two points have different x-coordinates. You don't know the value of w, but you can see from the graph that it is not 1, so you also know that the points have different y-coordinates. Since the endpoints don't have a common coordinate, you must use the distance formula.

    Plug into the distance formula to solve for w:

    $$d = \sqrt{\left(x_1 - x_2\right)^2 + \left(y_1 - y_2\right)^2}$$
    $$10 = \sqrt{(9 - 1)^2 (w - 1)^2}$$
    $$10 = \sqrt{(8)^2 + (w - 1)^2}$$
    $$10 = \sqrt{64 + (w^2 - 2w + 1)}$$
    $$100 = w^2 - 2w + 65$$
    $$100 - 100 = w^2 - 2w + 65 - 100$$
    $$0 = w^2 - 2w - 35$$
    $$0 = (w - 7)(w + 5)$$
    $$w = 7$$
    $$w = -5$$

    You can see that endpoint $(9, w)$ lies in the second quadrant, where y-coordinates are positive. Therefore, the correct answer is 7, choice (C).

You also could have viewed this segment as the hypotenuse of a right triangle. If you sketch in the legs as shown, you'll see that you have a right triangle with one leg with length 8 and a hypotenuse with length 10:

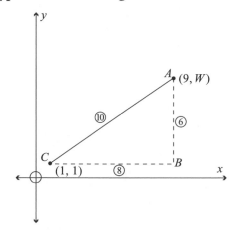

These measurements indicate that this is a 6-8-10 right triangle, and the length of leg $\overline{AB}$ is 6.

Point B has endpoints (9, 1) and point A has endpoints (9, w). Since they have a common x-coordinate, the difference between w and 1 must be 6: $w - 1 = 6$, $w = 7$.

If you didn't recognize the 6-8-10 right triangle, you could have used the Pythagorean theorem to solve for the length of $\overline{AB}$, and then proceeded as above.

Choice (C) is correct.

5. **The correct answer is (C).** Notice that since point G is to the left of the y-axis, its x-coordinate must be negative. Knowing this fact allows you to eliminate choices (D) and (E) right off the bat.

Segment $\overline{GH}$ is parallel to the x-axis so its endpoints have the same y-coordinate. Therefore, the length of the segment is the difference between its x-coordinates. The x-coordinate of H is 5 and the x-coordinate of G is r. Since you know that the length of $\overline{GH}$ is 7, you can solve for r:

$$\overline{GH} = 5 - r$$
$$7 = 5 - r$$
$$7 - 5 = 5 - 5 - r$$
$$2 = -r$$
$$-2 = r$$

So, $r = -2$.

6. **The correct answer is (D).** Since triangle XYZ is a right triangle, its area is found as $\frac{1}{2}$(leg$_1$ × leg$_2$) Use the endpoints to find the lengths of the two legs. The endpoints of leg $\overline{ZY}$ have the same y-coordinate. That means its length is the difference between its x-coordinates:

$$2 - (-3) = 2 + 3 = 5$$

The endpoints of leg $\overline{XY}$ have the same x-coordinate. That means its length is the difference between its y-coordinates:

$$3 - (-2) = 3 + 2 = 5$$

So, the area of right triangle XYZ is:

$$\frac{1}{2}(5 \times 5) = \frac{1}{2}(25) = 12\frac{1}{2}$$

Choice (D) is correct.

7. **The correct answer is (B).** You're asked to find the coordinates of the midpoint of $\overline{ST}$. Notice that the question states that the figure is not drawn to scale. Therefore, you can't just look at the graph and guesstimate where the segment's midpoint is.

The midpoint formula is:

$$\text{midpoint} = \frac{x_1 + x_2}{2}, \frac{y_1 + y_2}{2}$$

Plug the coordinates for $S, (-3, -4)$, and $T, (1, 5)$, into this formula. It doesn't matter which point you use as (x_1, y_1) and which as (x_2, y_2). You get the same result either way:

$$\text{Midpoint} = \left(\frac{1 + (-3)}{2}, \frac{5 - 4}{2}\right) = \left(\frac{-2}{2}, \frac{9}{2}\right) = \left(-1, \frac{1}{2}\right)$$

So the midpoint of $\overline{ST}$ has coordinates $(-1, \frac{1}{2})$.

8. **The correct answer is (E).** Be careful here. This question gives you the coordinates of one endpoint and the coordinates of the midpoint. If you didn't read carefully, you might have plugged in both pairs of given coordinates as endpoints, and come up with incorrect choice (B), $(\frac{1}{2}, 1\frac{1}{2})$. To solve correctly, plug in $(-1, 4)$ as (x_1, y_1), and $(2, -1)$ as the midpoint:

$$(2, -1) = \left(\frac{-1 + x_2}{2}, \frac{4 + y_2}{2} \right)$$

$$2 = \frac{-1 + x_2}{2}$$

$$4 = -1 + x_2$$

$$5 = x_2$$

$$-1 = \frac{4 + y_2}{2}$$

$$-2 = 4 + y_2$$

$$-6 = y_2$$

This is how the segment $\overline{HJ}$ and its midpoint, K, look when sketched on a coordinate grid:

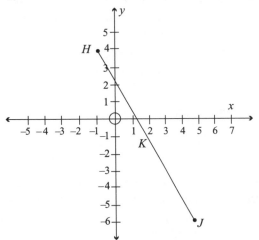

The coordinates of J are $(5, -6)$.

ADDITIONAL PRACTICE QUESTIONS

1. **The correct answer is (D).** Plot the point $(2, -3)$ by moving 2 units in the positive x direction and 3 units in the negative y direction:

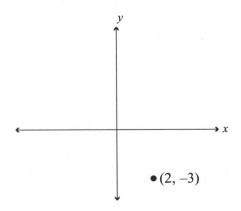

From the graph, you can see that the point $(2, -3)$ lies in the fourth quadrant. Choice (D) is correct.

2. **The correct answer is (B).** In order to find the midpoint, you must use the midpoint formula:

$$mdpt = \left(\frac{x_1 + x_2}{2}, \frac{y_1 + y_2}{2} \right)$$

Plugging the two given points into the formula, you get

$$mdpt = \left(\frac{3 + (-1)}{2}, \frac{4 + 2}{2} \right)$$

$$= \left(\frac{2}{2}, \frac{6}{2} \right)$$

$$= (1, 3).$$

3. **The correct answer is (B).**

    In order to find the distance between two points, you must use the distance formula:

    $$d = \sqrt{(x_2 - x_1)^2 + (y_2 - y_1)^2}$$

    Plugging the given points into the formula gives you:

    $$d = \sqrt{(4 - (-2))^2 + ((-1) - 3)^2}$$
    $$= \sqrt{(6)^2 + (-4)^2}$$
    $$= \sqrt{36 + 16}$$
    $$= \sqrt{52}$$
    $$= 2\sqrt{13}.$$

4. **The correct answer is (A).**

    In order to find the slope of a line passing through two specific points, you must use the slope formula:

    $$m = \frac{(y_2 - y_1)}{(x_2 - x_1)}$$

    Plugging the given points into this formula, you get:

    $$m = \frac{(6 - (-2))}{((-4) - 8)}$$
    $$= -\frac{8}{12}$$
    $$= -\frac{2}{3}.$$

5. **The correct answer is (A).** In order to find the slope of a line passing through two specific points, you must use the slope formula:

    $$m = \frac{(y_2 - y_1)}{(x_2 - x_1)}$$

    Plugging the given points into this formula, gives you:

    $$m = \frac{7 - (-3)}{-1 - 5}$$
    $$= \frac{10}{-6}$$
    $$= -\frac{5}{3}$$

Note: Photocopying any part of this book is prohibited by law.

LINEAR EQUATIONS

1. Point D is located by beginning at point C, moving 3 units up and then moving 4 units to the right. What is the slope of line CD?

   A. $-\dfrac{4}{3}$

   B. $-\dfrac{3}{4}$

   C. $\dfrac{3}{4}$

   D. $\dfrac{4}{3}$

   E. $\dfrac{7}{3}$

2. If the point $(5, k)$ is on the graph of $2x + y = 12$, what is the value of k?

3. Line p crosses the y-axis at $(0, 3)$ and has a slope of $-\frac{1}{4}$. At what point does the line cross the x-axis?

   A. $(3, 0)$

   B. $(-4, 0)$

   C. $(12, 0)$

   D. $(0, -12)$

   E. $(0, 12)$

4. Line g crosses the y-axis at $(0, 8)$ and crosses the x-axis at $(4, 0)$. What is the slope of this line?

   A. -2

   B. $-\dfrac{1}{2}$

   C. $\dfrac{1}{2}$

   D. 2

   E. 4

5. Which of the following is the equation of a line with no slope?

   A. $x = -7$

   B. $y = -7$

   C. $y = -7x$

   D. $x = -7y$

   E. $xy = -7$

6. When drawn on the same set of axes, the graph of the equations $y = x + 1$ and $y + x = 3$ intersect at a point whose coordinates are:

   A. $(2, 1)$

   B. $(1, 2)$

   C. $(2, 3)$

   D. $(-1, 4)$

   E. $(-4, -3)$

Note: Photocopying any part of this book is prohibited by law.

7. What is the slope of line q?

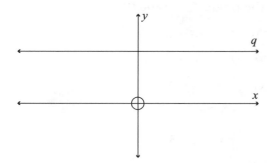

A. 1

B. 0

C. $\frac{1}{2}$

D. −1

E. undefined

8. What is the slope of the line identified by $-4y = 2(3x + 4)$?

A. −2

B. $-\frac{3}{2}$

C. 2

D. 3

E. 6

9. What is the slope of any line parallel to the line $3y - x = 4$?

A. −1

B. $-\frac{1}{3}$

C. $\frac{1}{3}$

D. 1

E. 3

10. In the xy-plane, what is the y-intercept of the line $8x + 3y = -12$?

A. −12

B. −4

C. $-\frac{8}{3}$

D. 0

E. 3

ADDITIONAL PRACTICE QUESTIONS

1. What is the slope of the line passing through the points (2, –4) and (1, 5)?

   A. –9

   B. $-\dfrac{3}{2}$

   C. $-\dfrac{1}{9}$

   D. $\dfrac{1}{3}$

   E. $\dfrac{3}{5}$

2. A line intercepts the y-axis at the point (0, –2) and has a slope of $\frac{2}{3}$. What is an equation for this line?

   A. $y = -\frac{2}{3}x + 2$

   B. $y = -2x + \frac{2}{3}$

   C. $y - 2 = \frac{2}{3}x$

   D. $y = \frac{2}{3}x - 2$

   E. $y = 2x - \frac{2}{3}$

3. What is the slope of the line passing through the points (6, 3) and (–5, 8)?

   A. $-\dfrac{11}{5}$

   B. –1

   C. $-\dfrac{5}{11}$

   D. $-\dfrac{1}{4}$

   E. $-\dfrac{3}{13}$

4. What is an equation for the line passing through the points (3, 0) and (0, 6)?

   A. $y = -2x + 3y$

   B. $y = -2x + 6$

   C. $y = \frac{1}{2}x + 3$

   D. $y = 2x - 6y$

   E. $y = \frac{1}{2}x - 3$

5. What is the equation for the line with slope $\frac{1}{3}$ and y-intercept 4?

   A. $y = \frac{1}{3}x - 4$

   B. $y = 4x + \frac{1}{3}$

   C. $y + 4 = \frac{1}{3}x$

   D. $y = -4x - \frac{1}{3}$

   E. $y = \frac{1}{3}x + 4$

ANSWERS AND EXPLANATIONS

1. **The correct answer is (C).** The fact that you're moving upwards and to the right to get from point C to point D indicates that the slope of the line is positive, so you can eliminate choices (A) and (B) right away. The formula for the slope of a line is $\frac{\Delta y}{\Delta x} = \frac{y_2 - y_1}{x_2 - x_1}$, so the number representing the change in y, 3 units up will be in the numerator of the fraction, and the number representing the change in x, 4 units to the right will be in the denominator of the fraction. So the slope of line CD is $\frac{3}{4}$.

2. **The correct answer is 2.** Since a point on a graph is marked by (x, y), the question is telling you that the point $(5, k)$ has an x-coordinate of 5. Plug 5 in for x in the equation, $2x + y = 12$ and solve for y:

$$2x + y = 12$$
$$2(5) + y = 12$$
$$10 + y = 12$$
$$10 - 10 + y = 12 - 10$$
$$y = 2$$

Since the y-coordinate is equal to 2, k is equal to 2.

3. **The correct answer is (C).** The point that is actually on the x-axis will always have a y-coordinate of 0. Knowing this fact allows you to eliminate choices (D) and (E) right away. The question provides the coordinates of points on a line as well as its slope, which is all that you need in order to calculate the point at which the line crosses the x-axis. Remember that the slope is the difference in the y-coordinates divided by the difference in the x-coordinates.

$$\text{Slope of a line} = \frac{\Delta y}{\Delta x} = \frac{y_2 - y_1}{x_2 - x_1}$$

You can plug the information that you have into the slope formula and solve for the x-coordinate of the point at which the line crosses the x-axis (remember that you already know that since the point is actually on the x-axis, it will have a y-coordinate of 0):

$$\frac{y_2 - y_1}{x_2 - x_1} = \frac{0 - 3}{x - 0} = -\frac{1}{4}$$
$$\frac{-3}{x} = -\frac{1}{4}$$
$$x = 12.$$

So, since x is equal to 12 and the point is on the x-axis and has a y-coordinate of 0, the line crosses the x-axis at the point $(12, 0)$.

4. **The correct answer is (A).** The question provides the coordinates of two points on a line, which is all that you need to calculate its slope. Remember that slope is the difference in the y-coordinates over the difference in the x-coordinates:

$$\text{Slope of a line} = \frac{\Delta y}{\Delta x} = \frac{y_2 - y_1}{x_2 - x_1}$$

Plug in the points $(0, 8)$ and $(4, 0)$ into the slope equation. Remember too, that you have to subtract in the same order between points.

$$\frac{y_2 - y_1}{x_2 - x_1} = \frac{8 - 0}{0 - 4}$$
$$= \frac{8}{-4}$$
$$= -2.$$

5. **The correct answer is (A).** Remember that vertical lines have no slope when graphed. This seems illogical at first, since it would seem as if a straight vertical drop would have about as much slope as you could possibly have. However, a vertical line is said to have no slope for mathematical reasons having to do with the slope formula:

$$\text{Slope of a line} = \frac{\Delta y}{\Delta x} = \frac{y_2 - y_1}{x_2 - x_1}$$

Each and every point on the vertical line will have the exact same x-coordinate, so when you take the difference between two identical x-values, you end up getting a zero in the denominator, which is undefined since it doesn't make sense to divide something up into zero parts.

So, basically the question comes down to this: What kind of equation will be a vertical line when graphed? One in the form of x = some number. The only equation among the choices that fits this criteria is $x = -7$.

6. **The correct answer is (B).** There are a number of ways to approach this question. Since the question itself is discussing the graph of the equations, your first inclination might be to graph these lines, but it is not necessary to actually graph them. This question is probably most easily tackled algebraically by using the substitution method. Since the question tells you that $y = x + 1$, you can substitute $x + 1$ for y in the equation $y + x = 3$ and solve for x:

$$y + x = 3$$
$$(x + 1) + x = 3$$
$$2x + 1 = 3$$
$$2x + 1 - 1 = 3 - 1$$
$$\frac{2x}{2} = \frac{2}{2}$$
$$x = 1.$$

Just knowing that $x = 1$ narrows your choice down to (B), since it is the only choice that has an x-coordinate of 1. If this were not the case, you would just proceed by plugging in the value that you just found for x into the first equation and solving for y:

$$y = x + 1$$
$$y = 1 + 1$$
$$y = 2$$

Alternatively, you could have answered this question by plugging in each of the answer pairs to see which one worked, but you would have to be sure to check the pairs against both equations.

7. **The correct answer is (B).** A horizontal line has a slope of 0. It makes sense logically that a flat surface has zero slope, but a horizontal line is said to have zero slope for mathematical reasons having to do with the slope formula:

$$\text{Slope of a line} = \frac{\Delta y}{\Delta x} = \frac{y_2 - y_1}{x_2 - x_1}$$

Each and every point on the horizontal line will have the exact same y-coordinate, so when you take the difference between two identical y-values, you end up getting a zero in the numerator.

A line with a slope of 1 would be a diagonal line with a positive slope. A line with a slope of -1 would be a diagonal line with a negative slope. A line with a slope of $\frac{1}{2}$ would be a diagonal line with a positive slope. A vertical line has a slope that is undefined. Since its x-coordinates will all be the same, the difference between them in the denominator of the slope formula will always be 0, which is undefined.

8. **The correct answer is (B).** Before you can identify information about a line, it must be in slope-intercept form ($y = mx + b$), meaning that y must be alone of one side of the equation with a coefficient of 1.

Begin by multiplying through the right side of the equation.

$$-4y = 2(3x + 4)$$
$$-4y = 6x + 8$$

Although y is alone on the left side of the equation it has a coefficient of -4. To undo the multiplication done to y, divide both sides by -4:

$$\frac{-4y}{-4} = \frac{6x + 8}{-4}$$
$$y = \frac{-3}{2}x - 2.$$

This question asks you for the slope of the line, or m.

Now that the equation is in slope-intercept form $y = \frac{-3}{2}x - 2$, you can see that $m = -\frac{3}{2}$.

Note: Photocopying any part of this book is prohibited by law.

9. **The correct answer is (C).** Before you can identify information about a line, it must be in slope-intercept form ($y = mx + b$), meaning that y must be alone on one side of the equation with a coefficient of 1.

Since x has been subtracted from $3y$, add x to both sides to undo this:

$$3y - x = 4$$
$$3y - x + x = 4 + x$$
$$3y = x + 4$$

Since y has been multiplied by 3, divide both sides by 3 to undo this:

$$\frac{3y}{3} = \frac{x+4}{3}$$
$$y = \frac{1}{3}x + \frac{4}{3}.$$

This question asks for the slope of any line parallel to the line with equation $3y - x = 4$. Parallel lines have equal slopes, so the slope of any line parallel to this line will also be m.

Now that the equation is in slope-intercept form $y = \frac{1}{3}x + \frac{4}{3}$, you can see that $m = \frac{1}{3}$.

10. **The correct answer is (B).** Before you can identify information about a line, it must be in slope-intercept form, meaning that y must be alone on one side of the equation with a coefficient of 1.

To isolate y, subtract $8x$ from both sides of $8x + 3y = -12$:

$$8x + 3y = -12$$
$$8x - 8x + 3y = -12 - 8x$$
$$3y = -8x - 12$$

Now, you have y alone on the left side, but it has a coefficient of 3. Divide both sides by 3 to undo this:

$$\frac{3y}{3} = \frac{-8x-12}{3}$$
$$y = -\frac{8}{3}x - 4.$$

For an equation in the form $y = mx + b$, b is the y-intercept. Therefore -4 is the y-intercept of this line.

ADDITIONAL PRACTICE QUESTIONS

1. **The corre6ct answer is (A).** Use the formula for finding the slope of a line:

$$m = \frac{(y_2 - y_1)}{(x_2 - x_1)}$$
$$= \frac{5 - (-4)}{1 - 2}$$
$$= \frac{9}{-1}$$
$$= -9.$$

2. **The correct answer is (D).** The equation for a line can be written in the form $y = mx + b$, where m is the slope and b is the y-intercept. Since the slope is $\frac{2}{3}$ and the y-intercept is -2, an equation for the line is $y = \frac{2}{3}x - 2$.

3. **The correct answer is (C).** Use the formula for finding the slope of a line:

$$m = \frac{(y_2 - y_1)}{(x_2 - x_1)}$$
$$= \frac{8 - 3}{(-5) - 6}$$
$$= \frac{5}{-11}$$
$$= -\frac{5}{11}.$$

4. **The correct answer is (B).** First find the slope:

$$m = \frac{(y_2 - y_1)}{(x_2 - x_1)}$$
$$= \frac{6 - 0}{0 - 3}$$
$$= \frac{6}{-3}$$
$$= -2.$$

Since we know that the y-intercept is 6, an equation for the line is $y = -2x + 6$. Choice (B) is correct.

5. **The correct answer is (E).** An equation for a line is where m is the slope and b is the y-intercept. Since the slope is $\frac{1}{3}$ and the y-intercept is 4, an equation for the line is $y = \frac{1}{3}x + 4$.

Note: Photocopying any part of this book is prohibited by law.

FUNCTIONS

1. If $f(x) = -3x + 1$, what is $f(-2)$?

2. If $f(x) = x^2 + 5x + 6$, what is the value of $f(2) + f(-2)$?

   A. 0

   B. 2

   C. 6

   D. 16

   E. 20

3. What is the value of $f(-3)$ if $f(x) = (x + 2)(x^2 + 2x - 1)$?

   A. -12

   B. -3

   C. -2

   D. 9

   E. 12

4. If $f(x) = x^2 - 5x - 7$, what is the value of $f(2) - f(-1)$?

   A. -20

   B. -12

   C. -5

   D. 1

   E. 3

5. For $f(x) = x^2 - 7x + k, f(5) = 0$. What is the value of k?

   A. -7

   B. -5

   C. 0

   D. 5

   E. 10

6. For $f(x) = \frac{x-5}{x-1}$. Which of the following cannot be a value of x?

   A. -5

   B. -1

   C. 0

   D. 1

   E. 5

7. If $f(x) = \frac{3x}{7}$, what is the value of $f\left(\frac{1}{7}\right)$?

   A. $-\dfrac{1}{3}$

   B. $\dfrac{1}{7}$

   C. $\dfrac{3}{49}$

   D. $\dfrac{7}{3}$

   E. 7

8. Which of the following ordered pairs satisfies the function $f(x) = 3x - 5$?

   A. $(-5, 3)$

   B. $(2, -1)$

   C. $\left(\frac{5}{3}, 1\right)$

   D. $(3, 4)$

   E. $(10, 5)$

Note: Photocopying any part of this book is prohibited by law.

ADDITIONAL PRACTICE QUESTIONS

1. If $f(x) = 4x - 6$, what is the value of $f(2)$?

   A. -2

   B. 0

   C. 2

   D. 10

   E. 14

2. The equation $f(x) = 2x + 3$ is a linear function. What is the slope of the line between the points at $f(4)$ and $f(6)$ in the xy-coordinate plane?

   A. -2

   B. $\dfrac{1}{2}$

   C. 2

   D. 4

   E. 10

3. If $f(x) = 5x^2 + 2x - 4$, what is $f(3)$?

   A. 23

   B. 32

   C. 45

   D. 47

   E. 55

4. The function $f(x) = 2x - 6$ is a linear equation. What is the slope of the line between the two points at $f(-2)$ and $f(2)$ in the xy-coordinate plane?

   A. -8

   B. 0

   C. 2

   D. 4

   E. 12

5. If $f(x) = 2^x - 6$, what is the value of $f(4)$?

   A. -2

   B. 2

   C. 3

   D. 10

   E. 22

Note: Photocopying any part of this book is prohibited by law.

ANSWERS AND EXPLANATIONS

1. **The correct answer is 7.**

$$f(-2) = -3(-2) + 1$$
$$= 6 + 1$$
$$= 7$$

2. **The correct answer is (E).** Begin by plugging in the given value in for x.

In this case you're given one function, and are asked to find the sum of $f(2)$ and $f(-2)$. Evaluate the function for each value and then add them.

To evaluate a function in the form $f(x)$, plug the value in parentheses in for x:

$$f(x) = x^2 + 5x + 6$$
$$f(2) = (2)^2 + 5(2) + 6$$
$$= 4 + 10 + 6$$
$$= 20$$

$$f(-2) = (-2)^2 + 5(-2) + 6$$
$$= 4 - 10 + 6$$
$$= 0$$

Finally, combine the values you worked out for $f(2)$ and $f(-2)$:

$$f(2) + f(-2) = 20 + 0$$
$$= 20$$

3. **The correct answer is (C).** Begin by plugging in the given value for x.

In this case, you're given a function that is the product of two polynomial expressions. Don't multiply these factors to find their product. It's easier to evaluate each expression for the given value and then multiply them.

Start by plugging in $x = -3$.

$$f(x) = (x + 2)(x^2 + 2x - 1)$$
$$f(-3) = (-3 + 2) [(-3)^2 + 2(-3) - 1]$$

Now, simplify:

$$f(-3) = (-1)[(9 - 6 - 1)]$$
$$= (-1)(2)$$
$$= -2$$

4. **The correct answer is (B).** In this case, you're given one function, and are asked to find the difference of $f(2)$ and $f(-1)$. Evaluate the function for each value and then subtract them.

To evaluate a function in the form $f(x)$, plug the value in parentheses in for x:

$$f(x) = x^2 - 5x - 7$$
$$f(2) = (2)^2 - 5(2) - 7$$
$$= 4 - 10 - 7$$
$$= -13$$

$$f(-1) = (-1)^2 - 5(-1) - 7$$
$$= 1 + 5 - 7$$
$$= -1$$

Finally, subtract the values you worked out for $f(2)$ and $f(-1)$:

$$f(2) + f(-1) = -13 - (-1)$$
$$= -13 + 1$$
$$= -12$$

5. **The correct answer is (E).** Start by evaluating $f(5)$. Then, use the fact that $f(5) = 0$ to solve for k.

$$f(5) = x^2 - 7x + k$$
$$= (5)2 - 7(5) + k$$
$$= 25 - 35 + k$$
$$= -10 + k$$

Now, substitute 0 for $f(5)$ and solve for k.

$$0 = -10 + k$$
$$0 + 10 = -10 + 10 + k$$
$$10 = k$$

Note: Photocopying any part of this book is prohibited by law.

6. **The correct answer is (D).** Choice (D), which is 1, cannot be a value of x, because it puts a zero in the denominator, which is undefined since it doesn't make sense to divide something up into zero parts. You can evaluate the function for any of the remaining values:

(A): $f\left(-5\right) = \frac{-5-5}{-5-1} = \frac{-10}{-6} = \frac{5}{3} = 1\frac{2}{3}$.

(B): $f\left(-1\right) = \frac{-1-5}{-1-1} = \frac{-6}{-2} = 3$.

(C): $f\left(0\right) = \frac{0-5}{0-1} = \frac{-5}{-1} = 5$.

(E): $f\left(5\right) = \frac{5-5}{5-1} = \frac{0}{4} = 0$.

7. **The correct answer is (C).** To evaluate a function in the form $f(x)$, plug the value in parentheses in for x:

$$f\left(x\right) = \frac{3\left(\frac{1}{7}\right)}{7}$$
$$= \frac{\left(\frac{3}{7}\right)}{7}$$
$$= \frac{3}{7} \times \frac{1}{7}$$
$$= \frac{3}{49}.$$

8. **The correct answer is (D).** Remember that function notation involves substituting "$f(x)$" for y. So, $f(x) = 3x - 5$ is the same as $y = 3x - 5$.

Substitute the values you are given for x and y in each answer choice until you find the pair that balances the equation.

Choice (A): $(x, y) = (-5, 3)$
$$y = 3x - 5$$
$$3 = 3(-5)-5$$
$$3 = -15 - 5$$
$$3 = -20$$

This equation does not balance when $(x, y) = (-5, 3)$, so choice (A) is incorrect.

Choice (B): $(x, y) = (2, -1)$
$$y = 3x - 5$$
$$-1 = 3(2) - 5$$
$$-1 = 6 - 5$$
$$-1 = 1$$

This equation does not balance when $(x, y) = (2, -1)$, so choice (B) is incorrect.

Choice (C): $\left(x, y\right) = \left(\frac{5}{3}, 1\right)$
$$y = 3x - 5$$
$$1 = 3\left(\frac{5}{3}\right) - 5$$
$$1 = 5 - 5$$
$$1 = 0.$$

This equation does not balance when $(x, y) = \left(\frac{5}{3}, 1\right)$, so choice (C) is incorrect.

Choice (D): $(x, y) = (3, 4)$
$$y = 3x - 5$$
$$4 = 3(3) - 5$$
$$4 = 9 - 5$$
$$4 = 4$$

The equation balances when $(x, y) = (3, 4)$.

ADDITIONAL PRACTICE QUESTIONS

1. **The correct answer is (C).** In order to find the value of $f(2)$, plug 2 in for x in the function:

$$
\begin{aligned}
f(x) &= 4x - 6 \\
f(2) &= 4(2) - 6 \\
&= 8 - 6 \\
&= 2
\end{aligned}
$$

2. **The correct answer is (C).** At $f(4)$, $f(x) = 2(4) + 3 = 11$ and at $f(6)$, $f(x) = 2(6) + 3 = 15$. You can rewrite the values as points $(4, 11)$ and $(6, 15)$. Now use the slope formula:

$$
\begin{aligned}
m &= \frac{y_2 - y_1}{x_2 - x_1} \\
&= \frac{15 - 11}{6 - 4} \\
&= \frac{4}{2} \\
&= 2.
\end{aligned}
$$

3. **The correct answer is (D).** In order to find the value of $f(3)$, plug 3 in for x in the equation:

$$
\begin{aligned}
f(x) &= 5x^2 + 2x - 4 \\
f(3) &= 5(3)^2 + 2(3) - 4 \\
&= 5(9) + 6 - 4 \\
&= 45 + 6 - 4 \\
&= 47
\end{aligned}
$$

4. **The correct answer is (C).** At $f(-2)$, $f(x) = 2(-2) - 6 = -10$ and at $f(2)$, $f(x) = 2(2) - 6 = -2$.

    You can rewrite these values as points $(-2, -10)$ and $(2, -2)$. Now use the slope formula:

$$
\begin{aligned}
m &= \frac{y_2 - y_1}{x_2 - x_1} \\
&= \frac{-2 - (-10)}{2 - (-2)} \\
&= \frac{8}{4} \\
&= 2.
\end{aligned}
$$

5. **The correct answer is (D).** Plug 4 in for x in the equation:

$$
\begin{aligned}
f(x) &= 2^x - 6 \\
&= 2^4 - 6 \\
&= 16 - 6 \\
&= 10
\end{aligned}
$$

NOTES

NOTES